BRILLIANCE

A Coaching Guide to Clearing
Inner Obstacles and Letting
Your Authenticity Shine

AMY LOMBARDO

LifeTree
MEDIA

PRAISE FOR *Brilliance*

"Amy's *Brilliance* principles are based on decades of coaching clients from every imaginable walk of life and societal background. Highly accessible and eminently pragmatic, the book's exercises awaken each reader's unique brilliance and teach them how to sustain growth over time. Part of a fresh new generation of self-help authors, Amy Lombardo illuminates the essential connection between self-fulfillment and giving back to family, community, and society at large. Highly recommended, this book is a healing antidote to the complex and divisive times that we live in."

— Gail Straub, Co-Founder of the Empowerment Institute and author of bestseller *Empowerment: The Art of Creating Your Life as You Want It*

"What a gem! As profound as it is practical, *Brilliance* synthesizes the wisdom of the ages into an elegant and effective system for self-transformation."

— Carolyn Murphy, model, actress

"*Brilliance* is like having a personal coach on speed dial (or in your purse) at all times. With an abundant mix of innovative strategies, new techniques, and easily relatable examples, this book gives you the power to turn your world around."

— Leanne Beesley, CEO of Coworker.com

"Lombardo has written the definitive guide to activate potential and stop self-sabotage so you can live from a place of personal excellence. *Brilliance* steers clear of any dogma or trendy new age clichés and instead provides a sensible and grounded step-by-step guide to living your best life. Don't miss this opportunity to seriously improve your 'A' game."

— Peter Rizzi, CEO and Founder of Rebel Health LLC

"Unlike so many self-help books that promise a just-add-water transformation so often promoted in our society, *Brilliance* takes us on a delicious ever-evolving life journey of self-inquiry and self-development."

— Lois Barth, human development expert, speaker, coach and author of *Courage to SPARKLE*

"*Brilliance* is a remarkable contribution from Amy Lombardo that provides a roadmap to clearing the cobwebs of confusion while empowering the reader to take the helm of their life and commit to owning their truest form of expression. Be prepared to be challenged and forever transformed."

— Mandana Mofidi, Executive Director of Audio, Gizmodo Media Group

Cataloguing data available from Library and Archives Canada
ISBN 978-1-928055-47-1 (paperback)
ISBN 978-1-928055-48-8 (EPUB)
ISBN 978-1-928055-49-5 (PDF)

Editor: Kendra Ward
Designer: Tania Craan
Typesetting: Kimberley Young
Cover photograph: Shutterstock/Tomertu
Author photo: Jill Sutherland

Published by LifeTree Media Ltd.
lifetreemedia.com

Distributed by Greystone Books Ltd.
greystonebooks.com

Printed and bound in Canada

Distributed in the U.S. by Publishers Group West

For Savannah,
the purest expression of brilliance I've ever known.
I love you always and forever, no matter what.

CONTENTS

PREFACE

I magine what would be possible if all of us unabashedly owned our greatness, not only to have more fulfilling lives for ourselves, but also so we could be of service to the greater whole in our own unique ways. Sound hokey? Well, maybe at first. But look a little deeper. I once had a wise mentor tell me that if I'm not being called naïve by someone, then I'm not thinking innovatively enough.

There's nothing foolishly romantic about believing in our capacity to be a force for good in this world. Emphasizing and believing in our potential for real brilliance is entirely strategic, especially in a world where we can be so easily seduced by others' and our own negativity.

At the time I wrote this book, I'd already been a practicing life coach and strategist in the field of human potential for over fifteen years, and I'd had thousands of clients literally from all walks of life—billionaires, creative entrepreneurs, social change activists in developing nations, yoga teachers, artists, celebrities, major philanthropists, millennial go-getters, high-powered lawyers, stay-at-home moms, and even individuals struggling with homelessness. Ever curious about the persistent patterns that exist in the human experience, I was not surprised to learn that no matter how varied my clients' backgrounds appeared to be, certain universal principles (what I now affectionately call the brilliance principles) always seemed to apply when it came to helping them ignite their potential. If we used the principles in our work together, we saw results.

Clearly, none of us is immune to the human condition or all the vulnerabilities that come with it, so it makes sense that there might be some common strategies that can help us address our inner obstacles and see the results we've been craving, no matter who we are. This idea isn't earth-shattering by any means and is perhaps in part why we have such an overabundance of self-help books nowadays. As humans, it seems we've been trying to codify a roadmap to success, happiness, and fulfillment for as long as we've been able to write.

So why did I choose to add yet another book to the already rich pot of wisdom out there? This is a question I considered very seriously before choosing to write this book. I was clear that I did not want to write a book just for the sake of it, or because it was a "smart business move." If I was going to put my heart and soul into a book, I wanted it to be of real value to its readers and to the field of empowerment overall.

As I reflected on this question, I knew I could use this book to promote the idea of empowerment as more than just achieving personal fulfillment. To me, when people are empowered and have truly activated their unique brilliance, they become a force for good in this world, a veritable change agent, if they want to be. With this definition of empowerment, we operate from a much more sophisticated context than when we're directed by the ego alone. We connect to our highest truth, and in that realm, feeling vulnerable is not viewed as a liability. Rather, vulnerability becomes an indication that we're leaning into a new edge of growth that can bring us to an even deeper level of authenticity and a greater expression of our true brilliance. I wish that there was more writing on empowerment that spoke of it with this bigger lens. Limiting the definition of empowerment to personal fulfillment alone is a disservice to us all.

I also decided to use this book as an opportunity to look more closely at the intersection where the universal and the personal meet, and where authenticity is birthed. Over the years, I've excelled at helping clients clearly identify, understand, appreciate, and embrace their authenticity as a guiding force for all that they do in their lives. As you explore how to apply universal principles in meaningful and unique ways in your own life, it's incredibly important to home in on your own authentic, individual essence. Yet I find this concept of authenticity so often goes the way of a New Age cliché. It sounds nice as a buzz word, so it's included in a lot of empowerment writing, but I've never found a satisfyingly detailed explanation of how to work with this concept in a practical way and to recognize when one is and is not in alignment with one's authenticity. In chapter 3, you'll be guided through a comprehensive process of defining authenticity, and throughout the book you'll be encouraged to return to that inner compass so that you can evaluate the best ways to activate the universal brilliance principles on your journey of personal empowerment.

Finally, I also wanted to use this book to offer a truly integrative approach to personal empowerment. In the coaching world, it's easy to get pigeonholed into a certain niche audience and to find your offerings starting to narrow themselves, as well, according to that audience's comfort zone. For example, executive coaches serving clientele in the corporate world may find themselves veering away from empowerment strategies that emphasize looking at emotions or accessing the body's intelligence and instead focus primarily on the intellect. Similarly, spiritually based coaches may rely more heavily on strategies such as meditation, yoga, or other embodiment modalities that are popular in their spiritual tradition. Because my client base has always been extremely diverse, I've never had the option of choosing just one approach to coaching. I've always had to think about new and creative ways to make the journey toward brilliance accessible to anyone.

This led me to create a comprehensive and multipronged approach toward personal growth that acknowledges that empowerment can be happening on the emotional, mental, physical, and spiritual planes of an individual all at once. The more ways you can engage with your understanding and experience of your personal brilliance, the more likely you are to learn how to live from that place in you. That's why you'll be prompted throughout the book to investigate your experience of brilliance through a variety of self-inquiry activities that speak to all parts of you—body, mind, and soul. At several places throughout the book, you'll even be guided to the complimentary *Brilliance Workbook: Resources for Clearing Inner Obstacles and Letting Your Authenticity Shine*, which you can download from my website, AmyLombardo.com/Brilliance. There, you can access additional options for self-discovery, including guided meditations, journal prompts, embodiment exercises, and more.

Having used this program with countless clients over the years, I can say with confidence that the journey you are about to embark upon is truly one of a kind, and it has the power to be deeply transformational. My hope for you is that by the end of this book, you will have the know-how, the confidence, and the tools you need to make your most desired dreams an inevitable reality. I want to support you in unleashing your brilliance so that not only will you thrive, but also those around you will ignite with possibility when exposed to your shine. Because, why not?

Far too many of us have settled for mediocrity. Or perhaps we have become very efficient at achieving "success" as it has been defined by someone else, and as a result, we have found ourselves left feeling empty and disillusioned. Not to worry. Whatever your current state, you are welcome here. And it is never too late to turn your ship around, so to speak.

The good news is, if you're reading this page now, then you've already begun the journey to truly owning your brilliance. It's not a journey for the faint of heart. It'll require a deep level of vulnerability from you, and I can guarantee it will take you out of your comfort zone. But it will also reveal to you an incredible process of remembrance—an intimate reintroduction to the brilliance in you that has been there all along, patiently waiting for you to claim it and make its beauty known to the world.

So, without further ado, let's turn the page and get started. Your brilliance awaits!

What Is Brilliance?

There is an adage that says, "If you don't know where you're going, how will you know when you get there?" We must start this magical journey by first understanding what we mean when we talk about brilliance.

Brilliance is probably best explained by using the metaphor of a diamond. Diamonds are known for their brilliance, their incomparable, sparkly, radiant shine that emanates from their very core. A diamond forms deep within the earth, about a hundred miles below the surface in the upper mantle, where it is incredibly hot and the pressure from the weight of the overlying rock is extreme. In these conditions, the hardest naturally occurring substance on the planet is created.

We can't drill to that depth, nor do we have another way to extract the diamonds from the upper mantle. Those closer to the earth's surface were brought there by a deep-seated volcanic eruption that predated scientific recording. When such eruptions reached the surface, they built up a mound of volcanic material that eventually cooled. That's where you find diamonds.

Brilliance Uncovered

What does this diamond metaphor suggest about brilliance?

Brilliance Is Within

You source brilliance deep from within you. Just like a diamond comes from the deep confines of Mother Earth herself, your brilliance is innate, not something you have to grasp, obtain, or cultivate from outside yourself. No one can make you brilliant. You have the natural ingredients for brilliance within you, and therefore you have the potential to live from that place within.

You Will Endure Trials

It's likely that in order for your brilliance to be revealed, you'll need to endure some trials—a burning away of impurities that are not really you—for the inner gem in you to be accessible and to shine. Living in your brilliance is not a one-dimensional, feel-good approach to life. Remember the intense volcanic eruption needed to bring the diamonds to the surface? You, too, will have your own process, sometimes intense and sometimes calmer, that will help you uncover your brilliance just like one might uncover diamonds when mining.

Others Will Benefit from Your Brilliance

Just like a diamond, your brilliance reflects the light, and all in your presence will benefit from your shine. Diamonds are great conductors and amplifiers of energy, and you, too, once in your brilliance, will be a conduit and a catalyst for others to own their brilliance. Light begets light. It's one of the most wonderful joys of being in your brilliance—that you can't help but make the world a better place when you are really living in your deepest truth.

With these basic concepts in mind, our working definition of brilliance becomes

The state of being when a person thinks, feels, and acts from their inner source of radiance, aligning themselves with the unlimited potential of the universe as it exists within them.

What isn't in that definition is the idea that you have to create brilliance. That's because brilliance is already fully formed within you. To reveal it, you must choose to align with the part of you that senses something extraordinary is possible for you and that already says a big, unequivocal and unconditional *yes* to life.

When you own your brilliance, you are connected to your true essence and to the whole universe. You have access to the deepest wells of wisdom and greatness inherent within you. Living brilliantly does not look the same for each person, just like no two diamonds look alike. Even within you, brilliance will show up in different ways in every area of your life as you continue to evolve, grow, and learn. It's possible that you may find it easier to access brilliance in certain areas of your life than in others. But rest assured, it is always there, and should you choose to, you can always be in a process of uncovering more of your brilliance to shine even brighter.

What Gets in the Way of Brilliance?

Now that we know what brilliance is and that we all have the capacity for it, the question is, why aren't we all living from that place? Many factors affect whether we are living in our brilliance.

Lack of Information
We may not know how to uncover our brilliance. This seems obvious enough. We may be fully aware that we have brilliance within us, and we may even actively yearn for it. But perhaps we haven't been taught the skills that can help us uncover our brilliance more easily. Without this know-how, it's like trying to mine for diamonds in your backyard with a shovel and a flashlight. Good luck! Uncovering your brilliance becomes far easier when you have the right support, knowledge, and skills. Good news for you, that's what this book is all about!

Uncertainty
We may not know what brilliance looks like in us. Sometimes you can be so used to living in the not-so-brilliant way that you lose touch with what makes you shine. You don't know what you want. You're not sure what would light you up and make you feel energetically engaged in your life. Maybe this stems from a lifetime of never being encouraged to pursue your dreams. Or perhaps you were taught to prioritize others' dreams for you instead of your own. Through my coaching career, I've met many clients who were fully successful at living someone else's dream for them. Perhaps their mom wanted them to be a doctor or their husband wanted them to give up their job. Whatever the case, and no matter how long you may have felt out of synch with your brilliance, rest assured, you can still access it. Uncovering brilliance doesn't have a time limit or expiration date. It's always there, just waiting for you to discover it.

Lack of Encouragement
Our world doesn't necessarily encourage brilliance. A sad but true reality is that living brilliantly is not always promoted in our world. Have you ever

been told "don't rock the boat" or "play it safe"? Or maybe you've been encouraged to do the minimum necessary to "get by." Or have you ever dared to dream big, only to find others calling you naïve or a Pollyanna? Add to this our media's tendency to propagate fear, and many of us are prone to adopt a stance that prioritizes comfort and safety over authenticity and shining bright.

Demonizing Pain

We've been taught to demonize pain. Have a headache? Just pop a pill for that. No need to feel the pain, and certainly no reason to do the self-investigation required to determine what might be causing that headache so that you can change your behavior in the future. This is not a condemnation of taking medicine, by the way. Sometimes you need it! Rather, it's a sober look at the problem of repeatedly and consistently demonizing or numbing the pain. If you do that, you cut off the feedback loop that your being is trying to share with you. You end up addressing only symptoms instead of dealing with the root cause of your problems. This approach also encourages a mere state of maintenance, rather than learning how to thrive. We're constantly running from pain instead of moving toward what we want to create. If we numb the pain, there's a good chance we're also numbing important insights and wisdom from within about how we can be more aligned with our highest truth, and that makes it very hard for us to live from our brilliance.

Prioritizing Instant Gratification

We prioritize instant gratification. The flip side of demonizing pain is putting the idea of instant gratification above all else. Even our self-help industry is inundated with resources perpetuating a belief that empowerment is somehow just about the pursuit of pleasure and fulfillment. But pleasure is just one facet of brilliance. When we really are committed to owning our brilliance, it means celebrating the entirety of our being, even the parts that don't feel so "instant" or "gratifying."

Aversion to Risks

Owning your brilliance takes a lot of courage. Brilliance requires commitment and a willingness to take risks—to jump into the unknown and perhaps even stand in direct contradiction to what the world around you suggests is appropriate or acceptable. And that kind of commitment takes courage with a capital "C." There's no guarantee of constant comfort or security. Your metaphorical mining for diamonds may result in just a bucket of rocks sometimes. But, as you continue to commit to your brilliance again and again, you get better at learning how to align with your inner truth, even in those times when it feels less clear than others. You won't always receive encouragement from the outside world. Others may not understand your quest or may not know how to support you. But once you've committed to owning your brilliance, it's a risk you're willing to take because the yearning in your heart is one you can no longer refuse.

Why Seek Your Brilliance?

Could you live a perfectly decent and good life without pursuing your brilliance? Sure, I suppose so. I'm not here to tell you that your life will only have meaning if you agree to pursue your brilliance. Committing to brilliance is a personal choice, and you have to be ready, willing, and able to make it. Nobody else can decide but you.

You may desire to embark on the journey to your brilliance for a variety of reasons. Here are a few examples:

- to move forward in an area of life where you feel stuck
- to manage life/work balance more effectively
- to renew or reenergize career goals
- to reconcile being "successful" with feeling "fulfilled"
- to put "someday" dreams into action now
- to bring your professional or personal life to the next level
- to conquer self-sabotage and move ahead with more freedom
- to bring an entrepreneurial vision to fruition
- to create a healthy and loving relationship
- to contribute to the greater whole
- to learn self-love and self-compassion
- to stop settling for "good enough" and start pursuing your greatest possibilities instead

How to Use This Book
....

At this point, owning your brilliance may seem as rare as a diamond in the rough, but the possibilities for brilliance lie all around us.

This book is designed to walk you through a step-by-step experience of uncovering your brilliance at every level. In Part One, we look very closely at some key brilliance principles and skill sets we need to understand and develop in order to navigate the journey toward our brilliance with the most ease and grace possible.

In Part Two, we take an in-depth look at how brilliance manifests in specific ways in your life, specifically how it corresponds with seven brilliance centers. Each brilliance center reflects an aspect of consciousness that is essential to your life. Considering the qualities at the heart of these different brilliance centers and how they influence your life provides a powerful tool for personal growth.

I've based the brilliance centers on the chakra system in yoga. "Chakra" is a Sanskrit word meaning "wheel" or "circle" and refers to seven energy centers positioned along the midline of the body. In the yoga tradition, chakras are considered part of one's energetic (subtle) body and denote a point of intersection, where mind and body meet. But you don't need previous experience with the chakra system to use the model of the brilliance centers easily and effectively. Nor do you need to believe in any specific tradition or religion to use this program. The brilliance centers are an organizing template to help you manage the journey in steps, looking at one area of life at a time. For those who know the chakra system, you'll notice that I start at the top, beginning with the seventh chakra and working our way down to the first.

The brilliance centers are like a map for the journey to our brilliance. Like the chakra system, they show us a formula for wholeness and how to maximize our energetic potential, physically, mentally, emotionally, and spiritually. Just like a map, the system won't tell you where to go, but it will help you navigate the journey you wish to take. By the end of Part Two, you'll have a clear vision of how to sustain your brilliance in all areas of your life, from work to self-care, finances, relationships, health, spirituality, and more.

Finally, in Part Three, we pull it all together for an integrated embodiment of brilliance. When you own your brilliance, you become a living, breathing example of what's possible for others too. You become a leader in brilliance. You are awakened to how your gifts can support the greater whole in big and small ways, and your radiance is infectious. The information in this section will help you learn how to sustain and continue to optimize your brilliance in support of a revolution in consciousness that starts from the inside out.

Additionally, to support you in getting the most you can out of this experience, I've created a *Brilliance Workbook* that can be downloaded for free at AmyLombardo.com/Brilliance. I highly recommend you do that right now. It will become handy to have all your self-inquiry exercises, affirmations, visualizations, and other pertinent insights located together in one space. A plethora of other resources at that web link will support you on your path to brilliance as well, including guided visualizations, videos of embodiment practices to help you fully integrate this work, and recommendations for further reading. I hope you visit the site frequently to take advantage of these resources.

Throughout the book, I provide multiple examples from my own life and from my coaching practice in order to provide a sense of how this work is realized in one's day-to-day experiences. The examples from my coaching practice reflect actual issues I've addressed in my years of coaching, but the people mentioned are composites of my clients. Any resemblance to a real person is inadvertent and coincidental. In cases where I use direct quotes from clients with their permission, I have changed the names of individuals and other identifying details in order to protect their anonymity.

I'd also like to offer an important disclaimer before we dive into this program together. This book is designed to help you access greater levels of your own potential to live your most brilliant life, but empowerment doesn't happen in a vacuum. We also need to look at the institutional systems and societies we create, since those structures invariably affect the way our world works. And more often than not, those structures are not an even playing field for individuals when it comes to pursuing one's brilliance. For example, because I am a white woman, I've clearly had access to certain things my whole life that have made it easier for me than it would be for a person of color to pursue personal empowerment, and certainly to pursue a career as a coach. This dynamic needs to change.

In writing this book, I tried my very best to remain aware of my position of privilege and of the limits that our societies and systems reinforce so that I could offer this material in a way that speaks to and supports any reader who would like to access it, no matter their circumstances. I've also aimed to offer this book up in the spirit of creating possibilities for each of us to have greater accountability and commitment to transforming our current systems and society. When we engage with our journey of personal empowerment with the understanding that we have the power to truly impact the collective, we develop an opportunity to create a new social fabric, one in which we all take ownership for the well-being of the whole and feel called to take action. It is my sincere hope that this book not only helps you to evolve for greater personal fulfillment, but inspires you to leverage your brilliance to support the advancement of the collective as well.

It's my belief that the health of the human psyche is inextricably linked to the health of the collective consciousness, and you cannot heal the whole without healing the individuals within it. So, from that standpoint alone, it's imperative that we all do the inner work to empower ourselves if we want to improve our world. This is what I hope my book will help you do.

With that said, here are a few important things to keep in mind before you get started.

It's Not About Perfection

You won't feel perfect at the end of this book. Please don't confuse brilliance with perfection. Perfection is an illusion of some arbitrary "right" way to do or be, whereas brilliance is aligning with your true essence and living from there. Owning your brilliance is a process, and though I can say with confidence that you will experience many deeply significant and positive shifts in your life if you commit to this program, the process will not end at the final page of this book. You will evolve into deeper states of brilliance throughout your life. And you will continue to have much to learn. That's true of everyone. So, be kind to yourself and remember to keep the long-term perspective here.

Some Things May Not Resonate

Not everything you read in this book may resonate with you, and that's okay. Brilliance is accessed in different ways by everyone. In this book, I humbly offer processes, strategies, concepts, and techniques that have supported me and the thousands of clients I've worked with over the years on the journey to uncovering brilliance. My advice is to keep an open mind, try all the techniques at least once, and do all the exercises. After that, you can decide if each is a technique or an idea that you want to keep with you for the road ahead.

Journaling Is Key

Get a journal. Throughout this book, there are many written exercises for you to engage in to keep moving you forward. It's helpful to use a journal to record all your answers and notes in one place. You can call this your Brilliance Journal and refer to it again and again throughout the years. I still have my first Brilliance Journal that I created when I was in my twenties, and it is chock full of wonderful insights. I am so grateful to have had this valuable tool with me on the path, and I still refer to it frequently.

Bonus Resources

Also, remember to download your complimentary *Brilliance Workbook*. You can print it out if you like and keep it alongside your journal for additional activities, exercises, and support throughout this journey.

It's time for us to get started. Let's prime the pump with some exploratory questions to get the creative juices flowing.

♦ SELF-INQUIRY EXERCISE: Looking Within

Please record your answers in your journal.

1. What do you currently love about your life?
2. What are you tolerating in your life right now?
3. What's something your soul yearns for?
4. List three things you could do to feel more energized about your life.
5. If money were no issue, what would you do to occupy your time?
6. What's one thing you could do to improve your relationship with your body?
7. What motivates you to succeed and evolve as a person?
8. List some of the things that make you feel most loved.
9. In what areas of your life do you feel most out of alignment, and why?
10. What's something you want to stand for in this world (for example, a cause, a way of being, or a characteristic)?

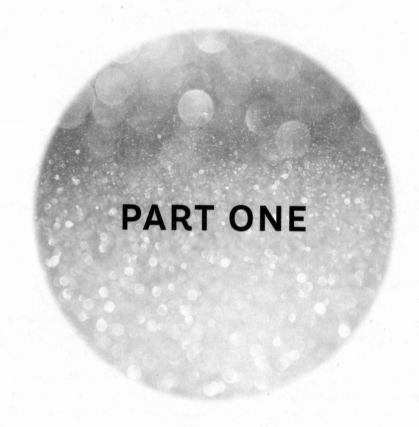

PART ONE

CHAPTER 1

Let the Journey to Your Brilliance Begin!

Nature has always been one of my biggest inspirations. In fact, nature's brilliance in some ways is so abundant that it might get overlooked and mistaken for being commonplace. So that we don't fall prey to such insensitivity, let's take a closer look at one of nature's most magnificent beings—the giant sequoia tree.

For those of you not familiar with these beauties, giant sequoias are found in the Pacific Northwest of the United States and are the world's largest trees. They are also among the oldest living organisms on earth—the oldest was dated at over thirty-five hundred years old! Sequoias grow to an average height of three hundred feet and a width of over thirty feet in diameter. These towering redwood evergreens are truly a sight to behold. On occasions when I've stood in a grove of sequoias, I've felt as though I was in one of Mother Nature's most sacred cathedrals. They inspire awe like few other things can.

But I think what makes their enormous size and splendor even more remarkable to me is the seed that gives life to one of these giants is the size of a dime. Even more fascinating, this little seed won't germinate unless it's been heated to an extreme temperature, one possible in its environment only when a raging forest fire blazes through the landscape and leaves the soil extra fertile and ready for new sprouts to take root. How's that for a brilliant adaptation?

It's mind-boggling to think that the largest and oldest trees on our planet began as unexpressed potential in the tiniest of seeds. It's a fine example of the first concept we need to understand on a journey toward our brilliance: intention.

What Is Intention?
. . . .

Well, in a word, intention is everything.

Like a sequoia seed holding the potential of a whole tree, your intentions are the seed energy from which all your actions arise. Intentions give meaning to everything we do. Let's look at an example.

Imagine I am in a room with you and I cut you with a knife. Is that a bad or a good thing? If I'm a robber and my intention is to steal your valuables and kill you, then the action is a harmful one. If I am a surgeon and I intend to save your life by making a specific incision, then my action is definitely life-affirming. Notice how the intention behind the action is what determines its true value and meaning.

From time to time, you may have had a version of the thought, "I'll just change 'X,' and then everything will be all right." There's a problem with this logic, though. Even if you succeed at changing "X," you often still feel unfulfilled. Why? Because it's not only *what* you aim to do that matters, but also *how* you aim to do it. In other words, to feel fulfilled and empowered in life, both our expectations *and* our intentions count. Let's take a closer look at what each of these things means.

A Critical Distinction
. . . .

Our results-oriented world tends to focus almost exclusively on expectation, which is what we aim to accomplish. Inherently, there is nothing wrong with this, but if we neglect to look at the intention, or how we want to be, then we're missing a key component to our brilliance.

Expectation: The specific goal you hope to accomplish
Intention: How you want to be on the journey

An interesting thing to note is that you can be wholly successful at living your intention even if you don't end up achieving your intended goal. Let's look at some examples.

Expectation (My Specific Goal)	Intention (How I Want to Be on the Journey)
Save $20,000 this year.	I want to be more mindful when it comes to my finances.
Get a new job.	I want to be patient while I search for the best career for me.
Run a marathon.	I want to be more disciplined when it comes to taking care of my body.

If we look at the first example, we see that if I don't fully achieve my goal of saving $20,000 this year, I can still be successful at being more mindful about my finances. Perhaps I learn to save more, spend less, and be more aware of situations in which I waste money. Even if I don't quite make it to my goal yet, I am still aligned with my true intention and make progress in the right direction.

Read through the chart again. Notice how the intentions are contextual, while the expectations are narrower in scope. Intentions activate the feeling part of our brains. They create space in our minds (and hearts) and open us up to our creativity and our innovative side. As a result, it's important for us to know that we need to use both our feeling and thinking capacities as we move toward our goals.

Energy Goes Where Intention Flows

Your intentions have an impact on your beliefs. Imagine I have a goal to lose ten pounds. Let's explore a few of the intentions that may motivate me and affect how I feel about myself.

One possible intention I could have is to be more attractive so that others will like me more. Do you see how this intention could affect my self-esteem? Even if I lose the weight, I'm still likely living with the fear that I have to behave and appear a certain way to be worthy of love. This keeps me in a constant battle to "maintain" myself so that I can be accepted. Not only is this mentally exhausting, but also the intention will probably propel me to constantly compare myself with others.

Now let's imagine I have a different intention behind my goal of losing weight. Let's assume my intention is to be kind and compassionate to myself by being more conscious of the diet and exercise choices I make. Think about how dramatically different this journey to weight loss could be. In this instance, I take the focus off the pounds and off meeting others' expectations. Instead, I make the intention about self-acceptance and self-love. In this scenario, I'll not only be addressing the weight loss, but I'll also be supporting myself to change underlying belief patterns that may have led me to make poor choices about diet and exercise in the first place. Which journey do you think is going to feel more empowering?

Now that we understand the important distinction between expectations and intentions, I want to share with you the first of fourteen brilliance principles we'll explore throughout the first part of this book.

BRILLIANCE PRINCIPLE #1
Be Firm with Your Intention and Flexible with Your Form

Brilliance Principle #1 asks us to be clear and firm with our intentions but also understand that life demands we be flexible at the same time. It's important to note, however, that being flexible doesn't mean you have to compromise your values. You can certainly hold true to your values, even if how those values are outwardly expressed looks different from moment to moment.

Here's an example. I have a firm intention in my life right now to be more patient. A few of the forms that intention may take are

- not honking my car horn in a traffic jam;
- not interrupting my husband when he's talking; and
- not freaking out if I don't get an email or text response right away.

No matter the action, I am clear on the quality of energy I want behind it: patience. The intention stays the same, but the expression of it looks different, depending on the scenario. You get the idea. Now it's your turn to practice.

♦ SELF-INQUIRY EXERCISE: Clarifying Intentions and Expectations

For each of the following areas of life, list any specific expectations (goals) you have in that area. Then note one overarching intention that describes how you want to be while moving toward those goals. If you're not sure of all your goals, just do your best to write what you know. This exercise will help you focus on your path (and the way you want to be on it) for the journey ahead.

Example: In the area of spirituality, one expectation (specific goal) I have is to meditate every morning. My intention (how I want to be) in this area of my life is to be more calm and centered, no matter what's happening in my life.

Now you try. Good luck!

Life Areas

- Spirituality
- Profession/livelihood/career/studentship
- Finances/prosperity/abundance
- Intimacy/sexuality
- Body (physical health and well-being)
- Mind/intellect (mental health and well-being)
- Emotions (emotional health and well-being)
- Friendships/family/personal community
- Environment (home/personal space)

CHAPTER 2

The Road to Brilliance

When I was twenty years old, during my senior year of college, I had the great fortune to work in Tanzania for six months. This was my first time traveling internationally, and I knew it was going to be an epic adventure. Before heading out on this transformative journey, I poured over every guidebook I could find (this was before the internet existed!) so that I could prepare myself for the experience. I wanted to know what types of situations, cultures, and opportunities I might encounter, and what I should pack for my trip. I also wanted to know how to be a smart, sensitive, and responsible traveler and to avoid any unnecessary challenges during my stay. The preparation for my trip was essential to making the most of my experience abroad.

In a similar way, preparing for the journey to uncover your brilliance will allow you to embrace the experience wholeheartedly as it gets underway. To that end, let's think of this chapter as a guidebook to the Land of Brilliance.

The journey to the Land of Brilliance is really one of evolution, from unconscious to conscious choice. You are choosing to connect with the part of you that already aligns with your highest potential and intentionally live from there. When you orient to life from your brilliance, the negative patterns and habits you've struggled with become a lot less compelling, and your true essence can start to emerge more organically. This might sound great, but indeed, how does one prepare for such a journey as this?

In chapter 1, I discussed the first brilliance principle, "Be firm with your intention and flexible with your form," so that you could clearly outline your intentions and goals in the different areas of your life. This exercise gave you an idea of where you want to go in the Land of Brilliance.

In this chapter, I'll outline Brilliance Principles 2 to 14. These introduce the major themes you're likely to encounter on the path ahead, time and again. You'll have the opportunity to do self-inquiry with each principle so that you become more aware of where you, specifically, are likely to get tripped up on your journey.

For example, your self-inquiry might reveal that you've been making a lot of choices for your life based on what other people want and not on what you want. Or you might discover a harsh inner critic that keeps preventing you from pursuing your dreams. Or perhaps there's a part of you that can't feel safe unless you're "in control" and this keeps you stuck in your tracks. Whatever happens, it's important to know what these potential obstacles might be before getting started so that you can be a savvy traveler in the Land of Brilliance. It might help to think of these principles like trail markers on the path, giving you guidance about which direction to take when you encounter a proverbial fork in the road on your quest for personal empowerment.

In my coaching practice, my clients have often found this part of the journey to be the most revelatory. In this phase of the process, we're developing greater self-awareness about how we might be contributing to our own unhappiness or lack of fulfillment. The information we uncover in this chapter will support us throughout our journey, helping us to stay the course and not fall victim to old patterns of self-sabotage once again.

A word of caution: When we do a deep dive into self-awareness like this, we might become painfully aware of all the places we feel completely out of alignment with our brilliance. That discovery can sometimes feel disheartening. Have faith. It's natural and common to feel this way at this point. Remind yourself that this is the beginning of the journey, and it's entirely appropriate not to feel completely secure in your way forward yet.

As in any guidebook, there is indeed a lot of information to digest in this chapter. Some of what you reveal may be old news for you, and other insights might be quite groundbreaking. Do yourself a favor and ease off the pressure to have it all figured out right away. All we are aiming to do is to become aware of these principles so that we can refer to them, so we can steer clear of obstacles and move toward what we truly want to create in our lives.

So now, fellow traveler, it's time for us to dive in. Get a pen and your journal ready, and let the adventure begin!

BRILLIANCE PRINCIPLE #2
Go Forth with a Beginner's Mind

The second brilliance principle reminds us of the importance of staying open and being mindful of how our preconceived notions may prevent us from seeing the possibilities ahead.

The concept of beginner's mind is from Zen Buddhism. In that tradition, a popular story tells of a well-educated and high-profile Western man visiting a Zen master during his travels. The Zen master is a renowned teacher in the tradition, and the westerner comes in pursuit of learning the secret to enlightenment. As the master begins to teach the westerner, the visitor constantly interrupts the master to tell him about the ways he is already well versed and skilled in this or that technique. So, the Zen master stops talking and instead starts to pour the man a cup of tea.

He fills the man's cup to the brim and keeps on pouring. As the tea spills over the edge and onto the table, the man insists the master stop: "The cup is already full! Why do you keep pouring? It cannot hold anymore."

The master gently replies, "You, too, are like this cup. How can I show you Zen if you will not first empty your mind?"

When you practice beginner's mind, you are aware of the biases you bring to your experience that might prevent you from being fully open to receiving new wisdom and insights. Beginner's mind inspires a stance of curiosity and humility, keeping you expansive in the field of possibilities and ever a learner of life.

When you don't "empty your cup," you take all your pre-conditioning with you on the journey, and this affects how you show up in the here and now. Without beginner's mind, you might hold an attitude of "been there, done that" that can keep you stuck in the past and unable to break free from old negative patterns. For example, imagine that up until now, every experience you've had with intimate relationships has suggested that they are not safe and that you shouldn't bother with them. You believe you'll just get hurt. As long as you are unwilling to let go of that metaphorically full cup, it's going to be very hard to create a future with a successful intimate relationship. You have to be willing to let go of past perceptions, preconceived notions, and even your first habitual reactions to things if you want to be innovative in the way you think about yourself and what's possible for you.

♦ SELF-INQUIRY

Are there people or situations that you tend to react to automatically, as if you already know what to expect from them? What possibilities might you be missing out on because of this?

BRILLIANCE PRINCIPLE #3
Practice Discipline and See It as Devotion

Brilliance Principle #3 asks many of us to relate to discipline in a new way—as an act of devotion. Sadly, the concept of discipline often conjures up images of strict rules, stern commanders, and the promise of punishment if one falls out of line. When we orient to discipline in this way, we end up coming from a place of "should," "must," or "have to," such that many of us neglect this extremely important brilliance principle. Or, if we tend to the need for discipline, we do so begrudgingly.

Fortunately, there is another way to orient to discipline. What if you could think of it as devotion to some higher cause or purpose that is deeply meaningful to you? When you see discipline in this way, your actions are no longer required but are inspired. To be sure, you still have to make a conscious choice to be disciplined. But when it becomes about devotion instead of a "should," you can align with your higher truth and with the realm of possibilities, even when you have to engage in activities that you're not enthusiastic about.

An area where I've used this principle successfully time and again is self-care. Incredibly passionate about my work, I often find myself brushing off important self-care regimens and getting swept away in the excitement of another work project. To motivate myself to be more diligent and responsible about exercise, sleep, and eating habits, I decided to see each act of self-care as an act of devotion to my daughter. More specifically, I dedicated myself to setting a good example for her about how you can take care of yourself in a healthy way, no matter what other demands life places on you.

Making this perceptual shift was transformative. All of a sudden, the act of dragging myself to the gym became an opportunity for me to connect with how much I love my daughter. When I thought of it that way, it became easy to follow through on my choices. Nothing about it felt like a "should" anymore. It just felt like a pleasant opportunity to express gratitude and love for my daughter. When we tap into discipline as devotion, energy flows effortlessly, and brilliance comes forth much more easily.

♦ SELF-INQUIRY

In what areas of life do you need to connect to discipline more strongly? What could you devote yourself to that would make you more successful at following through on your intentions for discipline in that area?

BRILLIANCE PRINCIPLE #4
Choose Self-Responsibility over Blame and Shame

Brilliance Principle #4 asks us to take responsibility for ourselves rather than focus on blame and shame. Sometimes things don't work out the way you want. How you choose to perceive those situations is really where your power resides.

The path of blame and shame focuses on judgment and looks backwards. We're seeking to find fault with someone or something. Sometimes we pin the blame on others, perhaps to shirk our own responsibility. It might make us feel good to do this temporarily, but over the long term, it can lead to feelings of victimization and disempowerment. Other times, we may choose to blame ourselves and use it as a reason to feel even worse about the situation and subsequently lower our self-esteem.

In my coaching practice, I have often encountered clients in situations with a lot of unresolved hurt getting trapped in the blame game. Whether it's a nasty divorce, being overlooked for an expected promotion, or an estranged relationship with a parent, for example, our story about blame is an excellent vehicle for discharging some of our pain. Every time we tell the story, we get a temporary release of the hurt inside. It feels good to let some of the venom out, so to speak. The problem is this is only a quick fix and does nothing to truly remedy the hurt. If we just keep repeating our story of blame, we simply avoid any real reflection on the matter and any accountability for how we may have contributed to the situation in question. Sadly, we can get stuck in this mental cycle for years, literally.

There is another way. The path of self-responsibility is more forward thinking and focuses on accountability. We don't beat ourselves up for being wrong, and we don't focus on others. Instead, we stay curious and inquire about what we may be able to do differently if this experience were to happen again. We focus on where we could align more with what we know is possible for ourselves. We also learn to accept what is out of our control. Self-responsibility feels empowering. It allows us to take challenging experiences from the past and learn from them so that our future actions more accurately reflect the reality we want to create for ourselves.

♦ SELF-INQUIRY

What are some situations in your life where you typically play the blame and shame game? What self-reflections might you be avoiding by doing this?

BRILLIANCE PRINCIPLE #5
Seek Personal Excellence instead of Perfection

Brilliance Principle #5 asks us to surrender the illusion of perfection and instead seek our own personal best. We all have a vision of our perfect selves. It's great to have goals and aspirations, but when we pursue perfection, we imply that unless we achieve that assumed state, something is wrong with our lives or with us. Even when we make progress toward that arbitrary goal, it's still not good enough because there's always something more we could do to make things even better.

This is a no-win battle. Research has shown that those who dedicate themselves to a pursuit of perfection are far more likely to end up unhappy than those who do not. Some of us are so paralyzed by our image of perfection that it even catapults us into a constant state of procrastination. We dare not even try to achieve something because if we do it less than faultlessly, we'll be considered a failure. This is no way to live.

If you are to reveal your brilliance, you must first understand that there is no empowerment in the pursuit of perfection. There *is* empowerment in the embracing of your humanity. This means accepting all of you, including your imperfections. The more you do this, the more likely you will be to express the fullness of your potential. You can replace the old paradigm of perfection with a new idea of personal excellence.

With personal excellence, you see yourself as a soul, a being constantly in evolution. You acknowledge that you are on a continuous journey of moving toward deeper states of your fullest truth. Knowing this, the most you can expect of yourself in any given moment is to do the best you can with whatever your capacities are at that time. My childhood summer camp had a great motto for this: "To be my own self at my very best all the time."

With personal excellence, the process is not linear, and you have a more realistic view of failure. You realize you are going to make mistakes, and you cherish these opportunities for the deep learning they provide. You don't expect results immediately, and you understand that sometimes things will work out differently than you thought. You have a renewed interest in the journey and know it has value unto itself.

Most importantly, you understand that your seeming imperfections are what connect you to every other person on this planet. We are all human, and we are all less than perfect. And, if we let them, these vulnerable points of human-ness can connect us in more meaningful and authentic ways with one another than putting up a facade of perfection does. Wouldn't that be refreshing? Our imperfections give us precious opportunities to learn self-acceptance and practice courage, if we're willing to take the risk and accept our human-ness.

♦ SELF-INQUIRY

Where does your inner perfectionist currently sabotage you? How can you change this?

BRILLIANCE PRINCIPLE #6
Stay Connected to Your Lightness

Brilliance Principle #6 asks us to stay connected to an open, light-hearted attitude, or our lightness. Perhaps Kermit the Frog said it best: "Don't take life too seriously. It's not like you're going to get out alive!"

Over-seriousness can be a major buzz kill. It cuts off your creativity and imagination. Life is sometimes intense and seems to demand a kind of solemnness and respect. But too much seriousness can add undue stress, worry, and anxiety to your life for no good reason. Could you get through all the same obstacles you're facing today, but with a little more spring in your step or playfulness in your heart? Might it even make the journey easier for you?

Robert Tennyson Stevens, the creator of Conscious Language, has a great motto that nicely supports a stance of lightness: "I choose to make this fun and easy." A simple attitude shift like this is sometimes all you need to get past the typical overthinking and over-seriousness that plagues so many of us. Resist the temptation to overcomplicate this. Ultimately, lightness is just a choice we need to connect to, and when we do, things are a lot more fun and flow with much more ease and grace.

♦ SELF-INQUIRY

In what areas of your life could you make lightness a closer ally on your journey to brilliance? Describe what you might do differently to make this happen.

BRILLIANCE PRINCIPLE #7
Give Up Comparison and Commit to Your Own Authenticity

Brilliance Principle #7 asks us to keep returning to our inner sense of authenticity as the compass that guides us. Imagine for a moment a herd of zebras on the plains of Africa. Now picture one of those zebras thinking to himself, "Oh my, that zebra's stripes are much more handsome than mine. I am a worthless zebra. No zebra will want to be with me as long as that zebra's around! I may as well not even go to the watering hole."

Ridiculous, right? But transpose this same scenario into a human context and somehow it's not only very plausible but also widely accepted that we might repeatedly and frequently compare ourselves with others. We are taught to do this by our families, societies, culture, and the media. Because the pressures to compare are so prevalent, uprooting the habit of comparison usually requires a no-tolerance policy for it. You need to make a conscious and deliberate decision every day to choose authenticity over comparison.

When you choose authenticity, you focus inwardly on your alignment with your highest truth. You do not concern yourself with how you measure up against others or society's standards. Reorienting like this takes practice, but the more you do it, the more you'll learn to ground yourself in a place of self-acceptance, where you'll be a lot less concerned with getting approval from others.

♦ SELF-INQUIRY

Where in your life are you most prone to compare yourself with others? How does this make you feel?

BRILLIANCE PRINCIPLE #8
Be Courageous and Take Risks

Brilliance Principle #8 encourages us to access courage and take risks, even in the face of fear. Look up the Latin root for the word "courage," and you will find *cor*, which means "heart." Coincidence? I think not. Courage requires you to stand in your vulnerability with an open heart. When you display courage, you are willing to risk exposing yourself to new obstacles or hurts and to move forward with no guarantee of security.

At first, your more conservative side might think, "Now why would I want to do that?" Well, for starters, when you are courageous and willing to take risks, that's when you really feel alive. You connect with your vitality in a way that you can't experience when you "play it safe."

Suppose you sign up to take a trapeze class. Imagine, when you go, that you grab onto the first bar and just stay there, swinging back and forth saying, "Nah, I'm good." Will you be safer? Yes, but you certainly won't experience the exhilaration, empowerment, and liveliness of letting go and reaching out for that next bar.

So many of our meaningful growth experiences and a-ha moments happen in the space "between the bars," when the ground beneath us is uncertain and all that we know has been released. That stepping into the great expanse of possibility is what courage is all about, and it's where we are most likely to encounter our brilliance.

♦ SELF-INQUIRY

Recall a time when you felt especially courageous. Take a few minutes to write about the experience. How did you feel? How did you behave? What insights did you discover?

BRILLIANCE PRINCIPLE #9
Being Is Just as Important as Doing

Brilliance Principle #9 reorients what we value, so we understand that being is as integral to our life objectives as doing. It's easy to see how one might think that doing is more important, valid, or powerful. After all, if you want to see results, then you should take action, right? You don't have to look far to see how our culture pushes this idea. A quick internet search on "being versus doing" will bring up results like these:

- "Just do it."
- "Actions speak louder than words."
- "Small deeds done are better than great deeds planned."
- "Actions always prove why words mean nothing."
- "Stop wishing and start doing."

Certainly, the act of doing is absolutely critical on the path to brilliance. But in our zest to accomplish, succeed, and achieve, many of us overlook the subtler art of being. One might also call this the art of receptivity.

The power of receptivity is not to be understated, and it would be a gross misunderstanding to think of receptivity as passivity. That could not be further from the truth. The best example I can think of to illustrate the immense power of receptivity and how it can open us up to deep levels of potential and transformation is to use the example of a pregnant woman.

A pregnant woman is able to achieve one of the most miraculous things on the planet—she uses the vehicle of her body to help create another human life. Let's think for a moment about how this is accomplished. This woman doesn't get into doing mode during her pregnancy. For example, she does not sit down and write a to-do list:

Week One: Make my baby's nervous system.
Week Two: Grow my baby's limbs.
Week Three: Start separating the hemispheres of my baby's brain.

Of course she doesn't! Instead, she surrenders to a larger process that's happening within her and through her. She literally and figuratively makes space in her body (both emotionally and physically) to let the magic of life happen. She may find herself listening more deeply to the messages she gets from her body as she becomes attuned and sensitive to the processes happening within her. She may slow down and seek more stillness and silence in her life. She may desire more time for self-reflection, and she may feel a lot more vulnerable, in many ways, than she normally does. This deep receptivity results in the profound outcome of a new human life. That result did not come from her efforts as much as it came from her surrendering and allowing. Yes, she still needed to do many things, such as eat well, rest, and take vitamins in order to have a healthy pregnancy. She was not passive, but at the heart of this great process was a stance of receptivity.

The next time you feel worn down by the overachiever in you, remember this example and see how you might do less and allow more.

♦ SELF-INQUIRY

In what ways could you practice "being" more in your life? List at least three ways and be specific.

BRILLIANCE PRINCIPLE #10
Embrace Not Knowing and Learn to Live in the Question

Brilliance Principle #10 asks that we let go of our need for surety so that we can open up to the potential that comes from not knowing. Perhaps you've heard the advice of Rainer Maria Rilke, from *Letters to a Young Poet*:

Be patient toward all that is unsolved in your heart and try to love the questions themselves... Do not seek the answers, which cannot be given to you now, because you would not be able to live them. And the point is, to live everything. Live the questions now. Perhaps then, someday far in the future, you will gradually, without noticing it, live your way into the answer.

Life's only certainty is uncertainty. What if instead of coloring the place of "I don't know" with panic, anxiety, shame, fear, or concern, we chose curiosity, excitement, enthusiasm, and awe? How would we experience uncertainty then—as our enemy or our ally? Interestingly, research has found that those willing to embrace ambiguity with a positive attitude are more likely to innovate thought and behavior and learn something new. When we admit we don't know, we begin to discover our own innocence again, and this allows our unexpressed brilliance to come forth.

This requires us to admit that we don't have nearly as much control over some things as we would like. I used to suffer a lot at the hands of my inner control freak. So, to short-circuit her powers and remind myself how ridiculous it was to assume that I had control over most of the things I stressed about, I gave my inner control freak a character. I pictured her as a ridiculous-looking cartoon superhero wearing a bright red cape and a spandex suit with a big letter "C" on her chest for "Control Girl." I pictured her flying over Manhattan, where I lived at the time, trying to control the subway system, the traffic lights, even the weather. It may seem a bit silly, but that was the whole point. Connecting to this image in my mind precisely when I felt the desire to control the unknown allowed me to reorient and remember the beauty of just admitting that I don't know everything. It was totally okay not to have the answers. It took a tremendous amount of pressure off me and allowed me to be more open to receive from others. It also reminded me to be open to learn from as yet unknown experiences. What a relief to just embrace the uncertainty instead of fighting it all the time.

♦ SELF-INQUIRY

When you're not in control of a situation or you don't have an answer to a problem, what are some of the things you could do to stay more curious?

BRILLIANCE PRINCIPLE #11
Be Willing to Value Truth over Comfort

Brilliance Principle #11 requires that you are willing to live your truth, even when doing so feels scary or uncomfortable. If you are on a quest to reveal your brilliance, then there's something you need to accept: you have to be willing to align your actions with your deeper truth even when you don't feel like it.

Prioritizing comfort at all costs will kill your brilliance. How many times have you found yourself staying in a certain situation not because it feels fulfilling, empowered, and aligned, but because it feels familiar and safe? A bad marriage? A dead-end job? The wrong apartment or living situation?

No need to make yourself feel bad about it. As humans, we have a natural tendency to seek comfort, and sometimes it's entirely appropriate to do so. However, if we always use comfort as our default, breaking out of unhelpful routines and patterns, even after we've long outgrown them, will be difficult.

Taking a stand for your truth can be scary. It might feel lonely. It might make you unpopular with your friends and loved ones who are used to seeing you behave in a certain way. You might disappoint others, and they might disappoint you. You might even make a mistake from time to time. There are no guarantees, and chances are you are going to feel a lot more vulnerable.

The upside is that you will be energetically engaged in the journey, learning and evolving as you move toward greater alignment with your brilliance. You will feel alive at every level! And remember, you don't have to do it all at once. The "comfort zone" is always there if you ever need to pop back in for a quick visit. But I invite you to experiment with no longer making it your permanent residence.

♦ SELF-INQUIRY

How comfortable are you with being uncomfortable? Are there certain areas of your life where you are more willing to tolerate being uncomfortable than others? Why?

BRILLIANCE PRINCIPLE #12
Deeply Commit to Regular and Deliberate Self-Inquiry

With Brilliance Principle #12, we commit to regularly reflect on our lives, our actions (or non-actions), and our motivations so that we can shine the light of awareness where we need to see. Suppose an Olympic athlete went into training with the attitude of being willing to practice only occasionally, when she felt like it or when she needed an extra boost. It seems ridiculous because it is! No athlete could get to the Olympics with sporadic commitment. Olympians bring their "A" game and steep themselves so thoroughly in their sport that it becomes almost second nature to them. Intimately aware of their strengths and vulnerabilities, they are devoted to the journey to its end. This willingness to go all in is what makes them champions.

It's very similar for a traveler on the path to brilliance. If you only commit to your self-inquiry practices when it's convenient or when you are in dire straits, the quality of your relationship to self will only go so deep. A casual practice of self-inquiry becomes about mere maintenance, not about thriving.

You have to get to know your own ego very well, including the unconscious parts of yourself that may sabotage you. (By the way, these are also frequently the parts of you that require the most acceptance and self-love in order to heal.) It's far easier to recognize those parts of yourself when anchored in a regular and deliberate practice of self-inquiry. It essentially teaches you how to align with your brilliance no matter what's happening externally. This alignment creates an extraordinary sense of integrity and freedom—a freedom from your past and from your limiting beliefs. Whatever type of self-inquiry practice you choose—prayer, meditation, journaling, yoga, and so on—committing to it wholeheartedly is essential in order to gain any real traction on your path to brilliance.

♦ SELF-INQUIRY

What does your self-inquiry practice currently look like? Is it consistent? Daily? Would you like to make changes to it so that it feels more intentional? If so, what?

BRILLIANCE PRINCIPLE #13
Seek Community That Supports Your Conscious Evolution

Brilliance Principle #13 highlights the value of having a community that supports our evolution. There's an African proverb, "If you want to go fast, go alone. If you want to go far, go together." The road to brilliance is not an express trip. It's a journey that lasts a lifetime, and seasoned travelers know they need trusting companions to support them along the way.

A community of support is about more than just company on the path. We are social creatures and always take cues from one another. Having a creative, social relational matrix amplifies our evolution. In other words, we really need to keep each other accountable. We need to challenge each other, inspire each other, and support each other's brilliance. There will be times on the path when you stumble, become confused, feel doubt, and need support. Having a community to fall back on during those times, one that understands where you are going, is crucial.

If you find yourself surrounded by individuals prone to living from their comfort zone or perpetuating a cynical or pathological (problem-based) view of the world, the path ahead can feel lonelier and much more daunting. Think carefully about whom you choose to surround yourself with, and ask yourself if this community feels like one that will bring out the best in you. If not, it may be time to seek new support.

If you don't have much in the way of a community around you and the thought of finding one feels entirely overwhelming, fear not. It may take a little time and patience, but now more than ever before in our history, a plethora of tools can connect us quickly to like-minded and supportive community members. For example, when I first moved to Los Angeles by myself, with no community to speak of, I relied heavily on meet-up groups, yoga classes, and networking events that I found listed on Facebook to quickly immerse myself in situations where I might find people I could connect with in a meaningful way. Of course, it took some time and courage (especially for my introverted self), and the activities I attended weren't always home runs, so to speak. But, ultimately, it paid off and then some. It was at one of these events that I met my husband and several of my closest friends.

List the five people you spend the most time with. Would these people support your brilliance even when you falter? If not, who might?

BRILLIANCE PRINCIPLE #14
Embrace Being a Force for Good in This World

Brilliance Principle #14 asks that you embody your innate ability to be a force for positive change. Your brilliance is already in tune with the larger collective. This part of you knows that your healing is inextricably linked to the healing of the whole. This part of you doesn't privatize your love, making it only available to those in your immediate circle. When you are in your brilliance, you understand that you truly have the power to be a force for good in this world, and you embrace this possibility completely.

I am not suggesting that to live in your brilliance you have to become an activist for some noteworthy social movement. You don't have to start a non-profit or become a spokesperson for a charitable cause. That may indeed be how some people's brilliance manifests, but it is possible that the way you contribute to the greater good is "quieter." It may not make headlines on the evening news, but when you get in touch with your brilliance, perhaps you start extending your compassion and love well past where you thought possible before. Or maybe you open yourself to new levels of vulnerability that allow your children or youth from the next generation to see a fine example of someone owning their brilliance.

I can't tell you what brilliance will look like in you. I can tell you, though, that when you uncover it inside, you discover your ability to advance the evolution of the collective consciousness in big and small ways. You feel compelled to serve and spread the infectious vibe of brilliance to even more as you celebrate this part of you.

One of my favorite quotes that expresses the sentiment of this principle beautifully is attributed to George Bernard Shaw:

I am of the opinion that my life belongs to the whole community, and as long as I live it is my privilege to do for it whatever I can.

I want to be thoroughly used up when I die, for the harder I work the more I live. I rejoice in life for its own sake. Life is no "brief candle" for me. It is a sort of splendid torch which I have got hold of for the moment, and I want to make it burn as brightly as possible before handing it on to future generations.

How could you become a deliberate force for good in this world? How could you love even more? How can you serve others? What would that look like?

Putting It All Together

Congratulations! You just finished a major component in your journey to brilliance. My hope is that with your new awareness of the brilliance principles and the insights you uncovered in your self-inquiry exercises, your road ahead is going to be a lot more smooth. Granted, you'll need to revisit these new discoveries from time to time to remind yourself of what you need to do to stay on the path. Each time you do, it will become more natural to integrate these lessons into your daily life. Let's keep going and see where our adventures take us next.

CHAPTER 3

The Most Important Tool to Bring on Your Journey

You've read through the guidebook to the Land of Brilliance and taken detailed self-inquiry notes on what to watch out for on your adventures. Now it's time to pack your bags. But what should you bring with you on the journey of a lifetime? The most important tool to pack is your inner compass.

Your Inner Compass

Okay, let's imagine you've just landed at your destination, the Land of Brilliance. Woohoo! Excitement is high, and you're eager to get off the plane and get started on your adventure. But first, you've got to pick up your luggage.

Suppose for a moment that as you go to the baggage claim, you not only pick up your own luggage, but you also grab several other people's bags too. Maybe your mother was on the plane with you, and you take hers. Or maybe you're towing the luggage of your colleague, your best friend, and your long-lost lover. Now, imagine lugging all that with you wherever you go on your journey. Sounds cumbersome, yes?

There's a reason why, when you go on a trip, you don't pick up everyone's luggage at the airport. You need only your own, and even then, sometimes you pack too much. Similarly, you also don't need anyone else's mental or emotional "baggage," but for some reason, many of us have a nasty habit of taking it anyway. Heck, some of us even end up being an out-and-out Sherpa for our families or communities. Sigh.

There's another way to travel. With your inner compass, you can direct your journey and be driven by a vision that comes through you, for you, without being clouded or confused by the views of others. Let's take a closer look at what I mean.

Your inner compass is your personal GPS—an internal navigating system to guide you on the path ahead. More specifically, your inner compass is a clear, direct understanding of your core values. How would your life look if you 1) knew very clearly what your values were; and 2) were authentically living your life in accordance with those values?

As humans, we crave meaning in our lives. We're hardwired to want opportunities for personal growth and to realize our potential. Fulfilling this desire in us is called self-actualization. If you've done the work to determine your core values and have clearly defined your inner compass, it becomes much easier to navigate the path toward self-actualization and to create a life with a deep sense of purpose.

Your core values are the backbone of your vision for your best life. When the things that you do and the way that you behave reflect your values, you are aligning your external life with your inner brilliance. In my coaching practice, I frequently see clients have epiphanies about certain life decisions after getting crystal clear about their values. Distinctly defining and affirming our values is sometimes just the thing we need to do to have the confidence, courage, and faith to take those scary leaps in life. Whether it's to leave a dead-end job, to say a full, committed yes to the next level of a relationship, or to finally take the risk of pursuing your long-held "someday" dreams, with your inner compass in hand, things that once seemed impossible might start to seem inevitable. Aligning with your values can be that powerful.

On the other hand, when you are unclear about your values or fail to align your actions with them, things just feel wrong and inauthentic. And because things feel off, you may start seeking guidance elsewhere or looking for directives from others about the "right" thing to do or be. You also become more susceptible to picking up other people's baggage, which takes you even further off track. To prevent this, you need to do another deep dive in self-inquiry, this time to claim your inner compass.

It's time to break out your journal again and get ready for more exploration with this multistep exercise.

Step 1: Review the list of common personal values included with this inquiry. Put a check mark next to any values that resonate with you. If other values that feel important to you pop into your mind but aren't listed, write them down too. This list is by no means exhaustive!

Step 2: Of the values you choose, in your journal list in clusters those that seem similar and combine them into one main value. For example, you might cluster "adventurousness," "exploration," and "truth-seeking" into one new, main value you call "curiosity." Narrow your list down to no more than five top values that are the most important for you, the ones you want to live by.

Step 3: Once you've chosen your top values, complete the sentences below for each value.

One of my top values is _____.
I know I am living in alignment with this value when _____.
(*Psst*...think about what happens, how you behave, and how you feel when you are in alignment with this value.)

You don't want your values to just be "buzz words" or clichés. You want to really know what they look and feel like when you activate them. That's why Step 3 is so important. Here's an example of how one might flesh out these sentences:

One of my top values is *family.*
I know I am living in alignment with this value when *I take at least four weeks of vacation each year and spend time with my extended family in different parts of the country. Also, I prioritize having dinner around the kitchen table with my husband and daughter, every night, no matter what my work schedule is like. When I am living in alignment with this value, I feel loved, nurtured, and supported because I am connecting to the people who matter the most to me.*

Take your time with this exercise, as it will be central to your commitment to your brilliance. Have fun and good luck!

VALUES

Accountability	Curiosity	Fluency
Accuracy	Decisiveness	Focus
Achievement	Dependability	Freedom
Adventurousness	Determination	Fun
Altruism	Devoutness	Generosity
Ambition	Diligence	Goodness
Assertiveness	Discipline	Grace
Balance	Discretion	Growth
Being the best	Diversity	Happiness
Belonging	Dynamism	Hard Work
Boldness	Economy	Health
Calmness	Effectiveness	Helping Society
Carefulness	Efficiency	Holiness
Challenge	Egalitarian	Honesty
Cheerfulness	Elegance	Honor
Clear-mindedness	Empathy	Humility
Commitment	Enjoyment	Improvement
Community	Enthusiasm	Independence
Compassion	Equality	Ingenuity
Competitiveness	Excellence	Inner Harmony
Consistency	Excitement	Inquisitiveness
Contentment	Expertise	Insightfulness
Continuous	Exploration	Intellectual Status
Contribution	Expressiveness	Intelligence
Control	Fairness	Intuition
Cooperation	Faith	Joy
Correctness	Family	Justice
Courtesy	Fidelity	Leadership
Creativity	Fitness	Legacy

Love	Resourcefulness	Structure
Loyalty	Restraint	Success
Making a difference	Results-oriented	Support
Mastery	Rigor	Teamwork
Merit	Security	Temperance
Obedience	Self-actualization	Thankfulness
Openness	Self-control	Thoroughness
Order	Self-reliance	Thoughtfulness
Originality	Selflessness	Timeliness
Patriotism	Sensitivity	Tolerance
Piety	Serenity	Traditionalism
Positivity	Service	Trustworthiness
Practicality	Shrewdness	Truth-seeking
Preparedness	Simplicity	Understanding
Professionalism	Soundness	Uniqueness
Prudence	Spontaneity	Unity
Quality-orientation	Stability	Usefulness
Reliability	Strategic	Vision
Religiousness	Strength	Vitality

Using Your Inner Compass to Live Authentically

You've discovered your inner compass. Congratulations! Nothing will help you lead a more brilliant life than that. Now the work is to embody these values so they inform your actions, words, and thoughts. When you do this, you start to live authentically. To truly live an authentic life and embody your values, you need to understand what I call "The Four A's of Authenticity."

The Four A's of Authenticity	Main Affirmation
Awareness	I am present in this moment.
Alignment	I know what I believe in, and I align with those values.
Action	I act from my inner compass and bring my truth to the world.
Allow	I allow myself to be changed by the journey and continue to embrace my personal evolution.

If you have trouble activating any of the Four A's of Authenticity, it's going to be difficult to embody your values and live from your inner compass. Let's take a look at each component to understand its role in maintaining authenticity and learn how we can connect with that part more fully, even if we are feeling stuck.

COMPONENT 1: Awareness

Every journey must first start with awareness, and awareness requires presence. You need to be willing to show up, stay curious, and make yourself available to the present moment. If we're not present, it's going to be very hard for us to assess whether we are aligning with our values. Connecting with awareness also opens the door for us to choose an orientation toward brilliance in any given moment, so that we can actualize our potential in the here and now.

For example, I've taught group yoga classes for years, and very early on in my teaching career, I developed the habit of taking a moment of silence for myself before each class begins. During that moment, I intentionally connect to my higher self, that place of brilliance within, so that I can let it flow through me and guide the class through a meaningful experience. In that moment, I am no longer a yoga teacher trying to perform for or impress anyone. Instead, I become a vehicle for some larger wisdom to flow through me. I become present, aware, and open to the possibility of something wonderful happening in the class.

Taking a simple pause of intention before you begin an activity can be a profound ritual that allows you to more deeply connect to your authenticity. It can be as simple as closing your eyes, drawing a deep breath, and saying the affirmation, "I am present in this moment." If you're having trouble connecting with your awareness, try a more active phrasing in the form of a question: "Am I fully here and present to the potential for brilliance in this moment?"

COMPONENT 2: Alignment

After becoming present and aware, if you want to be authentic, your next job is to determine the quality with which you are showing up. Are you in alignment with your values? If not, what might be getting in the way, or how might you need to shift things so that you can line things up more closely? The affirmation for this component of authenticity is "I know what I believe in, and I align with those values." With it, you calibrate your inner compass and set the course to orient in the direction of your authenticity. When you have trouble activating this component of authenticity, you can ask yourself this: In this situation, which values of mine would I like to align with?

By slowing down what's happening in your head, you can consciously choose which of your values you want to activate and express. This seems obvious enough, but so many of us don't take the time to do it. Imagine how your day-to-day interactions with others might change if you did. How would this affect the quality of your relationships and the way you show up in them?

One of my clients, Cassandra, had such a busy life as a single mother of two with a high-powered job in the entertainment industry that she often lost sight of her intentions and ended up in reaction mode while tackling her never-ending to-do list. Her reactions were beginning to influence the quality of her relationship with her children. So, I encouraged her to start every day with a small adjustment. Every morning as she reviewed her to-do list, she was to also make a "to-be" list in which she would note the values she wanted to align with that day, no matter what she was doing. For instance, she might have a to-be list that reminded her that no matter what was happening, she wanted to act from a place of compassion, kindness, and enthusiasm—three of her core values.

This simple ritual became a stronghold for her and allowed her a sense of calm and centeredness even on the busiest of days. As a result, she was able to be more present with her children, and their relationships improved. They even started doing the ritual together every morning! If it's easy for you to get swept up in the details and lose sight of your values, this might be a good tactic for you as well.

COMPONENT 3: Action

The third "A" of authenticity is action. The affirmation here is "I act from my inner compass and bring my truth to the world." We don't live in a vacuum. It's wonderful to be aware and to internally align with our values, but for authenticity to really take root, the way we *act* in the world must reflect what we truly believe. Otherwise, we're not really owning our truth fully. Perhaps we behave in ways that we think will please people, or maybe we hide parts of ourselves that we are afraid others won't approve of. We might take on certain roles because they feel familiar and comfortable, not because they feel true to us. These are just a few of the ways we compromise our authenticity and, therefore, our brilliance.

It can be quite scary to act from our true values, especially if we haven't been in the habit of doing it consistently. But it can also feel very freeing, releasing you from the limitations of the old story you have about yourself. This is where values get expressed in tangible form, where we can start to make a positive impact on others and the world around us.

If you feel clear on your values but often have trouble performing actions that accurately reflect them, you may benefit from asking yourself, "How would I act in this situation if I were acting from [insert value]?" or "What's one tangible action I could take in this situation to reflect [insert value] accurately?"

Most of us want to act according to our values, but sometimes we get caught up in the momentum of things. Take, for example, the schedule of an ethical investment adviser who came to me for coaching. Joe wanted to break the habit of chronically overscheduling his work life, which he did so often that he couldn't attend to his relationship with himself or his partner or family. Though he intended to be a good spouse and parent, he was absent more than he wanted to be. I'm sure many of us can relate to this. We can end up falling short of what we intend, in many different ways. It happens. Try not to beat yourself up when it does. Consider using the questions above as a way to slow down and discover when and how things get off track for you. That way, you can activate a different decision next time.

COMPONENT 4: Allow

The final "A" of authenticity is to allow. The affirmation here is "I allow myself to be changed by the journey and continue to embrace my personal evolution." Here, we aim not only to expect evolution on the journey to brilliance but also to welcome it. Otherwise, we can end up in a pattern of resistance, cutting off possibilities for our growth.

One thing is certain in life, and that is change. Circumstances will change, and you will change. Your core values as a teenager were probably different than they are now. Or you may think you have a strong grasp on your core values, only to find that, when you start living by them, it doesn't feel the way you anticipated it would. To be skillful at empowering yourself, you need to be clear on who you are and what you want, and you need to be prepared for the journey itself to change you.

If you find yourself resisting change or clinging to old beliefs or ways of being, you may benefit from asking yourself, Are there places in my life where my values don't "fit" me anymore? Do I need to upgrade my inner compass?

If we are truly honoring our authenticity, it's likely we will come upon a time when we need to upgrade our values. This happens frequently during big transitions in life. For instance, when I met Gwendolyn, she was a beyond burnt-out executive who by society's standards had achieved the height of success already, even though she was only in her mid-thirties. She wasn't sure what she wanted next for herself, but she knew something needed to change.

When she first did the inner compass self-inquiry exercise, she identified her core values as hard work, integrity, service, loyalty, and community. True to those values, she consistently put others first and expressed loyalty to a fault by working with certain clients, even when doing so started to put a strain on her energy. Inadvertently, her values had guided her to a pattern of neglecting her self-care and repeatedly treating herself as an afterthought. She had become overly serious about her life, depressed, and disconnected from her true passions.

Upon reassessing her values, she decided to upgrade and replace "loyalty" with "self-compassion," and "hard work" with "balance." She also added a value of "lightness." These upgrades in her values paved the way for her to start anew. She ended up leaving that job and successfully pursuing a long-held dream of being a professional artist. Anything is possible when we are willing to seriously commit to our own authenticity.

My hope is that you will use the affirmations and questions I've introduced to tune into the Four A's of Authenticity. They will help make living by your inner compass a reality. To support you in practicing these at home, I've created quick reference sheets on the Four A's of Authenticity. Please print them out and put them up where you'll see them frequently. You can access them in your *Brilliance Workbook*.

Charting Your Course
. . . .

With inner compass in hand, you are ready to chart your course—but where do you want to go? It's time to create your vision for brilliance!

A powerful, clear, and compelling vision will keep you motivated on the path, and it will support you in making the most aligned decisions to bring your dreams to fruition. Learning how to craft your vision for brilliance is an essential part of your journey. Without it, you may fall prey to the influences of a culture prone to focus on problems, not vision.

Have you ever noticed how often we are taught by parents, teachers, religions, cultures, and societal messages to look at what doesn't work in our lives? We contemplate disease, bad economics, emotional wounds, mental blocks, and shortcomings in our mental and physical bodies, and so on. Sometimes, it feels like we "fit in" better if we embrace this dominant way of thinking in our culture. The world of our problems may not be glorious, but we're accustomed to it, and so many of us stay there out of habit, never bothering to venture out to see what other alternatives exist.

Clearly, there is value in knowing our obstacles, challenges, and problems. But the journey to brilliance doesn't stop there. To truly empower ourselves, we need to learn how to identify our biggest hopes and boldest visions and gain the skills to bring them into reality. With a visionary approach to life, the strength of your dreams motivates you, rather than the pain of your wounds. You may still be challenged on the road ahead, but you have the power of a clear and intentional vision to move you from obstacles to outcomes.

Creating Your Vision
. . . .

A powerful vision expands your context, opens your mind, and helps you step into the unknown. It emboldens you to take risks as you continue with your self-awareness and self-discovery. We are most willing to release old beliefs, emotional pain, and other baggage when we can see what we want to replace them with. The clearer the vision, the more we will be attracted to it and the less we will need to hold on to self-limiting beliefs. Before you do the exercise of crafting your vision for brilliance, there are some important things to keep in mind.

Focus on What You Want to Create, Not on How to Create It

As adults, when we get creative and imaginative, it's all too easy to criticize, analyze, and judge. When visioning, you may be tempted to quickly make yourself wrong, thinking, "I can't do that," "Who am I to think that's possible?" or "It'll never work." These thoughts and others like them will most certainly suck the life out of any vision. The role of the vision is to awaken what's possible in you. It's designed to stimulate the dreaming self. Let it have free rein. We have many more chapters in this book, and you'll learn a lot more about mastering the "how to" of actualizing your vision. But right now, press pause on the analytic mind, the judging one, and the inner critic. Just let yourself enjoy the freedom of an uncensored creative self.

Get Specific

Do you want vague results? Then create a vague vision. But I don't recommend that! Powerful visionaries aren't afraid to be specific. Though you may not know all the details of what you want out of life, it's important to challenge yourself to get as clear as you can be. Let's take a few examples of specificity in a vision:

- **Vision 1:** I want lots of money.
- **Vision 2:** I want $100,000 in savings by the end of next year.

- **Vision 1:** I want to feel good in my body.
- **Vision 2:** I want to be able to run the NYC marathon next year.

Which visions feel more real? More compelling?

Include Yourself in Your Vision

Metaphors and images can be fantastic components of a vision, but you don't want to leave out the most important ingredient—*you*! Make sure you have the starring role in this new reality.

Choose Words and Images That Light You Up

This is your vision for brilliance, after all. Add some spice. You want your vision to speak to your heart. You want to be so attracted to it that you can't help but think about it all the time, reaffirming it with each thought. For example, instead of the word "happy," could you use "ecstatic," "overjoyed," or "blissful"? What about using strong, magnetic images or metaphors that really capture the "wow" factor for you? This vision is for you. No one else has to see it or know about it. Make it as colorful and creative as you like. Let your imagination have fun.

Be Logical, Too

As much as you want to create an inspirational vision that speaks to your heart and soul, you'll get more buy-in from yourself if it also appeals to your intellect. Are there places where a literal description of something specific might give you a big *yes* around your vision? Then add it in! In certain areas of your life, you may have more direction and be ready for a literal vision. For example, you may know exactly how much money you would love to make this year, and so you can include that number in your vision. Or maybe you just need to work on thinking of your world as more peaceful and so use a beautiful image of a sunset in nature to depict this feeling. Trust your gut to decide what type of description makes the best sense for you.

Construct Your Vision Based on Your Core Values

The work you did on your core values will now set the tone for your vision. It's time for your imagination to take it to the next level, creating a picture of what your life will look like when you are living in alignment with those values. Feel free to refer back to your core values for reference, but also let yourself play and see what comes up.

Allow yourself approximately forty-five minutes to do this exercise. You will need your journal and a writing utensil. For more dimension, you may enjoy doing this exercise with colored pencils. Find a comfortable seat in a quiet space where you will not be disturbed. Turn off your phone and turn on some soft, inspirational music. Perhaps light a candle or make a cup of tea. Treat this exercise as a ritual, an act of reverence for your highest self. Start by taking several deep breaths to help you sink into a relaxed state. When your mind feels quiet, begin reading through the questions below.

This vision is broken up into eight sections. After you read each question, take a few moments to close your eyes so that you can firmly connect with your imagination and answer the questions from there. When you have received your answer, gently open your eyes and record it in your journal. Feel free to draw, write, or both. If you would prefer an audio guide to lead you through this visualization, you can access a complimentary mp3 version of this exercise, "Visioning Your Brilliant Life," on my website.

1. Imagine it is five years from now, and you are living your most brilliant life possible. It's no longer just a dream. It's a reality, and you are living it. Take a deep breath and picture this.

See yourself in the morning, just waking up to your day in this brilliant life you've created. It's another glorious morning, and you've just awakened in the comfort of your bed in the home of your dreams. This bed and this home are so beautiful and completely ideal for you. You can't help but thrive in this kind of home.

Take a few moments to describe this home now. What style is it? Where is it located? What does it look like? What furniture is it filled with? What colors do you see? What smells do you smell? What images, words, feelings, and sensations come to you as you think of this amazing home? Close your eyes to connect with this image for a moment, and when you feel ready, begin to write or draw any insights in your journal.

2. Take another deep breath and see yourself once again in your home of your dreams. You've eaten breakfast and are all ready to begin your day, but first you take one last look in the mirror. You catch your own gaze, and you are filled with an unstoppable confidence. Every cell in your body feels wonderful!

What do you see in the mirror? How does your body look? How does it feel? What are you wearing? Take a few moments to close your eyes and connect to this experience. When you are ready, jot down or draw the images, words, feelings, and sensations that come to you as you confidently look at your brilliant self in the mirror.

3. Once again, take a deep breath and call forth your visionary self. Start to feel the fantastic energy of your future life come alive once more. This time, imagine yourself at your computer screen, casually looking over your last bank statement. You look carefully at your balances in your checking and savings accounts. And there, staring back at you on the screen, are the exact numbers you hoped for.

See those numbers clearly now. They make you feel relaxed, safe, and entirely comfortable in your abundance. You are thriving financially and are excited about the possibilities this abundance affords you. You feel free of any financial woes and are filled with gratitude for the abundance in your life. As you look at those numbers, what other sensations, feelings, images, thoughts, and ideas emerge? Jot down or draw your insights in your journal.

4. With another deep breath, see yourself in your future life in the midst of your day. Everything is truly brilliant. What is it that you are doing? How are you occupying your time? Do you have a certain career? Are you doing something different than you are now? What values and gifts are you expressing? Who and what are you surrounded with? How are people acknowledging you for what you do? How do these activities make you feel? How do you handle any challenges that come up during your day? Is your schedule full or is there room for spontaneity in your day? Write down or draw any words, thoughts, sensations, feelings, or ideas that arise as you think of how you spend your days in your most brilliant life.

5. This time as you take a deep breath, you see yourself in your future life opening a letter telling you that you've just won an award acknowledging you for the extraordinary ways you've been bringing your brilliance to the world and helping others. What are you winning an award for? What ways are you bringing your brilliance out to the larger whole? How does your brilliance affect others? How does it make them feel? How does it make you feel? Describe or draw anything at all that comes up for you as you contemplate how your brilliance is unfolding in your future life.

6. Take a moment to connect to your imagination yet again. This time, see yourself in your future life toward the end of the day. You are enjoying a dinner with the people you love the most. Who is with you? Describe your relationship with these individuals. How do they make you feel? How do you make them feel? What bonds exist between you? What activities do you like to do together? Do you travel to places with these individuals? Where do you go? Write down or draw anything that comes up in terms of phrases, thoughts, sensations, feelings, or ideas as you think of the people you surround yourself with in your brilliant life.

7. One last time, take a deep breath. You are still in your future life, five years from now, and it is the end of your most brilliant day. You are taking a little time to connect with *yourself* and celebrate another wonderful day. What are you doing? How are you taking care of yourself? How are you connecting to your spirit and your intuition? Are there certain practices or rituals you use to stay connected to your truth? How does this special day end in your future brilliant life? Describe or draw any thoughts, sensations, images, feelings, or words that come up when you think about the relationship you have with yourself in your future brilliant life.

8. Now, before you come out of this visualization, add anything you need to round out and make your vision for your most brilliant life totally complete.

Working with Your Vision

Congratulations! You created your first vision for your brilliant life. Take a few minutes to really absorb the power of what you just created. With a few deep breaths, close your eyes and see if you can access how that vision feels in your body. Imagine it is true right now. How does your brilliance feel? Bring this reality into your being—into your mind and heart. Let every cell download it like a new software program for your consciousness to run. Drink it in! Say *yes* to the possibility of this vision becoming a reality.

It's possible that after this exercise you will feel quite excited, expanded, and connected to another realm of your being. It may have confirmed some things you already knew about your brilliance, or maybe it opened you up to a whole new world of possibility. You may feel you have a clear idea about how to proceed with creating this vision starting tomorrow, or you may feel you need more clarity about what to do next. Whatever you're feeling, it's all good!

This is just your first umbrella vision, your overarching view, of your brilliant life. Over the following chapters, you'll be looking again and again at your vision for specific areas of your life. You will be able to work off this umbrella vision and break it down into bite-sized visions that you can refine to see progress toward your dreams. In the meantime, here are a few tips on how to keep working with this vision you just created.

TIP 1: Make a Vision Board

Use your answers from the "Visioning Your Brilliant Life" exercise to make a powerful vision board. Vision boards are a tangible reminder and further affirmation of your dream and are an excellent way for you to connect to the potency of your vision on a daily basis. Place your vision board somewhere in your home where you can look at it every day, connecting with it consciously and deliberately, helping you keep the passion alive. Vision boards are entirely personal. You may choose to draw your board, or you may use magazines from which to cut out images and words that build upon what you've uncovered in this exercise. Or, if you're digitally inclined, you may choose to use Pinterest as your digital vision board that you look at on your computer every day.

TIP 2: Purposefully, Frequently Connect with Your Vision

Remember that when you connect with your vision, you don't just want to look at your answers or your vision board. You want to *feel* your vision. After you've reviewed your vision, take several deep breaths and close your eyes. Let the reality of the vision drop into your cells. Notice how they feel. Are they tingling with excitement? What other sensations arise in your body as you visualize your dreams as reality? Try to hold the feeling of your vision for at least thirty seconds. This is a very important step in the visioning process. The longer and more frequently you hold a feeling in the body, the sooner new neuro-pathways can start to establish themselves in your brain to support that feeling. These neuro-pathways support new positive thought patterns and help make your vision a reality. The more you affirm the new feeling pattern, the less of a grip the old feeling patterns will have on you. If you practice feeling the vision regularly, your reality will start to shift more quickly to align with that vision.

TIP 3: Treat Your Vision as Sacred

Treat your vision as sacred and consider keeping it for your eyes only. In the yoga tradition, there's an old story that teachers used to pass on to students to demonstrate the importance of this. Imagine that you are a new tree seedling planted in a pasture of cows. With no barrier around you, the cows will most certainly trample on you, and you will not be able to grow into all your glory. Now, let's suppose we place a fence around you in those early stages of your growth so that you are protected from harm. Years later, you will become a fully grown, magnificent tree. In fact, you will be so large that all the cows that once were a threat to you will now rest in your shade. It's a very similar experience as you tend to the growth of your vision. In the early stages of tending to your dreams, you can be particularly vulnerable. It's important to provide yourself with the boundaries you need to protect yourself from other people's cynicism, projections, or negativity. This is your time to connect with you and your dreams, not with other people's opinions of your dreams! You don't have to share your vision with anyone. But if you want to, choose thoughtfully about whom you let into your inner circle. Keeping good company in this way can really make a difference.

TIP 4: Let Your Vision Evolve

Remember that your vision is ever-evolving. Frequently, the road to brilliance is a less than direct path, to put it mildly! There are many turns and creative cul-de-sacs along the way. One of my mentors, Gail Straub, used to refer to this as the "beautiful mess" of life. We each have our own beautiful mess to navigate, and it requires patience and compassion toward the self. Imagine that you are tending to a garden in your backyard. Would you scold your seedlings and demand that they be better? Would you deprive them of the water and nourishment that they need to keep growing and expect them to grow anyway? I hope not. But, for some reason, this is often what we do to ourselves when we are tending to the seeds of our dreams. Choose to be kind to yourself, and you will set the foundation for a smoother, happier ride. It won't be a linear path, but you *will* get there.

What's Next?

With a clear, overarching vision now articulated, you are on your way to brilliant living. But, even with an amazing vision established, you will still encounter obstacles on the path. That's to be expected with an organic process of growth. Remember our beautiful mess?

How do we handle those obstacles? Or, if we're going to be brilliant about it, how do we leverage those obstacles and turn them into opportunities? That's what our next chapter is about. So, let's keep going.

CHAPTER 4

Turning Obstacles into Opportunities

Even with the best intentions, a masterfully tuned inner compass, and a deeply inspiring vision, there can still be obstacles on the path. If you are truly engaged in your conscious evolution, you will be challenging yourself with new ways of being and thinking that will often brush you up against obstacles as you push forward to new growth.

In this chapter, we take a look at our internal obstacles, specifically our limiting beliefs. Metaphorically, you can think of limiting beliefs as the things you pack in your "baggage" that make it a lot more difficult for you to get where you want to go. To understand what I mean by limiting beliefs, let's take a closer look at another foundational concept first—core beliefs.

Core Beliefs
. . . .

A core belief is one that seems so basic to the way you relate to the world that you never stop to question the validity of it. You assume it to be true and live in a way that reflects that belief.

Many of our core beliefs become established in childhood, well before we are aware of what is happening. Children don't have the same sophisticated mental filters to distinguish between helpful and unhelpful beliefs that adults do. Therefore, whether you like it or not, a lot of the core beliefs you developed in childhood are heavily influenced by your culture, religion, parents, family, friends, and community. Sometimes we don't even know what our core beliefs are! They act like sneaky stowaways in our baggage.

Unfortunately, many of these stowaways are unconscious beliefs, and they're not helpful. Thoughts like "I'm not good enough" or "I can't trust anybody" can be imprinted in your consciousness at such a young age that you don't think to question them. Like an old vinyl record with a scratch, these beliefs will just play on "repeat" in your head well into your adult life, causing all sorts of challenges for you.

Your core beliefs literally shape your worldview. They directly affect your behavior, the way you think about yourself, and how you show up in the world. They even influence what you think is possible for you when you root into your potential for your brilliance. Essentially, if I can't believe in the possibility of my brilliance coming forth in my life, the chances that I'll succeed at manifesting it are nil.

Creating Our Reality
. . . .

I have to establish a belief on the inside first if I wish to manifest something new in my life on the outside. Sounds easy, right? Just create a new belief, and then your life will change! Unfortunately, a lot of popular new-age offerings have perpetuated this oversimplified view, making it seem as if all we have to do is think a new belief hard enough and long enough and our life will change.

As I've already mentioned in the introduction to this book, it's a lot more complex than that. We have a lot of institutional systems, societies, and cultures in place that don't always support an equal playing field to make it possible for everyone to manifest their desires. And we are products of these societies and cultures, so we too might be perpetuating and internalizing the negative beliefs or unsupportive realities existing in these systems on an unconscious level.

Yikes! So, what are we to do? If we can't change societies and systems overnight, and we are often unconscious of some of the negative beliefs that we hold, then how can we get any traction to change our reality?

Whenever I think about this particular conundrum, I slow it down a bit in my mind. Otherwise, it's all too tempting to settle into overwhelm, stay cynical and skeptical, and do nothing. But, when I pause, I remind myself of something Howard Zinn said: "You can't be neutral on a moving train." In other words, life is going to move forward nonetheless, whether or not I take an active role in trying to create a better reality for myself and others.

Knowing this, I choose to stay intentional, aware, authentic, and engaged in my journey to brilliance even with no guarantees, rather than be complicit in keeping things the way they are.

It's important to remember that you are a co-creator of the universe, part of the whole. You matter, and you can *and do* change the world with your beliefs, words, and actions. You may not always see how your choices affect others, but rest assured, you are having an impact.

Although the path to brilliance is not as straightforward as "you create what you believe," this does not negate the fact that indeed we are powerful beings, and what we choose to believe is entirely relevant to pursuing our brilliance. Even more importantly, what we believe is something that is totally within our ability to change. With a little conviction, faith, and courage, we can see the challenges in our lives as opportunities for our creativity to emerge. Our tensions can become drivers for our own evolution toward a higher self. And as for those unconscious beliefs, those stowaways in your baggage? They too can be uncovered and transformed into opportunities for intentional, purposeful action. Let's take a closer look at how we can do that.

Choose Beliefs That Support Your Brilliance

In this section, I outline a helpful six-step process for clearing a limiting belief pattern and replacing it with a new vision. It is one of many tools in this book to help you upgrade your inner talk so that you can choose your beliefs consciously to support your brilliance.

Please understand that although I've described this technique in a series of linear steps, in truth, this process is much more organic than that. When clearing your limiting beliefs, you exercise creative, non-linear thinking. You step into the realm of possibility, staying curious and being willing to try out new thought patterns that open you to the promise of your brilliance.

In my coaching practice, I often tell my clients that, in addition to packing their inner compass for the trip, they also need to pack an open mind and heart. If we want our lives to be different than they are now, we have to be willing to act, think, and believe differently than we do now. For many, this is a process of trial and error, and it requires a lot of courage, patience, and self-compassion.

If you commit yourself fully to this process, you will get tripped up on old beliefs that you thought you had already uprooted. Don't worry. You are not doing anything wrong if that happens. Some beliefs are just more stubborn than others, and these setbacks are part of the natural clearing process. You might have to repeat this process a few times before the new belief pattern sticks.

Throughout these steps, I provide an example from my coaching practice of how this might work in your life. After you've read through this section in its entirety, you'll have an opportunity to do your own test drive of this technique with another self-inquiry exercise. But for now, just take this in. As you read through this example, let it start to soften your mind and heart so you become open to the possibilities of brilliance that lie ahead. Let's start the process now with Step 1.

STEP 1: Identify Your Limiting Belief

We must start with awareness. This seems like an obvious statement, but there are so many times when we are really not aware of what we believe in. To uproot a limiting belief, we must first be able to clearly articulate it and see it for the obstacle that it is. So, how do we recognize a limiting belief when it arises?

Though each limiting belief is unique, what all limiting beliefs have in common is that when you think about them, you don't feel good. Are you feeling scared, ashamed, anxious, depressed, or hopeless? Make note of what you're thinking in those moments, because those thoughts will often represent your limiting beliefs.

Take, for example, the situation Jessica found herself in. She had recently graduated college and had gotten a highly respected and sought-after job in technology. At first, she was excited about this possibility. It paid well, and it would also look excellent on her resume. Everyone was complimenting her on her great success at landing a job at a hot new start-up. Though Jessica wasn't particularly passionate about her tech job, she had a sizable amount of student debt, and staying at this job felt like the responsible and logical thing to do. But, as time went on, Jessica was increasingly bored with her responsibilities and overwhelmed with deadlines and stress. So, she sought out my support as a coach.

As Jessica talked about her job with me, we discovered that Jessica felt trapped and depressed. When I asked why, we uncovered her limiting belief right away: I have to choose either a job I'm passionate about or a career where I make a lot of money. I can't have both. By simply following the trail of her negative feelings, we uncovered a story about financial abundance and career passion not being possible at the same time. As long as she held this belief, Jessica had only two options: stay in a well-paying job that she didn't feel passionate about or pursue her passion and make no money. Neither felt like a viable option to her.

Limiting beliefs often do this. They create a situation of "either/or" thinking. There is no room for creativity. Also, when you think a limiting belief, your body will often respond with physical sensations that reflect the negativity of that thought. You might frown, furrow your brow, or feel a pit in your stomach. You might experience feeling your body freeze, or you may even have a bad taste in your mouth. These sensations can be clear indicators that you're operating with a limiting belief. Once you've identified it, you're ready to move on to Step 2.

STEP 2: Connect to Choice

Once you are aware of your limiting belief, your next step is to connect to choice. Stay open and curious, and remind yourself that this belief is not happening to you. It is something arising from your internal thought process, and you can change it. By connecting to choice, you put the power to change the experience of your reality back in your hands.

To activate choice, first feel into your limiting belief. Once you have a clear experience in your mind and body of the limiting belief, repeat this:

> I created or adopted this belief, and it no longer serves me. At any time, I can choose to create or adopt a new belief, a far better one to replace this one. Am I ready to do that now?

When you receive a resounding and authentic "yes" to that question, you have connected to choice. This seems simple, but it's not always. Connecting to choice means we have to give up our stories of victimhood or blame and shame. It means we also have to look at the ways we may have been perpetuating a negative belief and sabotaging ourselves. It means being vulnerable as we step into the unknown. If we connect to choice, we might make a mistake, and that can be scary.

In Jessica's case, connecting to choice meant she'd have to be honest with herself and her family. Jessica was scared to tell her parents how miserable she felt at work because they had worked so hard to send her to a good school so that she could get a well-paying job just like this one. She didn't want to disappoint them. She also felt scared about taking the risk of pursuing another career. After all, she wasn't entirely certain what that other career would be, and she still wanted to make enough money to be financially responsible. She just knew she wanted to be working with people and helping them instead of sitting in front of a computer all day.

By taking this step of connecting to choice, we show up with intention. In essence, we are pledging to take responsibility for the belief we want to create, even if it means we have to get uncomfortable and start acting and thinking in ways that don't feel totally natural to us yet. This is a crucial step to take in order to make transformation possible.

STEP 3: Expand the Context around the Limiting Belief

As I noted in Step 1, limiting beliefs can feel definitive and unchangeable, very black and white. They often elicit the feeling, "That's just the way it is." Because of this, it's imperative that we expand the context around limiting beliefs in order for us to make room for new possibilities to enter our consciousness.

The goal of this step is to break through the resistance of the old mental landscape so that we can carve out a path to a new reality. It's like clearing the weeds from a garden. Before we can plant a new seed thought, we must clear the mental weeds and be sure to pull them out at the root so they don't come back. If we skip this step and try to jump right to creating a vision or an affirmation for a new possibility, our mental weeds are likely to sabotage the whole process.

So, how do you expand the context around a limiting belief? When you notice a limiting belief in your mind, press pause and upgrade your negative self-talk on the spot by replacing it with an *empowering declaration*. Empowering declarations are very effective tools to use in clearing your mental weeds. They free up the imagination and create space for creativity by moving away from either/or thinking. They inspire a sense of ownership and responsibility in you and build upon your current strengths, resources, skills, and talents. They also help you focus your positive thoughts on yourself, instead of distracting you with things or people you can't control. And, most importantly, empowering declarations acknowledge where you are at and speak to what's possible for you right now, instead of postponing a feeling of empowerment to some future date. Let's take a closer look at what I mean.

When Jessica uncovered her limiting belief, "I can't make a good living doing something I am passionate about," I wanted her to step back from that belief for a moment and see what else might be possible, if she changed her self-talk about this situation. To stimulate a new inner dialogue, I gave her a sentence to complete with a new thought:

Even though I feel scared that I can't make a living doing something I love, I am an intelligent, creative, and resourceful person, and I know that...

After taking a few minutes to free-write her response in her journal, here's how Jessica finished the sentence:

Even though I feel scared that I can't make a living doing something I love, I am an intelligent, creative, and resourceful person, and I know that I could reach out to others who have figured out how to make money doing something they love to see if they can help me in my quest. They may have some ideas about where to start searching for other options. I may not have all the answers yet, but I know starting to look for other possibilities will make me feel better than just staying in my job now and not doing anything.

Notice how Jessica's empowering declaration acknowledges the reality of her fear in the first part of the sentence, but *also* presents her with the positive reality of asking for help in the latter part. What she did is move herself from "either/or" thinking to "both/and" thinking. She freed up her imagination with this change, and she created a stepping stone to get to a new vision. Her empowering declaration didn't need to be super concise or polished. It took the form of stream-of-consciousness thinking, and that's appropriate since its goal was to upgrade her self-talk and connect her to her strengths and possibilities.

When I checked in with her about how this empowering declaration made her feel, she said she felt a lot more relaxed. She felt she could even breathe easier, as if there was somehow more space in her body now. Though she was still scared, she felt some of her power come back by focusing on a concrete step she could take next. She also felt relief because she didn't have to quit her job or decide about it right away.

That would have been inauthentic to where she was currently at in her process. But she was also happy to start exploring options. Doing nothing would have felt like she was checking out and not honoring the truth of where she was at.

The empowering declaration helped her access a sense of possibility that wasn't present in her original belief, and it helped her identify her next best step in moving toward her brilliance. Empowerment trainers David Gershon and Gail Straub call this next step toward brilliance the "growing edge"—the point at which our personal evolution is currently most activated. Like a bud primed to blossom on a flowering plant, the growing edge marks that place within us where our greatest potential for possibility lies. It can feel quite vulnerable and maybe even challenging to live on our growing edge, but it is also the place where we are most energetically engaged in our personal growth process. Now on her growing edge, Jessica was ready to start crafting a vision for what she really wanted.

STEP 4: Create a New Possibility

With the context expanded around the original limiting belief, your mind can now open up to create a new possibility. In other words, you've done your mental weeding, and there is now space in the garden of your mind to plant whatever new seed thoughts you like. When you create a new possibility, you can anchor it into your body and mind by developing an affirmation and a visualization that support the new reality you'd like to create.

When creating an affirmation and a visualization, it's important to focus on the belief you want to create, not just the external vision you want to manifest. Let's take Jessica's situation, for example. As she started to ask for help from others who had discovered ways to make a living doing what they love, Jessica became increasingly aware of how hard it was for her to trust that this could also be possible for her. She knew that if she wanted to create the job of her dreams, she'd first have to be willing to work on her trust.

Knowing this, I asked her, "When you think about the new belief you'd like to create, how do you want it to make you feel?" She told me she wanted to feel relaxed, hopeful, and secure. She wanted to bravely explore new job options without the stress around potentially losing money. She wanted to trust in her intuition to guide her through this process. It also became clear that she didn't want to feel rushed into making any decisions. She needed to acknowledge that she was on a journey of self-exploration, and she wanted to give herself permission to enjoy that process.

With these insights, Jessica and I began to craft an affirmation that she could use to encourage a new seed thought to take root in her mind. After some wordsmithing, we came up with this:

I am in a process of finding the career of my dreams. I stay relaxed and let my intuition guide the way. With every step, my trust in the process grows deeper.

You'll notice how the affirmation focuses on Jessica and what's under her control. It does not depend on someone or something else changing, like a boss or the job market. She also keeps it in the present tense and in the positive. She's careful not to talk about this new belief as if it will happen someday. It's very much a belief about the present. It also honors her current growing edge. She's not talking about quitting her job tomorrow, or even affirming that she's more certain than she feels right now. Those assertions would feel over her edge. Her edge right now is more about affirming her trust in herself and the process. So, that is what we homed in on for her affirmation.

With Jessica's affirmation determined, we turned our attention next toward creating a visualization that would evoke feeling and create emotional investment for Jessica in her new belief. I asked Jessica, "What will it look like when you are really feeling and living this belief fully and are inspired by it?" She closed her eyes for a moment before sharing that she saw an image of herself smiling, surrounded by mentors who were enthusiastically offering ideas about potential job opportunities. She smiled as she described this vision, and I saw her body relax. Jessica was fully invested in her new belief with her body and mind, and if she committed to using this affirmation and visualization daily, she would start to see this new belief transform her reality.

When you work with your own affirmation and visualization, it's important to remember that these tools support you only if you connect with them intentionally and regularly. Practice not only saying and thinking your affirmation and visualization daily, but practice *feeling* them too. To merely think the new belief is not enough. Your body must also say a solid *yes* to this new energy. One good way to get the body to hold the potential of this new belief is to practice saying your affirmation out loud and then close your eyes for three long, deep breaths. As you breathe, picture your new visualization in your mind and imagine the new belief literally downloading into your cells. How does it feel to hold this new belief as if it were a reality right now?

Perhaps even commit your body to a certain posture that supports the type of energy you want this new belief to represent. When you hold the feeling of the new affirmation and visualization in your body for three deep breaths, you give your nervous system an opportunity to carve out the new neuropathways that you need to sustain this belief over the long term. Skip this step, and you may find yourself tripping up on old patterns that your body is still unconsciously holding.

STEP 5: Support Your Vision with Action

Once you've done the inner work of upgrading your self-talk and creating a new possibility, you are primed to take your new vision to the next level by supporting it with external action steps.

For Jessica, taking baby steps toward her vision of a more passionately fulfilling job would make her dream feel more real to her. It would also start lining up her actions with what she truly wanted to create for herself. So I asked her, "What next best step or steps can you take to support this new vision and belief?"

Jessica's action plan was two-fold. Her practical side wanted to set up some meetings with specific mentors to ask them questions about potential jobs in other industries of interest. So, we set a deadline for when to complete this. Mindful of the fact that she still had some work to do around her resistance to trust, however, Jessica also decided to journal about her feelings around trust. We agreed to explore the discoveries journaling would yield in a future coaching session. Both deliverables proved important for Jessica to stay fully invested in her process and moving toward her desired reality.

Every time you create a concrete action step, such as Jessica's plans to meet mentors and to journal, you are saying yes to your brilliance. As you complete more and more actions, the momentum builds, and so does your confidence. Along the way, the actions you take give you further opportunity to refine your vision and be aware of where any other limiting beliefs may be coming up on the path. With regular commitment, soon your vision becomes the new reality.

STEP 6: Sustain Your Motivation

As I mentioned at the beginning of this section, clearing a limiting belief and creating a new one is far from a linear process. More often than not, it can feel like taking two steps forward and one back. Or, as you forge ahead toward a new belief, you may uncover other unexpected limiting beliefs and need to take a left turn altogether into a different territory. Inevitably, there will be times where motivation can falter, even after you've created a new possibility and initiated actions steps.

So, in the final component of this process, we recognize that we are human and may encounter struggles from time to time, and we proactively create some strategies to help us get back on track if the old belief pattern kicks in again.

I asked Jessica what might help her feel motivated to get back on track, if she felt the overwhelm of her old belief arise again. After some discussion, we arrived at a few strategies that felt helpful to her. When her old belief was triggered, she would take a deep breath and put her hand over her heart while she closed her eyes. Then she would connect to an empowering declaration in her mind to break her negative thought pattern.

If that didn't work, she thought it would be useful to connect to a mental image of a particular role model she had, recalling the journey that a friend had taken to start a very successful career after leaving a job she disliked. Jessica would think of this role model and ask herself, "In this moment, what might Meaghan do?" This gave her the courage to connect once again to her new belief and stay on track.

Finally, she thought it might be helpful to create a vision board that captured the essence of her new vision. She'd keep a picture of this vision board on her phone so she could pull it up whenever she needed to feel motivated. She also made the image of this vision board her new computer screensaver. These strategies might seem simple or even trivial at first, but it's this level of detail that can make or break your ability to successfully turn obstacles into opportunities and to up-level your belief system.

Now that we've reviewed the steps in this process, it's your turn to give this technique a test drive. Take out your journal and a pen, and let's get started.

♦ SELF-INQUIRY EXERCISE: Upgrading Your Beliefs to Optimize Your Brilliance

As you jump into this exercise, please remember to be compassionate and patient with yourself. Learning to uproot long-held limiting beliefs takes time. This will not happen overnight, but you have the tools and the know-how in place to make progress. It's likely this process will feel a bit awkward at first. If you would like more support or more examples of how to work on each of the six steps, refer to the exercise "Upgrading Your Beliefs to Optimize Your Brilliance" in the workbook for additional complimentary resources.

STEP 1: Identify your limiting belief. Think of an area of life in which you are feeling stuck. Take a moment and zero in on a particular limiting belief you have in this area. Write down your limiting belief.

STEP 2: Connect to choice. Before you do the inner work on transforming this belief, take a moment to connect to choice. Repeat this:

I created or adopted this belief, and it no longer serves me. At any time, I can choose to create or adopt a new belief, a far better one to replace this one. Am I ready to do that now?

If you get an authentic "yes," you're ready to go to the next step. If not, you may not be ready to work on this belief, and you should go back to Step 1 and select another limiting belief.

STEP 3: Expand the context around the limiting belief. Create an empowering declaration around this belief by using the following sentence stem:

Even though (A), I am a (B) person, and I know that (C).

- In part A, state a challenge you experience related to this belief.
- In part B, list your relevant strengths that are important to connect to as you work on this belief.
- In part C, state a positive, new reality that you can also connect to as you move toward your vision.

STEP 4: Create a new possibility. Carefully review your limiting belief and your empowering declaration. Now, think about the new belief you'd like to create.

- Write down how you would like this new belief to make you feel.
- Note what it will look like when you feel and live your new belief fully. What's the vision you see?
- From these notes, create a specific affirmation and visualization that

address the root belief you are aiming to change. Choose an affirmation and visualization that are truly on your growing edge.

STEP 5: Support your vision with action. List three specific actions you can take to advance this new vision forward. Be sure to put deadlines on these deliverables.

STEP 6: Sustain your motivation. In your journal, answer the following question: If your old belief pattern kicks in again, what small thing could you do to motivate yourself and get back on track? Identify three specific strategies.

You did it! Great job! This foundational exercise offers a key way to overcome limiting beliefs. We'll now move into the seven brilliance centers that govern various aspects of brilliance in our lives, but we will return to this exercise in each center to deepen the journey inward to brilliance.

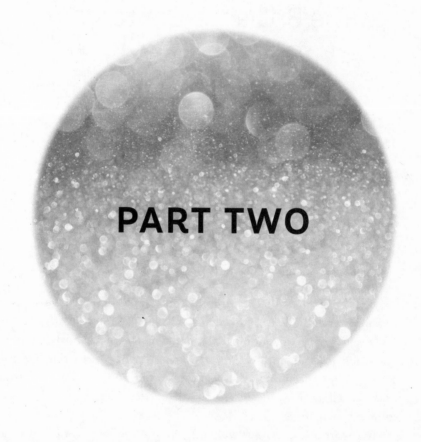

PART TWO

CHAPTER 5

The Brilliance Center of Consciousness

*When you touch the celestial in your heart, you will realize
that the beauty of your soul is so pure, so vast and
so devastating that you have no option but to merge with it.
You have no option but to feel the rhythm of the universe in
the rhythm of your heart. —Amit Ray, Meditation*

Having completed the first part of your journey, you know how to set powerful intentions that can inform your expectations. You've learned the principles for skillful travel in the Land of Brilliance. You've clearly defined your core values to claim your inner compass and crafted a captivating overarching vision for your future. And you know how to turn your internal obstacles into opportunities so that you can start creating the life you really want for yourself. In the work ahead, you will practice using these tools, skills, and mindsets many times over.

The next part of the journey will take you into the specific areas of your life, through the lens of what I call brilliance centers, to further refine the vision you have already created.

The Brilliance Centers

Within you lies not just one form of brilliance, but many! In fact, you have seven different vortexes of brilliance in your being that are associated with specific aspects of your personal power. These different vortexes, which are aligned with the chakra system from the yoga tradition, are plexuses of life-force energy. Each brilliance center is not only governed by particular themes related to your experiences, but is also part of your subtle (energetic) body. As a result, how you function in each area of brilliance influences the way your energy circulates and is experienced throughout your entire being. Please note that when I say energy, that can include physical, mental, emotional, and spiritual energy.

Each brilliance center reflects an aspect of your consciousness that is essential to your empowerment. The centers also hold detailed information (in the form of energetic imprints) about the underlying core beliefs and behavioral patterns that affect and shape your life. Learn more about these centers and you will be much more effective at embodying the various forms of your brilliance. As a whole, the system provides a profound formula for integration, connecting you in body, mind, and spirit so that you can orient yourself from a place of wholeness and interact with the world from there. To begin the journey through these brilliance centers, in this chapter, we will look at the Brilliance Center of Consciousness, which is associated with the crown chakra in yoga.

Understanding the Brilliance Center of Consciousness

The crown, or the seventh chakra, to which this brilliance center relates, is also called the *sahasrara* chakra. In English, *sahasrara* translates as "thousand-petaled lotus," and it's often symbolically depicted as a lotus flower blossoming from the crown of one's head and dripping the sweet nectar of consciousness into one's being. This is a beautiful image that accurately captures the role of this brilliance center in our energetic system: *to connect us to the universal or divine knowing within ourselves.* This brilliance center is literally the seat of our consciousness.

In the Brilliance Center of Consciousness, we reach understanding and reveal the deeper meaning of our lives. This center gives us the ultimate context. It's the place in us that sees the world as if from the perspective of the creator. If we had to choose one action statement that sums up the power of this brilliance center, it would be

I know.

The Brilliance Center of Consciousness holds the wisdom of the body, mind, and spirit combined into one. In many traditions, this energy center is deemed to be the seat of enlightenment. (For the purposes of our journey, when I speak of enlightenment, I mean the progressive understanding of greater wholeness.)

When the brilliance in this center is activated, you still have emotions, but you are no longer emotional. You still have thoughts, but you are no longer just the thinker. You are still an individual, but you are no longer limited and bound solely by the body or the mind. You understand that there is something larger than all of that. You connect with the universal identity.

There have been a few times in my life that clearly reflect when this brilliance center was fully activated for me. One was during the birth of my daughter. After ninety-six hours of labor and being wheeled into the operating room for an unexpected emergency cesarean, my stress level was through the roof and my exhaustion complete. But the moment I heard my baby cry for the first time, it was almost as if I had left my body and was watching everything happening in the room from above. All the emotions, the exhaustion, and even the noises present in the room just stopped, except for the sound of my daughter's voice. I was in complete awe at the miracle of life that I had just witnessed happening through me. It was a divine moment, and I felt completely connected to the whole of the cosmos in that one instant. Perhaps you too have had an experience where the mundane fell away and you felt completely connected, even for an instant, to a much bigger reality that we're all part of.

The Witness: Accessing the Brilliance of Universal Consciousness

At this level of consciousness, we encounter the "Witness," the ultimate observer. Though we can't see, measure, or isolate it, we know that the Witness exists. In his book *A New Earth*, Eckhart Tolle describes the Witness as "conscious connection with universal intelligence. Another word for it is presence, or consciousness without thought." It is a place that is beyond thought, emotion, and judgment. It is totally detached from outcomes. It is the eternal guide.

In terms of our journey to brilliance, this center is crucial for giving us a larger perspective to inform our individual lives. When you are activated at this brilliance center and take the seat of the Witness, you understand that you are not separate from the universe. You are an intricate part of it, and so *you are* it. Since that statement can feel a bit abstract, I find it's helpful to use a few metaphors to describe the incredible potency of the Witness and to exemplify why it's such an important part of our empowerment journey.

Pie, Anyone?

You can gauge how a whole pie must taste from a bite of one slice, yes? In the same way, even though you appear to be this individual unit, separate from other beings around you, you are really a small piece of something larger. And it so follows that just like the piece of pie contains the same ingredients that make up the whole, so, too, do you contain the same energy as the rest of the universe. You are the universal energy, just expressed in your own unique way. You are a small piece of the divine!

An Ocean of Consciousness

If each of us were represented as different waves in the ocean, we would understand ourselves as very distinct individuals. We would, quite literally, have our own ups and downs to deal with throughout the course of our existence. We would experience ourselves as separate, but still we would be inherently linked to one another. That's because each wave is also really the ocean.

You cannot have waves without the ocean, and you cannot have the ocean without the waves. Even as a wave crashes and ceases to exist, the water molecules and energy that compose that wave don't cease to exist. They just enter back into the whole, only to appear again in the form of another wave. You are at once simultaneously the wave and the entire ocean. As the Indian mystic poet Kabir said, "All know that the drop merges into the ocean, but few know that the ocean merges into one drop."

Taking the Perspective of the Witness

We sometimes get the experience of the Witness in little tastes when we have a profound moment of transcendence. In these moments, we feel deeply connected to all that's around us, but remarkably totally detached at the same time. There are so many ways we can experience awe and transcendence, and these are necessary experiences to have on our path to brilliance. They allow us to access the wonderment of life, however brief it may be, and help us to distance ourselves from the grip of human dramas and the chatter of our egos.

It is difficult to describe a moment of transcendence—it is an experience beyond the capacity of words. Many have experienced transcendence while witnessing moments of birth or death, but it can also be experienced in less extreme situations. For example, basking in a quiet moment in nature, dancing to powerful music, being in the zone while playing a sport, or making love sensually to your partner can all lead to transcendence. Deep states of meditation can also lead to transcendence and an experience of the Witness.

Why would taking the perspective of the Witness be a useful strategy on our journey to brilliance? Let's go back to our ocean metaphor to find out. Imagine for a second that waves in the oceans had feelings, and imagine they tended to compare themselves with other waves. Maybe they would start to feel bad about themselves when their wave-self was at a low point or they didn't look or feel as robust as the next wave. Now, suppose that wave thought it was only a wave and not the ocean. Its mood, and perhaps even its sense of self-worth, would be at the mercy of whatever its current state of existence was. If it was at a high point, then the wave would feel happy and confident. If the wave was at a low point, then it might feel distraught, hopeless, and depressed. Since the wave would not understand that it also was the ocean, it would suffer a lot in its lifetime. It would constantly be in a cycle of ups and downs, and it would feel quite isolated. And it certainly wouldn't know the brilliance of its true nature—its ocean self.

Perhaps this is a goofy metaphor, but I think it gets the point across. Learning to take the seat of the Witness (the ocean self in our example) is a critical skill to have when seeking an empowered life. With Witness consciousness, we understand that we are more than our thoughts, we are more than our bodies, and we are more than the emotion of the moment. We are able to detach from the suffering that can come from solely identifying with our ego or our individualistic understanding of self. This is a very powerful knowledge to have!

The good news is we all have the capacity to experience life from the seat of the Witness. Though, as with most things on this journey, we have to choose to activate this ability within ourselves. Let's take a closer look now at what happens when we do choose to optimize our brilliance at this level.

Optimization at the Brilliance Center of Consciousness
. . . .

When we are optimized at the Brilliance Center of Consciousness, several possibilities exist for us. Here are a few of the more common ones.

POSSIBILITY 1: You Know How Your Spirit Informs Your Life

For the purposes of this journey, "spirituality" is how you make sense of your connection to the whole. No matter your religious affiliations or personal beliefs, when you feel you have clear guidance on how to align with your higher truth, the path to your brilliance is unobstructed. When you understand that you are connected to the whole, you also know that when you work to heal your own consciousness, you are also healing the consciousness of the whole. Knowing that can be deeply meaningful and provide you with a profound sense of purpose in life.

When you connect to the universal consciousness within, you often have a much better understanding of what "being a force for good in this world" looks like for you. In other words, you have more clarity about what in the yoga tradition is called your "dharma"—your sacred duty on this earth.

If that last sentence just caused you to feel instant overwhelm, thinking, "I don't know what my purpose is," fear not. It's easy to get lost in the idea that we need some big, epic vision of how we are going to change the world. I invite you to keep in mind something Mother Teresa believed: rather than doing great things, we should do small things with great love. Your sacred purpose on this earth can take many forms, big and small. Even the big things only result from doing a lot of little things. So, try not to get caught up in a "size matters" game.

Your dharma may coincide with your profession, but it could also be linked to how you choose to show up in your personal relationships. Your dharma could be to be the most loving parent possible, or it might be to be an incredible, innovative architect that revolutionizes low-income housing facilities. Your sacred purpose might even be to develop a more compassionate and loving relationship with yourself so that you can be a role model for others. The ways in which your dharma can unfold are endless. And by the way, it's very likely that the understanding of your dharma will continue to evolve throughout your lifetime.

I remember receiving a powerful lesson about dharma when I traveled to New Orleans after Hurricane Katrina. At the time, I was co-leading and organizing a yoga and service trip to support and work alongside individuals affected by the storm. On one particular day, our volunteer group was invited into the temporary housing trailer of a hurricane victim, Bonnie. Bonnie had lost her job, her home, all her belongings, and even one of her family members in the storm. She took great pride in her family, her home, and her career as an elementary school teacher. She was living her dharma before the storm happened and feeling quite aligned with her brilliance.

It would be totally understandable for Bonnie to go into a place of collapse, depression, or devastation after taking so many blows. But when we walked into her trailer, we found out that Bonnie, a woman who had no physical possessions left to her name, had prepared and laid out a full lunch for our group of twelve on her small table. On the wall of her new temporary home, a lone picture was hanging. It was a needlepoint work she had recently completed, and it had just one word on it: "Simplicity."

Bonnie talked to our group about how losing everything she identified her sense of purpose with was a profound lesson for her in what the meaning of her life really was. She explained that after the storm, she'd found out that her ultimate dharma was to serve. Whether that service happened through her role as a mother, a home provider, or a teacher mattered not nearly as much as she thought it did. She just knew that as long as she was able to use her life for service, she would be in alignment with her truth. And in that spirit, she invited us to sit at her small table and feast on her delicious meal.

As Bonnie's story illustrates, when you are optimized at this level of brilliance and are in an ongoing process of living your dharma, the journey denies you nothing. It celebrates your everything, even the dark underbelly of life, the parts you would rather avoid. The opportunities for healing here are unlimited.

POSSIBILITY 2: You Find the Spiritual in the Mundane

If we associate our Brilliance Center of Consciousness only with those things that feel or look spiritual according to cultural norms, we miss out on the true essence of this brilliance center. Our ability to feel connected to the whole and find spiritual meaning in our lives is not limited by what we do or experience. Optimization at this brilliance center is available to us in every moment.

What if you could see your most annoying tasks during your day as acts of devotion to your higher self? A financial mentor of mine once suggested that when I could pay my bills with as much enthusiasm in my heart as I had when

I deposited a paycheck into my account, then I would have made some progress on letting my spirituality penetrate my day-to-day living. Opportunities to connect with the larger meaning of life are always there. We may just have to orient differently than we are used to in order to feel them.

POSSIBILITY 3: You See All as Divine

Another benefit of activating this brilliance center is that it opens your eyes to seeing everything as divine. Why would this be helpful on your journey to brilliance? Let's revisit our metaphor of the wave and the ocean. If I act from a place of knowing that I am truly the ocean (I am part of the divine), then this knowledge can be motivation for me to be the best wave I can be. I can move from a place of love, acceptance, and connectedness, and this allows me to be a powerful unifying force of peace and healing in the world.

I am no longer afraid of whether I am a "good enough" wave because I know at my essence I am actually the ocean. I no longer feel the need to compete with other waves because I understand that I have my own unique gifts to bring to the whole. As long as I stay connected to the ocean energy running through me, I constantly strive for my own personal best in this wave-life. I am less likely to get derailed by the lows—or attached to the highs—that this life offers me. I have the power to be a unifying force in this world, if I choose to recognize it.

Let's extend this idea even further. If I see myself as the ocean (the divine), then can't I also choose to see all the other waves as the ocean too? Yes, I can! When I choose to see the divine in others, I expand my capacity for compassion and empathy exponentially. Suddenly, there is room for their faults, and I no longer have to judge them or take their shortcomings personally. When we relate to others from our "divine self" and choose to see their "divine self," amazing shifts and connection happen.

This practice of seeing the divine was brought to life with a simple strategy shared with me by a fellow yoga teacher. She suggested that, when in an argument with someone or feeling challenged, while extending compassion toward the other, I could look in their eyes and seeing the wounded child version of them staring back at me. In other words, I could choose to see that they too are just an imperfect wave, like me, trying to remember their ocean self. And if I can remember that in a heated moment, then I am a lot less likely to be reactive. Ironically, by remembering we are all divine, we make room for the humanity in one another too.

POSSIBILITY 4: You Surrender to a Higher Process

Another benefit of optimization at this brilliance center is having the ability to surrender to a higher process. Often the idea of surrendering is associated with a feeling of weakness or failure. On the contrary, when we surrender to a higher process, we remind ourselves that we are in a constant dance of co-creation with the universe. We are not passive in this lifetime, with things just happening to us. Nor are we the ones calling all the shots. We are truly in partnership with the universe in creating our reality, and the only thing we are really surrendering is *the illusion of control.*

I like to think of surrendering as "offering up" all the things I don't know what to do with to the part of me that is all-knowing. For me, this happens through prayer and meditation. I might ask the universe for guidance when I feel lost on the path. Or if I feel strong emotions around something, pleasant or unpleasant ones, I might "offer them up" to my higher self and ask for the clarity to see without the veil of my attachments or aversions. Surrendering takes many forms, and it doesn't happen all at once. It's a process, one that cultivates a healthy sense of humility and opens the door to you receiving more support from the universe than you previously thought possible.

I have witnessed countless examples of surrendering to a higher process in my coaching practice, but one that particularly stands out is the story of Justin. He experienced a major disruption in his life when a motorcycle accident left him bedridden for six months. Justin was an enthusiastic, highly active twenty-nine-year-old with big plans for international travel. He was in high demand as a freelance event producer, and he threw himself headlong into every project that came along. The accident changed all that. Overnight, it became impossible for him to perform his work, and he had to cancel plans to travel to Brazil for volunteer work and eco-adventures in the Amazon. Perhaps even more jarring for him was the fact that he had instantly become dependent on others for basic daily tasks like bathing and eating—quite a humbling experience.

If he didn't want to spend the next six months miserable, Justin had no choice but to surrender to a higher process. I encouraged him to double down on a fledgling meditation practice and see if he could dig deep to find the lessons that this experience was here to teach him. It wasn't easy, as you might suspect. There were a lot of feelings to process, but ultimately Justin was able to uncover some powerful insights by letting himself surrender any sense of control over his situation.

As a result, he realized how out of whack his life had become, with his intense work schedule and always-on-the-go attitude. His relationships with his family and friends and his girlfriend had been suffering, and he had started to feel increasingly isolated by his busy schedule. Getting injured forced him to look more closely at his priorities. Years later, Justin is now happily married to his former girlfriend and in a career that affords him a lot more time with his loved ones. He's still able to pursue his passion for travel, but now he does it with his wife and daughter. Looking back, Justin feels grateful for his accident because he knows it was that time of surrender that allowed him to open up to a deeper layer of brilliance within him.

POSSIBILITY 5: You Strike a Balance between Being and Doing
A final way in which the Brilliance Center of Consciousness can inform our lives is by helping us strike a healthy balance between being and doing. One of my teachers, Andrew Harvey, explains that within each of us there are two fires—the fire of the mystic and the fire of the activist.

The fire of the mystic is the part of you that has a sacred passion for the divine. This part just likes to "be." When this fire goes into overdrive, you can become addicted to transcendence and seek out peak experience after peak experience to "escape" from life. The fire of the activist, on the other hand, is the part of you that has a sacred passion for action. When this fire is out of balance, you can become addicted to "doing" because you believe it's the only thing that gives you meaning or a sense of self-worth. This is what happened to Justin. Always on the go, he neglected his inner life and personal relationships.

Clearly, we need both fires, and we need to know how to balance them. Interestingly, when they are balanced, Harvey calls this the fire of sacred activism—a place where we are able to surrender to divine guidance and use it to inspire radical actions in the world to fulfill our dharma. In other words, when we've awakened the fire of sacred activism, we have also ignited our brilliance.

Obstacles to the Brilliance Center of Consciousness

In this section, we'll look more closely at some of the obstacles that can arise at this level so we can learn to recognize when things are not optimized at this brilliance center.

OBSTACLE 1: Spiritual Bypassing

Spiritual bypassing is when a person uses their spiritual practices as a way of *escaping* their current reality. When I first started getting into yoga seriously, right after college, I fell into a trap of spiritual bypassing without even knowing it. At that time, I was suffering from depression caused by years of avoiding painful feelings from my past, and I didn't have the tools or the understanding to deal with my challenges appropriately.

When I discovered yoga, I quickly became obsessed with it. After years of depression, the "high" of yoga and the feel-good energy it gave me after a class or a deep meditation was addictive. As I dived more fully into my yoga practice, I'd still experience bouts of depression from time to time or feel the grief of my old wounds festering inside. But as soon as I'd notice any of those unpleasant feelings, I'd hop right on my mat and move, chant, or meditate my way out of the pain and discomfort. Conveniently, the more I devoted myself to my yoga practice, the more I could cleverly avoid really looking at or dealing with my uncomfortable feelings. It was a very sophisticated and socially acceptable way to stay in denial about how unhappy I really was.

Eventually, with the support of a good therapist, trusting friends, and a few wise yoga teachers, I was able to see the illusion I had created. My dedication to yoga was being masked as transcendence and spirituality, but it was effectively keeping me "frozen" in a state of arrested development. As long as I was using yoga to avoid life, I was missing the true intent of these practices—to bring about a deeper state of integration with the wholeness of my own humanity. In essence, my spiritual bypassing short-circuited my ability to activate my brilliance at this center. Unfortunately, as New Age techniques, wellness practices, and spiritual traditions like yoga become more mainstream, this phenomenon is becoming common in Western cultures.

OBSTACLE 2: Spiritual Materialism

Another way this brilliance center can be blocked is by spiritual materialism. Spiritual materialism is when we use our spirituality as a means for giving us an ego-boost by presenting ourselves as more realized or holier than others. We use our spirituality as a badge of pride, and it becomes co-opted by the desires of the ego. This is a significant self-deception that presents a big obstacle to brilliance. We may believe we are on our spiritual path, but we are strengthening egocentricity through our spiritual techniques. This can lead to attitudes of self-righteousness and narcissism and to rigid belief systems, and it can perpetuate a need to be right.

Sadly, there are abundant examples of spiritual materialism in the stories of "gurus" of various spiritual traditions falling from their pedestals in very public ways. Embezzlement charges, sex scandals, abusive relationships with students, and drug trafficking are examples of some of the abuses of power that have happened when a respected and well-known teacher falls prey to the temptation of spiritual materialism. The negative consequences can be significant and far-reaching.

OBSTACLE 3: Being Hyper-rational

Another way we obstruct ourselves at this brilliance center is by clinging to the hard-and-fast linear reality of rationalism at all costs. Often when people demonstrate this behavior, they have a significant fear of being out of control. They may also be uncomfortable with the "messiness" of emotions and want a more structured world dominated by rationality.

When you feel this way, you need to "see it to believe it." Having faith in something is difficult without solid, tangible proof. You cannot figure out what to do with the unknown, so you choose to deny its validity. Have you ever felt yourself in a state of hyper-rationalism? Did it feel empowering? Often, this way of thinking offers a temporary feeling of security, but over the long term, it can increase anxiety and fear of the unknown, shutting down brilliance indefinitely.

OBSTACLE 4: Being Cynical

To be sure, it's important for us to exercise discernment and show a healthy amount of skepticism as we evaluate new ideas. However, when a pattern of skepticism leads to a habitual state of jaded negativity, we enter the realm of cynicism. This can lead us to a perpetual state of distrust in others and the universe. It can cripple our ability to let go and leave us feeling isolated and powerless.

Sometimes people take a posture of cynicism as a form of protection. For example, Martha had experienced so much hurt in her relationships with men that over time she shut down altogether and unconsciously became cynical about all men. By the time I met her, she was a self-proclaimed "man-hater" and was afraid that if she didn't learn how to stop being so cynical, she was never going to find a partner. Martha and I worked together on finding alternative ways for her to tolerate her feelings of vulnerability around men, and we also worked on enhancing her current meditation and prayer practice to strengthen her connection to her "ocean self." With regular practice, she started to feel more comfortable releasing her armor of cynicism and began making herself more available to the possibility of brilliance in her love life.

Unleash Your Power at the Brilliance Center of Consciousness

....

I've discussed a fair bit about the Brilliance Center of Consciousness and the critical role it plays in your journey of empowerment. So that you can make use of the information you've gathered, let's now look at specific strategies you can use to unleash your power at this particular brilliance center and align more fully with your truth.

STRATEGY 1: Have a Daily Spiritual Practice

I cannot overstate the importance of regular and deliberate connection with your highest self. The more I practice orienting to my life from my higher self, the more I intuitively know the feeling and experience of this place inside me. After years of regular practice, I can access that space in an instant. One deep breath and the close of my eyes, and I can be there. This makes me less and less susceptible to being tossed around by daily dramas. Certainly, I still have my ups and downs, but underneath them is this ever-strengthening current of inner calm that permeates my being.

All of us are capable of nurturing and growing our connection to that space within, but it takes regular commitment to accomplish this. Choose a spiritual practice that feels true for you and commit. By the way, don't overcomplicate this. You don't have to do something for hours a day. Your spiritual practice might be five minutes of prayer and deep breathing in the morning. Start where you are at, and let it evolve organically. Make it your special time of the day, where the only goal is to connect with yourself and no one else.

STRATEGY 2: Approach Each Day with Reverence

In the yoga tradition, there's a saying, "Without reverence, there is no practice." Reverence is deep respect for the sacred in all things. When we orient to reverence, we are less likely to get hung up on the ego's judgments. We see more beauty. We embrace "imperfections" with ease, and we are less likely to "sweat the small stuff."

Simply put, treat every day as sacred, and open yourself up to the possibility of seeing the divine in all. For example, you might take time each day to appreciate your family and friends, literally breathing in a feeling of gratitude for them. Or perhaps you'll want to use a strategy of mine, which is making sure every room in your home has some living thing present in it at all times. It may just be a house plant in each room, something that reminds you to connect to the mystery and beauty of nature more readily throughout your day. Or consider creating daily morning and evening rituals where you set aside time to pray or just be in silence so that you can connect to your reverence consistently.

STRATEGY 3: Meditate

I could write a whole book on meditation—in fact, volumes of books. And many people already have! When I am public speaking or leading a workshop, I am often asked, "What is the one suggestion you would make for someone wanting to enhance his or her spiritual practice?" I always answer, "Start meditating." There are as many forms of meditation as there are people on this planet. The style you choose is less important than your willingness to commit to the process and to do it frequently and consistently.

Science is now beginning to "prove" what long-term meditators have known for years—that meditation can literally alter your brain chemistry and the way you see reality. There are even studies now linking regular meditation to anti-aging and the healing of one's DNA. The scope of this topic is beyond the reaches of this book. But, if you want to make a huge stride in the direction of your brilliance and you do not already have a daily meditation practice, I suggest you start one now.

STRATEGY 4: Spend Time in Nature

Mother Nature is the teacher of all teachers. She has the power to connect us to the mystery of life even in the most urban environments. Have you ever seen a spring flower take root in the crack of broken asphalt? Mother Nature is unstoppable and has an irrepressible yearning for life. She is constant inspiration, and she reminds us we are part of something larger than just our human experience. As John Muir so beautifully shares in Samuel Hall Young's book, *Alaska Days with John Muir*, "Keep close to nature's heart and break clear away once in a while. Climb a mountain or spend the week in the woods. Wash your spirit clean."

STRATEGY 5: Create a Daily "To-Be" List

You are already familiar with a "to-do" list. Why not complement it with a "to-be" list? Every day, at the top of your morning, you can get clear on your tasks for the day and also on your intentions. This is an excellent way to maintain an awareness of your two fires—the mystic and the activist—and become more proactive at keeping them in balance.

STRATEGY 6: Be of Service

Mahatma Gandhi is reported to have said, "The best way to find yourself is to lose yourself in the service of others." No truer words have ever been spoken. We are one another's teachers and mirrors. And we absolutely need one another's support in order to advance ourselves on our spiritual paths. You don't have to limit "being of service" to classic ideas of volunteerism, though those can be amazing and transformative. Being of service can happen in the most basic of actions: a smile to a stranger on the bus, paying for someone's coffee, or spending some extra time listening to your friend after she's had a hard day. Opportunities to serve, and therefore to connect, exist everywhere.

STRATEGY 7: Explore Different Spiritual Traditions

There are so many fascinating ways of connecting to the whole. What would it be like for you to explore some of the ways people do this? The goal is not to judge, compare, or analyze the different options. Rather, it is to create an opportunity to be in the seat of the seeker, a pilgrim on the path. It's likely you will encounter some ideas that resonate with you more than others, and that's great. Perhaps you'll decide to explore new communities in which people have an intention of supporting each other on the spiritual path. Practice your beginner's mind and expose yourself to new spiritual ideas with frequency. You never know what insights may arise for you.

STRATEGY 8: Create a Sacred "Altar" in Your Home

Do you have a space in your home, no matter how small it may be, where you can honor the sacred? It could be as small as a corner of a table just big enough for a candle or an incense burner. Or maybe it's an entire room in your house. Size doesn't matter, but when you create a space for you to intentionally honor the sacred in life, that place starts to hold potency. It acts as an anchor to connect you with your higher self. Many people use this space as their regular meditation spot.

STRATEGY 9: Practice "Namaste"

Perhaps you've heard of the word "namaste" (pronounced *nah-mah-stay*). In the yoga tradition, this word means, "the divine in me sees and honors the divine in you." Practicing "namaste" means seeing everyone, including ourselves, as divine. This is particularly powerful when we interact with people whom our ego finds challenging. When we can see everyone as divine, we are far less likely to be judgmental, critical, negative, and petty. We are more compassionate and more forgiving of our own and others' imperfections. Try it! Ask yourself, How would I act in this moment if I was seeing the divine in this person and in myself? How would our communication change?

STRATEGY 10: Practice Saying, "I Don't Know"

Ah, the power of these three small words, "I don't know." For many of us, they can be terrifying to utter. If we are attached to the illusion of control, we have probably spent much of our lives avoiding and denying what we don't know. But learning to use those three words when they're true is a powerful practice for connecting with brilliance at this center. And, pausing after saying them helps build up our tolerance for what the unknown feels like. Don't qualify it. Don't apologize. Don't backpedal. Just claim your "not knowing" and experience it.

For example, when I first moved across the country after ten years in New York City, I was in a state of disarray and didn't know what direction I was headed in life. All I knew was that I was completely burnt out and needed a break. The uncertainty of this reboot made a lot of my family and friends uncomfortable. They would lovingly ask me, "What are you going to do for a job? What are you going to do about money?" I sincerely didn't know at the time, and when I just started to own that reality instead of pushing it away, something shifted.

Saying "I don't know" gave me the permission to rest. Eventually, things became quiet enough internally that I could receive the guidance I needed from the universe about my next steps. Saying "I don't know" also gave me the space to start some emotional processing that I had been putting off for years. Now, I look back at that time of "not knowing" as one of the richest personal growth periods of my life.

♦ SELF-INQUIRY EXERCISE: Your Spirituality

We've covered a lot in this chapter! It's time to put this new information to use. Take out your journal and carve out about half an hour
to answer these questions related to your spirituality so that you can
increase your awareness about this area of your brilliance.

1. What is your current spiritual practice? Is it a daily practice? Does it
   support you the way you want it to? What, if any, changes would you
   make?

2. Where do you have trouble letting go of control or trusting the
   universe?

3. Describe an experience of transcendence that you have had in the
   past. Take a few minutes to write in detail about it and how it made
   you feel.

4. What do you know about your dharma, or your sacred purpose on
   this earth? What do you believe it to be?

♦ SELF-INQUIRY EXERCISE: Optimize Your Brilliance Center of Consciousness

As you jump into this exercise, please remember to be compassionate and patient with yourself. You are still learning how to use these
tools, and it takes some practice!

To upgrade your potential for brilliance at this center, it's time to
put what you've learned into practice:

1. Review the insights you gathered from this chapter and the self-inquiry
   questions you answered to identify a place in your life where you are
   experiencing an obstacle or holding onto a belief that blocks your
   Brilliance Center of Consciousness from full optimization. Specifically,
   try to identify a limiting belief in the area of spirituality.

2. Return to the self-inquiry exercise "Upgrading Your Beliefs to Optimize Your Brilliance" on page 62, in chapter 4. Follow Steps 2 to 6 for clearing a limiting belief pattern and replacing it with a new vision, applying these to the limiting belief you've identified at your Brilliance Center of Consciousness.

If you feel stuck with identifying a limiting belief or would like examples of common limiting beliefs in this area, refer to the exercise "Optimize Your Brilliance Center of Consciousness" in the workbook for additional support.

CHAPTER 6

The Brilliance Center of Perception

*[Let] the mind be enlarged...to the grandeur of the mysteries,
and not the mysteries contracted to the narrowness
of the mind. —Francis Bacon,* De Augmentis

As we continue on our journey, we now move from the Brilliance Center of Consciousness to the Brilliance Center of Perception. This is the command center of the mind, and it correlates to the sixth chakra in yoga's chakra system. This is the place from which all our thoughts arise and where all our beliefs first take root in this reality.

In the yoga tradition, this brilliance center is called the *ajna* chakra. *Ajna* translates as "to perceive and to command." This is a dynamic pairing. We all know we have the power to perceive. This is a power no one can take away from us. The most horrible things can happen in my life, but whether I will suffer has largely to do with how I choose to perceive the situation.

If taken a step further, what if I could perceive how I wanted things to be in my life? Does it then follow that I might be able to command my thoughts or my flow of energy to turn such perceptions into a reality? Yes, this is possible. Of course, this kind of leap from perception to commanding thoughts requires skill and practice, which is in the domain of the Brilliance Center of Perception.

This brilliance center is often referred to as the third eye, the eye that looks within. The action statement that encapsulates the power at this center is the declaration

I see.

The Brilliance Center of Perception relates to the functions of seeing both with your physical eyes and with your mind. This includes the development of intuition. This brilliance center gives us the ability to see inwardly and outwardly. Our physical eyes give us a way to internalize and make sense of the outer world. The inner third eye gives us a way to create a symbolic language that helps us articulate our inner experiences. Furthermore, because we can recall things that happened long ago and imagine the future, it stands to hold that consciousness at this brilliance center also transcends time and space.

This center of brilliance is a powerful place indeed. Many call it our "sixth sense." All of us have this sixth sense, but many of us are not familiar with using it in a conscious, active way. In this chapter, you will learn more about how to do that so you can use the powers of this brilliance center to create the reality you truly want.

Who's Driving Your Car in the Land of Brilliance?

On your journey through the Land of Brilliance, there are two main passengers in your car. One is your *ego*, and one is your *soul*. These words can have many different meanings for people. Let's clarify what they mean in relation to one's brilliance.

Your Ego
Your ego identifies with your roles—parent, teacher, engineer, husband, dog owner, and so on. The ego is concerned primarily with the domain of expectation and survival, and this is not inherently a bad thing. For example, you need to make sure you get fed. You need to have money to pay your bills. It's important you behave appropriately so that you don't break the law and get thrown in jail. You need your ego so that you can function in this physical world. The ego has desires and dislikes, and it loves to get attached to some things and avoid others. Sometimes, the ego can lead you astray, but it is nonetheless an essential part of who you are. Without it, you would just be a disembodied spirit.

Your Soul
This is your energetic essence, your true being revealed once you remove all the labels, roles, expectations, and social masks. Your soul is your link to the universal whole and the divine wisdom within you. The soul is not concerned

with the nitty gritty of expectations. It does not seek reward or stimulation. Its deepest yearning is to align you with your highest truth, even if your ego strongly resists it. The soul exists in the domain of being and is experienced through the activation of your intentions. Many describe their soul as the place from which their intuition, also known as their inner knowing, arises.

Both passengers, the ego and the soul, must be in the car if you are to find your way through the Land of Brilliance. But it is quite important to think about who you put behind the wheel. Let's look at a few examples to see how these two aspects of your being can inform your experience.

The Breakup

Let's assume you had a bad break up with your partner. When your ego is in the driver's seat, you feel absolutely crushed. You really wanted this relationship to work, and you bent over backwards to try to make that happen. You feel so tired of being alone. As long as your ego is driving the car, you perceive this situation and yourself as being absolute failures. You are heartbroken, and you think life sucks. You experience a lot of pain and suffering.

Now, let's put your soul in the driver's seat. Remember that, above all else, your soul yearns to align you with your highest truth. So, when it starts to drive the car, the context of the situation becomes a lot more expansive, and your perspective shifts. You discover a deep knowledge that, although you are in a lot of pain, you are going to survive. You start to think that breaking up with your partner might have been a good thing. You see the ways you abandoned yourself in the relationship because you were afraid to be alone. With this new insight, you begin to feel a little lighter and more hopeful about moving forward. You know that whatever relationship you choose next will be a much better fit for you.

Overlooked for a Promotion

Imagine you are a top-level executive at a prestigious institution. You've worked at this company for decades, and you are up for a big promotion. Much to your surprise, your boss decides to hire a candidate from outside the company, and you are not promoted.

With your ego at the wheel, you are devastated. You feel betrayed and confused. You cannot believe that you've been denied this promotion after so many years of loyalty to the company. However, thinking about it more, you realize that the hired candidate was indeed more qualified, and that reality makes you feel even worse about yourself. This feels like a big blow, and you spiral into a depression about your whole life. You start to wonder what the point of anything is anymore.

After the initial shock wears off, you decide to speak to your coach about the situation, and together you discover that your soul has a very different perspective. As you talk about it, the realization dawns on you that for a long time, you've tied your sense of self-worth to your work. It felt good to do this for a while, as long as you were the top performer and receiving accolades. But this recent upset has revealed how much you've been neglecting your inner life and even your relationships at home. You start to see that you've been feeling empty inside for a very long time. You just haven't noticed it until now because you've been so focused on work. The upset at work begins to look more like an opportunity to reconnect with who you really are and what you want for your life.

In these two scenarios, notice how vastly different the journey becomes with a different driver. It's important to note, however, that the soul is not always going to be the best choice behind the wheel. Here's another example to consider.

Flying Too High

Imagine you are a yoga teacher, and you absolutely love your job. Yoga is not only your passion, it's your soul's calling. You've found what you are meant to do on this planet, and you are feeling grateful and blessed. In the excitement of feeling so aligned with your dharma, you decide to put the soul behind the wheel, and then you accidentally forget about the needs of the other passenger on board, your ego. Whoops!

Though you are still flying high, over time you realize that your passion for your work has blinded you to some important realities. You've been sloppy with your boundaries and have taken on a lot of gigs for free. Now, you can't pay your bills, and you are rapidly increasing your credit card debt. Your physical body is feeling tired from the long work hours, and you are emotionally drained because you don't have enough time for yourself. The journey ahead starts to look overwhelming, and you feel lost, burnt out, and confused. How did things veer so far off course? You were following your dream, after all! Shouldn't it be going smoothly?

As you can see in these three examples, both your soul and your ego have the power to perceive, and both perspectives will be valuable to you. Which perspective you choose at any given moment will greatly influence your experience and your feeling of alignment with your brilliance. Learning how to recognize and negotiate when to listen to your ego and when to listen to your soul is a foundational skill to master in your empowerment process.

Finding the Voice of Your Soul

Most of us have a pretty good grasp on accessing the voice of our ego. We simply get in touch with our desires and our dislikes, and we are there. But what about the voice of your soul? How do you know when that part of you is speaking? Some might describe this voice, the voice of your soul, as your intuition.

In Webster's dictionary, intuition is defined as our capacity for direct knowledge, immediate insight without observation or reason. Intuition is rapid and effortless, whereas deliberate thinking is critical and analytic. For example, we've heard about how a mother's intuition kicks in to know when something is wrong with the health of her baby, even if others around her don't see it. There is a felt sense inside, perhaps in her gut, and she just knows to trust it. She doesn't have to analyze or critique this feeling. She automatically knows it to be true in the very core of her being, and she acts on it.

To understand how intuition fits into the big picture of our brilliance, we need to understand what the spiritual teacher Osho calls the three I's:

- Instinct
- Intellect
- Intuition

Let's first look at instinct. Your instinct is your body functioning spontaneously. It's responsible for automatic actions, such as the blinking of your eyes. It's a deeper and older force than intellect, and for the most part, it's a lot more dependable too. Unless your body is in a state of disrepair, it's extremely likely your eyes will keep blinking, your heart will keep beating, and your inner organs will keep working without you having to think about it. Instinct is not prejudiced. It's natural.

Your intellect, on the other hand, is not spontaneous. It functions with procedure and methodology. Its domain is the realm of knowledge, and its roots are in philosophy, beliefs, and ideologies—not experience. Evolutionarily speaking, intellect is a much more recent arrival to the scene. It is situational and prejudiced, and it creates your interpretation of the truth—your reality, which could be vastly different from another's.

Finally, your intuition is your soul functioning spontaneously. It is a subtler, higher vibration than intellect. It comes from the full consciousness of your being. It doesn't need to grow. It is already fully intact—but your conscious connection to it can grow.

What does this have to do with your brilliance? Well, when you are aware and available to the information that all three I's have to offer, you are far more likely to have the knowledge and feedback you need to align with your deepest truth. Let's look at an example.

When Pilar was deciding between two fabulous job offers, she was very hesitant about which one to choose. She'd been a consultant for more than two decades, and she felt as though this was her chance to make one last big contribution in her career before retirement. She didn't want to choose the "wrong" job, and she wanted some coaching to help her decide.

Before we met, Pilar had completed the commonly used exercise of writing a list of pros and cons for each job to see if that would give her insight into what to do. This was the way her *intellect* approached the decision. Though the lists were helpful, she could still make a case for each job and thus remained stuck at a roadblock.

To help her access the realm of her *instinct*, or her automatic gut responses in her body, I asked her to pretend that she had made her decision to choose the first job. Then I instructed her to close her eyes and breathe, to experience what response her body had toward that decision. Next, I asked her to repeat the experiment with the second job in mind. The physical feedback she received was quite different for each job. When she "chose" the first job, her body felt an overall sense of expansion and butterflies of excitement in her stomach. Pretending to choose the second job gave her a sense of expansion, but there was simultaneously a feeling of tightness in her forehead and a locking in her jaw.

Finally, I encouraged Pilar to use these cues given to her by her body's instinctual response to guide her to the response of her *intuition*. Specifically, I asked her what she thought the tightness in her forehead and the locking in her jaw meant to her. She closed her eyes, felt those sensations again, and described them as a feeling of obligation. Feeling into her higher wisdom, or her intuition, she realized the second job fit the more traditional definition of "success" at this point in her career, and so she was feeling obligated to accept it. But the first job, though not as prestigious on paper, excited her more because it would have a more positive influence on the world. This felt much more in alignment with Pilar's dharma. After this exercise, she had clarity about what job to choose and has not regretted her decision since.

When harnessed correctly, the intellect, instinct, and intuition can work together in powerful ways to reveal the clearest and most aligned path to our brilliance. Combining their collective wisdom gives us the information we need to honor both the voice of our ego and the voice of our soul, keeping them in balance. Later in this chapter, we'll consider strategies for leveraging our intellect and instinct to better connect with our intuition. But first, let's take a closer look at how we might be showing up in the world if our Brilliance Center of Perception is fully activated and optimized.

Optimization at the Brilliance Center of Perception

We all have the power to perceive, but not all of us are masters at it. A master of perception is not in service to their thoughts. On the contrary, they are the *creator* of their thoughts and work with their perception to support their most desired reality. The following are some ways you can master the art of perception and maximize your brilliance at this center.

POSSIBILITY 1: You Practice Mindfulness

When you practice mindfulness, you support yourself in becoming a master of perception. In his book *Wherever You Go, There You Are*, Buddhist practitioner and teacher Jon Kabat-Zinn describes mindfulness as "paying attention in a particular way: on purpose, in the present, and nonjudgmentally." The practice of mindfulness allows us to be aware of when we orient from the ego or from the soul. With that awareness, we can then choose whether we need to reorient our perception accordingly. In essence, mindfulness is the *presence* we need in order to begin perceiving or commanding our thoughts.

Because of my years teaching yoga, I have had a lot of practice in mindfulness, and I am happy to report that practicing this skill pays off. Deliberately and intentionally watching and observing what's going on, including my thoughts, has greatly improved my ability to detect the instinctual cues my body sends me. These give me a lot of insight into whether I am in alignment with my truth. In other words, mindfulness has made me a lot more intuitive.

For example, if I'm falling into an old habit, workaholism, and I'm not minding my inner compass (my core values), my body will feel tense and rigid. If I look in the mirror, I'll usually see the creases on my forehead really pronounced because I've been over-thinking and neglecting my body. Years ago, I would not have noticed these things. But after practicing mindfulness for so long, I recognize these things as the early warning signs that I may be veering off the path.

Mindfulness enhances our skills of perception, and it can also improve our emotional regulation, task performance, and decision making. Being mindful can also make us more aware of how much information overload is present in our world, which brings me to my next point.

POSSIBILITY 2: You Curate Your Information Intake

When you carefully curate the type of information you take in each day, you improve your sense of perception. It's hard to hear your inner guidance, or master your perception, when you lack space, stillness, and quiet in the mind. Those who master the brilliance of this center know this and are proactive in clearing out the excess "noise." They practice consuming a good "brain diet" and feed their mind with healthy, nourishing options, instead of overloading on "brain junk food."

Take Eric, for example. Through our coaching work together, Eric realized that he filled his life with work, social media feeds that were often negative, and news media that brought him down. This had begun to affect his outlook. He felt stressed and cynical. So, I challenged him to make more conscious choices about what he was "feeding" his brain.

Never one to turn down a challenge, Eric downloaded a few wellness apps on his phone and started listening to short meditations every time he felt the urge to check social media. He also began reading novels, a leisure pursuit that had fallen to the wayside when he'd become distracted by social media. He even developed a daily ritual of reading prayers and inspirational poems before he went to sleep. The impact of his efforts, after just a few weeks, was noticeable. He seemed less distracted, more rested, and generally happier. Eric also noted that he spent more time exercising and connecting with friends. His willingness to upgrade his brain diet opened him up to a whole new world of possibilities.

POSSIBILITY 3: You Tame Your Inner Critic

Another type of "noise" that's noticeably absent when your Brilliance Center of Perception is thriving is the voice of your inner critic. Even with the healthiest of brain diets, you could still be ingesting a lot of brain junk food if you're continuing to listen to your inner critic. Someone with an activated Brilliance Center of Perception, however, has tamed their inner critic and learned the art of self-compassion. Their inner critic may still protest from time to time, but with their inner knowing intact, they no longer take it seriously. What's more, they can acknowledge the wounded part of themselves behind that voice that needs their love and support. And they take care of it. In other words, they are actively practicing self-compassion.

Consider Kara, for example. She is one of the most conscientious individuals I've ever met. She was meticulous about her brain diet, and yet she struggled at this brilliance center, falling prey to old, negative thought patterns that would sabotage her entrepreneurial dreams time and again. She was an expert at doing all the right logistical tasks to line up her nutrition and coaching business for success, but her inner critic had been sabotaging her with messages about how she was never going to be good enough, which stoked the fire of her perfectionist tendencies. This pattern kept Kara in a perpetual state of "not ready yet" as her inner critic came up with endless reasons why she should postpone launching her business.

After we homed in on her inner critic, we saw things shift. I suggested that Kara start working with the affirmation "Done is better than perfect" and asked her to practice a variety of self-compassion techniques every day. For example, I recommended she carry in her wallet a picture of herself as a child. Every time she opened her wallet and saw that picture, she would take a moment to send loving kindness to that little girl. With this and several other daily reminder tactics, the grip of Kara's inner critic loosened. With some time and a continued strong commitment to her new self-compassion practices, Kara began to feel a lot less pressure to be perfect. She focused instead on her excitement for serving people with her new business. Before long, it was up and running—and she even began teaching self-compassion techniques as one of her services.

POSSIBILITY 4: You Establish a Relationship with Your Intuition

Another way to optimize the Brilliance Center of Perception is to establish a conscious, deliberate relationship with your intuition. Sadly, many of us have only a haphazard relationship with our intuition. We make little to no effort to actively connect to it unless we are in a state of crisis and need support and direction immediately. Or, we may get a random hit of intuition, and we call it a coincidence. If we want to improve at recognizing how intuition is experienced in us, we must make a regular effort to connect to it. Otherwise, we are more prone to mistaking thoughts perpetuated by fear or wishful thinking for true intuition.

Brilliant individuals know the power of intentionally creating space to go within, and they prioritize it above the temptations of the external world. In the Samurai tradition, one of the fiercest warrior cultures known to date, there is a saying: "All great action arises from a point of deep stillness within." When we take the time to connect to inner guidance, we become capable of expertly directing our actions to align with our intentions. We hold our own metaphorical sword like the samurai, a sword of discernment to cut away all that is not essential to our vision for brilliance.

Sometimes, the prospect of creating a relationship with your intuition may be intimidating, especially if you don't necessarily think of yourself as an intuitive person. Try not to get attached to the labels. Start with something basic, such as carving out a few minutes every morning to practice silence or to ask the universe for guidance. In all my years of coaching, I have never had a client *not* benefit from that simple practice. And, who knows? You may be surprised about how in tune you are with your intuition once you create the space to listen.

POSSIBILITY 5: You Choose Your Stories

When you are a master of this brilliance center, you skillfully choose where your energy goes and carefully select the stories you tell yourself. Masters of perception know the power of a good story, especially the ones they tell themselves in their heads. As we discovered in chapter 4, when you feel aligned with your truth, your inner dialogue reflects a perspective that is positive, inspiring, and grounded in real possibility. Your story about your life or the world is not cynical, nor is it an artificial optimism candy-coated with platitudes. Instead, it's a story of empowered choice, one that lays the groundwork for the actions you take to create the reality you want for yourself. Your story is the first place where your brilliant life takes root in this world. That's why it's so important to choose the words of your inner dialogue wisely.

Brenda didn't fancy herself a storyteller, and she wasn't too keen about working with affirmations or empowering declarations. As a painter, she was much more of an "image" person rather than a "word" person. But we both knew that she needed to seriously improve her inner dialogue if she was going to have a fighting chance at making a living as an artist, so we improvised. I proposed to Brenda that she adopt a personal metaphor, starting each day imagining it was a blank canvas for her to paint. I reminded her that she was in charge of what colors to put on the canvas, how much of them to add, and how to compose the masterpiece of the day.

The metaphor clicked, and Brenda started to approach life with a renewed sense of enthusiasm by reminding herself that she was the artist (and creator) of her day. Tapping into her creativity in this way, she became a lot less critical of her work. She focused on the joy of giving herself over completely to her painting. Her new enthusiasm for life was infectious, and she began to attract more buyers for her work. And her new perspective on things made it easier for her to manage the behind-the-scenes of her business too.

Obstacles at the Brilliance Center of Perception

As we saw from the previous section, when our powers of perception are operating at peak levels, a world of possibilities can open up for us. But every brilliance center also has its potential saboteurs, and this one is no exception. In fact, since this brilliance center commands our thoughts, when we experience challenges here, it can literally stop us in our tracks before we even get started. Let's familiarize ourselves with some of the ways we might get stuck during this part of the journey.

OBSTACLE 1: Being Confused and Indecisive

We all get confused from time to time, but if you frequently find yourself in a state of confusion or indecisiveness, you may be unknowingly using these as a security blanket. Essentially, it becomes easier to stay in the indecision than to risk making the "wrong" choice. When I started coaching Amanda, she was forthright with me about her tendency to do this. She was so scared that she was going to make the wrong decision about something and miss out on opportunities that she often chose not to decide at all.

Ironically, this behavior is what was causing her to miss out on life. She was noncommittal about taking her relationship to the next level. She'd frequently talk about her desire to start a blog, but always came up with a reason for why it was better to wait. She had long thought about moving from Los Angeles back to her hometown of Boston, but she never explored the option.

To address this, I gave her an assignment: She was to change only one thing about her behavior. Every time she noticed herself being indecisive or confused about something, she was to declare, "I am *choosing* to stay confused" or "I am *choosing* to stay indecisive." I wanted to see if owning her pattern around this would shift her perception and allow her to get this brilliance center back online.

It turns out that after about a week of doing this, Amanda started to get fed up with herself and began to change her behavior. Much to my surprise, she came back the next week and reported that she had decided to leave her relationship, she had started her blog, and she was looking for jobs in Boston! She still uses this technique today, years later, to keep herself in check when this old pattern arises.

OBSTACLE 2: Giving Your Power Away

If you haven't been regular about checking in with your inner knowing, you may increasingly doubt your capacities. You lack trust in your intuition, and you think you don't know what to do and cannot visualize what you want. Because that feels uncomfortable, you may seek calculated guidance from outside yourself so that you can keep moving forward. Whereas there's nothing wrong with being open to support and insight from others, if you have a tendency to seek outside guidance frequently, then you are effectively in the habit of giving your power away.

Sometimes when we do give our power away, it's because it makes us feel safe. For example, Lexi had a great fear of abandonment and was scared that her boyfriend, Max, was considering leaving the relationship. On several occasions, she mentioned to me that she preferred to have Max "wear the pants" in the relationship so that she would know how to please him, and then he wouldn't leave. This strategy worked for her for a while, but eventually Lexi's tendency to give her power away backfired. Max left anyway, and Lexi was forced to look at the ways she had abandoned herself in the relationship. After a commitment to therapy and a lot of self-compassion, Lexi is now able to make much wiser decisions about her intimate partnerships.

OBSTACLE 3: Denying Intuition

Sometimes the Brilliance Center of Perception goes offline when we knowingly deny our intuition. Have you ever had a clear intuition about something, but for whatever reason you didn't follow through on it? How did that work out for you? The reasons for this conscious denial of our inner wisdom can vary. Maybe we're scared of what owning our truth will require from us. Look at how many people stay in bad marriages or unhappy jobs because they feel intimidated by the prospect of the unknown and would rather choose the comfort of familiarity over truth. Or maybe you were taught to deny your intuition because it can't be seen, touched, or understood by the rational mind, and therefore it was deemed impractical and foolish to listen to it. When you knowingly deny your truth, you get cut off from the wisdom of your soul, and your brilliance goes dormant.

A lot of my clients from the corporate world who manage others are inclined to use their intuition at work, despite popular beliefs that suggest otherwise. When I began coaching Adam, for example, he was in the midst of hiring a new personal assistant for his growing financial practice. He was considering two candidates, and at the last minute he opted for the one who had the "better" resume, even though his intuition clearly preferred the other. He chose the first because that seemed like the more logical choice, and he thought his boss would be more supportive of this decision.

Unfortunately, this new hire quit after only a week on the job, as soon as she found another job that paid better at a competing firm. After that experience, Adam made a point of more clearly checking in with his intuition regularly so he would know when and how to follow its guidance in the future.

OBSTACLE 4: Believing Someone Else's Story about You

As a child, you didn't have the filters to discern which stories were and were not in line with your truth. Some snuck into your consciousness, and they manifest years later as ammunition for your inner critic to use against you. Perhaps your father taught you that "real men don't cry, and if you cry, then you are a weakling." Or maybe you learned as a young girl that "if you wear tight clothes, then you're a slut and just asking for unwanted attention."

As an adult, you must exercise your power to choose where your energy goes, or else you may find your consciousness defaulting to those old stories you heard when you were younger. Those stories may start to seem like fact. In reality, they are only other people's perceptions, and they cloud your vision of what's true for you.

From time to time, reflect on the common stories you tell about yourself and determine where they first came from. For example, you can look at your beliefs around relationships and sexuality and see how many originated from your parents' beliefs or another source in your childhood. Then, ask yourself, Is this story still true for me? If not, create another one!

OBSTACLE 5: Resisting Letting Go

If you are not commanding your powers of perception skillfully, the negative stories you have about yourself can start to feel very seductive. They are like the low-hanging fruit on the tree. They are easy to pick, and once you get one taste, they can be very addictive. Suddenly, everything you think about seems to be further proof of why you are bad, and your life is all wrong.

A sneaky way that we make these negative stories more socially acceptable to share with others is to cast ourselves as sarcastic self-deprecators who love to poke fun at ourselves. This was me for a long time. Sarcasm was something I grew up with, readily used in my family to cut the tension of emotional moments. When I met my husband, he called me out on this behavior within the first month of dating. He told me that the word "sarcasm" meant to "tear the flesh," and it was a rather underhanded way to perpetuate violence toward ourselves and others while still appearing acceptable. We made a pact from that day forward to exclude sarcasm from our relationship.

As this example shows, though negative stories that have been with you a long time can be hard to let go, with the right awareness, intention, and support, you can turn these thought patterns around.

OBSTACLE 6: Denying Reality

All of us have periods of denial, and many times it's a natural phase within a grieving process. In most cases, we eventually move on. But denial becomes problematic for our brilliance when we repeatedly commit to it and avoid accepting what's really happening.

Another way denial can show up at this brilliance center is when we keep ourselves so busy that we don't have to think about how we really feel about our lives. In the Western world, so many of us have become the proverbial hamster in the wheel. We don't know how to stop "doing," and we may even feel like something is wrong with us if we stop.

When I lived in New York City, I readily adopted this way of existence, even though I wasn't totally aware of it at the time. I did whatever I could to keep busy because on some level, I knew that if I stopped being busy long enough to feel, I would realize how unhappy I was. So, I kept working and distracting myself, right into a major case of burn out with a glorious crash landing. I had to move across the country and start over from scratch to return to the guiding light of my inner compass. I learned the hard way that we can't run away from our truth. Sooner or later that voice within will demand we pay attention to it.

Unleash Your Power at the Brilliance Center of Perception

If, after reading this chapter, you're feeling a little shaky about your skills of perception, do not fret. Though there are indeed a lot of ways we can get derailed when it comes to the Brilliance Center of Perception, this is also an area where you can use ample tried-and-true strategies to get back on track. After all, as humans, we have been trying to master our perceptions for as long as we've been aware that it was within our power to do so. Here are a few useful techniques to get started with.

STRATEGY 1: Connect to Choice

Tony Robbins, the well-known life coach and entrepreneur, has a useful reminder that no matter what's going on in our lives, we always have the power to choose. Specifically, he talks about the three choices that are always available to us, regardless of our situation. We can always choose

1. where to focus our attention;
2. what meaning we wish to give to whatever we are focusing on; and
3. what actions we wish to take accordingly.

We can break things down to the brass tacks no matter what the circumstance may be. I find this technique to be especially helpful when I get stuck focusing on other people's baggage instead of tending to my own. Recall our brilliance principle of choosing self-responsibility over blame and shame. If you catch yourself blaming another for some negative experience you're having, press pause and try to employ this strategy instead.

When Rachel decided to come out as a lesbian to her parents and family, not everyone was supportive of her news. Rachel had to be crystal clear about choosing where she put her energy so that she didn't get lost in a sea of other people's judgments and expectations. She used this strategy to

1. focus on the fact that she was taking a first brave step to change her life;

2. think of this step in a celebratory way instead of focusing on the grief or pain about the disappointing responses she received from some of her family members; and

3. host a special gratitude party for all the people who had supported her through this difficult journey so that she could thank them for their love. It was a celebratory event indeed!

STRATEGY 2: Practice Mindfulness

Yes, we need to practice being present at this brilliance center too. (Indeed, mindfulness helps at each level of our being.) How many times have you found yourself in one place and time, only to discover that in your thoughts you're some place entirely different? This is probably the default for most of us. Remember, brilliance exists in the "now" moment and nowhere else. My friend Joanna, to remind herself of this fact, wears a watch that has on its face only one word, "Now," in big, bold letters. The watch doesn't even tell time, but as Joanna will be the first to proclaim, it's certainly serving its purpose of keeping her present.

STRATEGY 3: Ask Yourself Thought-Provoking Questions

The field of perception is an expansive one, and to explore it more, get in the habit of asking yourself questions that challenge your assumptions. Find questions that help you see the world from new perspectives, or choose questions that suggest that a different reality might be possible for you. Here are a few of my favorites to get you started:

• How would I behave in this situation if I went past my typical first reaction and created a new response?

• What if this thought I am having is not true?

• What would happen if I let go of this thought?

• What might happen if I chose a different action or thought?

STRATEGY 4: Practice Silence

Turn off your electronics, especially your phone. Clear your calendar and go out in nature. Have an information and technology "fast." Do you desire more moments of clarity? They are far more likely to appear when you press pause and create the space to listen and receive. If you feel bold, try scheduling a time for silence into every day or even consider attending a silent meditation retreat.

Sadly, in current research on the potential extinction of complete silence on our planet, scientists are literally searching for the quietest places on earth. As you can imagine, these are not easy to find, nor will they be easily maintained if they are in fact found at all. As the world and our minds fill with noise, we run the risk of losing a profound connection with ourselves and with *the* self (the collective whole, the universe, G-d, or whatever you like to call it). Regularly cultivating and abiding in silence is one of the most powerful things you can do to activate your Brilliance Center of Perception and keep yourself an open channel so your intuition can flow. If silence is indeed already "extinct" in your life, start small with a daily practice of silence for even five minutes and build up from there. Every bit of silence can make a difference.

STRATEGY 5: Slow Down and Declutter Your Schedule

This might sound utterly radical in today's day and age. What would happen if you took an honest assessment of what really needs to get done in your life? What could you let go of? Where could you just say no? Wanting more connection to your inner guidance won't happen just because you want it to. You need to carve out the space to make it a possibility. A teacher of mine used to say, "You need spirit, but spirit also needs you. Show it you're serious about being there for it by creating the space to connect."

Interestingly, after taking his words to heart, I doubled down on my meditation practice and spent more quiet time in nature to connect with myself. After years of an insane work schedule, these new openings I created in my day-to-day life to connect with my spirit were like nectar to my soul! It was these shifts that first allowed me to have the courage to explore therapy so that I could finally deal with the long-standing depression I had been ignoring for decades. I started to learn how to say no and realized that with each authentic "no" I claimed, I was saying a bigger and more authentic "yes" to myself. What a gift!

STRATEGY 6: Practice Asking for Guidance

Speaking of connecting to spirit, what if you started each day by asking your higher self for guidance? How might that change how you show up in your world? If it feels a little strange to talk to yourself in this way, try just being direct and ask, "Higher Self, please give me the guidance I need today to stay in alignment with my truth. I am open to receive." Then, take a deep breath and wait to receive whatever is offered.

Don't worry so much about how the "answer" comes to you, or even if any answer comes at all. Trust that just by committing to this ritual you are opening the door to a more intuitive and grace-filled relationship with yourself and further activating your Brilliance Center of Perception.

STRATEGY 7: Encourage Your Imagination and Stay Curious

Read poetry. Create music. Draw. Dance. Sing. Forget about whether you are coloring in the lines or if you sound good. Just let yourself be in the space of the non-linear. When we invite our imagination to play, we release ourselves from the grip of either/or thinking, and we expand the field of perception for a brilliant life. We start to foster our curiosity when we let our imagination play. We remember to ask why and to challenge our assumptions. We take nothing for granted, and we remember the art of learning about something through exploration. Life becomes an adventure again.

If you need support in this area, start hanging out with children. Toddlers can be the best for this. When I taught yoga to three-year-old children, I never knew where our adventures might take us that day—the jungle, the zoo, the Arctic, the circus, or who knows where else! Always present on our journeys, though, was the unbridled joy that came from embracing our capacity to dream and explore. Imagine if we held onto a fraction of that capacity as we moved into our adulthood. How would our world be different?

♦ SELF-INQUIRY EXERCISE: Your Perception

Congratulations! You've made it through another brilliance center, and with each step on this journey, you become ever more available to your full potential blossoming within you. Now it's time for you to take another deep dive into your unique experience of brilliance, here to get a detailed look at your center of perception. Record your answers to the following questions in your journal.

1. What's a story you've been telling yourself about yourself that's no longer helpful? Once you've identified a story, rewrite it as more positive and aligned with your brilliance. Reflect the possibility instead of the problem of the story. Make yourself the hero of your new tale, and then start sharing it with others. Watch how your mood, energy, and reality shift the more you adopt this new perspective.

2. Think back to a time when you felt really connected and listened to your intuition. How did it feel? What signs, signals, or sensations did you receive? How could you learn from this experience to create a more deliberate relationship with your intuition?

3. What's your current "brain diet"? What can you do to make it more nutritious so that you have the mental space you need to feel connected to your inner guidance? Are there things you want to remove from your brain diet? Are there things you want to add?

♦ SELF-INQUIRY EXERCISE: Optimize Your Brilliance Center of Perception

To upgrade your potential for brilliance at this center, it's time to put what you've learned into practice:

1. Review the insights you gathered from this chapter and the self-inquiry exercises you answered to identify a place in your life where you may be experiencing an obstacle or holding on to a belief that blocks your Brilliance Center of Perception from full optimization. Specifically, try to identify a limiting belief that influences your ability to be a master at perception.

2. Return to the self-inquiry exercise "Upgrading Your Beliefs to Optimize Your Brilliance" on page 62, in chapter 4. Follow Steps 2 to 6 for clearing a limiting belief pattern and replacing it with a new vision, applying these to the limiting belief you've identified in your Brilliance Center of Perception.

If you feel stuck with identifying a limiting belief or would like some examples of common limiting beliefs in this area, please refer to the exercise "Optimize Your Brilliance Center of Perception" in the workbook for additional complimentary resources to support you.

Excellent job! Remember to say your new affirmation and *feel* your visualization every day in your body to reinforce this new pattern. Start implementing the action steps, too. Your field of brilliance will start getting brighter and stronger with every day.

CHAPTER 7

The Brilliance Center of Communication

People may hear your words, but they feel your attitude.
— *John C. Maxwell,* Everyone Communicates, Few Connect

In this book, you've already done a lot of work to discover your brilliance and how you think about and experience it *internally*. This inner work will continue, but in this chapter, we add another dimension. We begin to look at how you share your brilliance with the world through the ways you communicate. When I speak of communication, I am referring to how you speak and the words you choose, but I am also referring to the *energy*, the vibration or attitude, behind those words too.

The Brilliance Center of Communication is the next stop on our journey, and it's known as the *vissudha* (*vee-shoe-dah*) chakra in the yoga tradition. *Vissudha* translates as "purification," which is rather fitting since, in order to find your own voice and speak your truth, you must first clear out all that is *not* your truth. Only then can you speak from a pure place of authenticity and integrity and reveal what is uniquely you.

Not surprisingly, the action statement that encapsulates the energy of this brilliance center is the declaration

I speak.

This is the first place on our journey where we bring our brilliance into manifest form beyond thought. What we do at this brilliance center can make or break the foundation for the actions we wish to take. Words are a potent expression of our energy, and they are one of the first places we get to express our creativity too. Knowing how to use them wisely and with reverence is a key skill to master when we desire to own our brilliance. To understand a little bit more about the power of words, let's first look more deeply at the power of vibration.

The Power of Vibration

If you've ever stood in front of a loud speaker when music was playing, you have probably felt the bass vibrate the floor and the room around you. You may even have felt that vibration penetrate your belly. We cannot see the sound waves, but as the music blasts through the speakers, we can feel it in a very real way.

Not all vibrations are that intense. Many may go unnoticed by us altogether. However, vibrations are everywhere. Everything on this earth holds a certain vibration: you, me, the space around us, everything. Furthermore, as vibrations interact, they can and do affect each other. Think of how your body cringes when you hear a high screeching sound. Now think of how your body feels when you hear a beautiful, melodious tune that soothes the ears. Not only are you affected on the superficial level, but your own vibrational frequencies are literally influenced by the interaction with that other sound.

Why is this relevant to owning our brilliance? Well, when we become more attuned to the vibrational realm, we acquire useful information about whether something feels in alignment with our truth. Recall that your body's instincts often support you in connecting more fully with your intuition. In a similar vein, as we become more skilled at interpreting vibrations, we gain more knowledge about how to respond to such vibrations in a way that aligns with our brilliance.

Let's take a mundane example to explore this idea more deeply. Suppose I am in a conversation with my husband, and I appear to be expressing love and support to him through my words. Also, suppose I'm also communicating a passive-aggressive vibration to him through my tone, my facial expressions, and my body posture. My words sound nice, but what my vibration is really saying is, "I'm only being nice to you so that you'll do what I want." My husband is going to feel the authenticity of that vibration no matter what words I use, and that's what he is going to respond to.

Often we aren't even aware of when our vibrations and words are out of synch with each other until we have interactions like this one and someone calls us out on it. As we've already discussed, sometimes we are blind to the ways we might be sabotaging our own brilliance. Fortunately, my husband is a supportive partner, and he and I are committed to communicating in an open and loving way so that both of us can improve our brilliance at this level. Though it helps to have supportive people in your life to advocate for you like this, you certainly don't have to be in a relationship to better your awareness or skill at this brilliance center. Being an effective communicator requires a certain level of attentiveness and a sensitivity to more than just the words being said. You need to stay open to the feedback you receive from the vast realm of vibrations. Keep this in mind as we move ahead. We'll learn more about how to improve your skill set here, but first let's dive into the Brilliance Center of Communication and see what it looks like when we are thriving here.

Optimization at the Brilliance Center of Communication

Certain habits and actions are in place when you are optimized at the Brilliance Center of Communication. A master of the center of communication will embody many of the following actions.

POSSIBILITY 1: You Communicate Honestly with Yourself

As you might suspect, the first place you need to learn how to be a brilliant communicator is with yourself. More specifically, you need to have an *honest* relationship with yourself in order to thrive at this brilliance center. This seems obvious enough, but many of us struggle with it. We may settle for a less honest version of ourselves to fit in or be liked by others, or even just to feel more comfortable with ourselves.

Even with the best of childhoods, many of us experienced something along the way that led us to believe that it is only acceptable to show certain parts of our personality to others, because if we showed people who we "really are," then bad things might happen. We might get rejected, humiliated, abandoned, shamed, or disappointed or be misunderstood. So, we learn how to compartmentalize, hold back, fake it, hide our true selves, and pretend. Sometimes, we pretend so well that we even fool ourselves!

When you learn to be honest with yourself, the charades and excuses stop, and your Brilliance Center of Communication becomes an open channel for your truth to be expressed. You become clear about who you are, even if you are still a work in progress. Knowing yourself means that you no longer indulge in the little white lies that keep you in your comfort zone—for example, saying, "I don't have time," when you know you really do. With deep honesty, you stop saying yes when you really mean no. You stop behaving in ways just to please others. You get more comfortable saying what you mean, even if it might disappoint another or cause conflict.

There's a fierceness about this level of self-honesty. It requires perseverance and a willingness to accept your imperfections. I think that is why many of us do not choose it. Instead, we choose the more familiar and "safe" option. We wear metaphorical masks to appear more politically correct or allow ourselves to hide our true feelings and vulnerability.

When you establish a no-tolerance policy for lying to yourself, it can be quite a liberating experience and positively affect your relationships with others too. An interesting side effect to being more honest with yourself is that you become far less concerned with others' opinions. Let's take a closer look at what I mean here.

POSSIBILITY 2: You Stand in Your Truth

When this brilliance center is optimized, you stand in your truth, and you are much less likely to consider someone else wrong for standing in theirs. You are able to see that everyone has their own perceptions, and you choose to focus on yourself and your process, rather than concern yourself with what you judge to be the shortcomings in others. When we accept others in this way, we create a real foundation for healthy communication to come forth. We can engage in dialogue about our differences and encourage each other to grow, but not from a place of expectation or judgment.

I knew Meredith was making progress in this area when our sessions together focused a lot more on herself and a lot less on the stories she told herself about her mother. Meredith had a complicated relationship with her mother, as many children do. She loved her deeply, but she was often upset about the way her mother played the victim in life, blaming others for her problems. To be sure, her mother had experienced a lot of disappointment and challenges. But Meredith also knew her mother to be very strong, and it frustrated her when her mother didn't see her own strength and take responsibility for her happiness. Instead, she seemed to continually focus on past hurts and dwell there. Whenever Meredith tried to intervene, her mother clung even more strongly to her stories, and Meredith felt disconnected and exhausted.

Things shifted for Meredith when I asked her to focus on her relationship with herself and specifically see if she could identify places in her life where *she* was playing the victim. Taken aback by this question at first, upon further reflection Meredith saw the truth of the matter. Once prompted, she easily identified the ways in which she blamed her boss for her unhappiness at work, and she saw the parallels between this behavior and how her mother acted. Meredith saw that in part she blamed her boss for things to avoid having to look at how she felt she had let *herself* down at work. This caused her to wonder about the real reasons why her mother might be hiding behind her victim stories too. In other words, Meredith was able to become more compassionate with her mother and significantly improve their relationship, all by putting the focus back on herself and choosing to be more honest about her life.

POSSIBILITY 3: You Engage in Self-Expression

At this brilliance center, another way you can recognize when you are thriving is when you regularly engage in healthy forms of self-expression, even if it scares you. Isn't it ironic that there are more ways to communicate than ever before, and yet so many of us still fear expressing who we really are? We are afraid to be judged, ridiculed, or worse. So, we suppress our creativity and neglect to speak our truth because of fear. One of my favorite authors, Elizabeth Gilbert, wisely points out in her book *Big Magic* that fear is almost always one of the travel companions of creativity. If we are truly willing to go out on an edge and express ourselves creatively, no matter what the world thinks of us, then it's very likely we're going to feel a little (or a lot) scared. The goal is not to be fearless. Rather, the goal is to feel the fear and do it anyway. Fear can be a guide. It reminds you that you are in the creative zone, but it does not have to dictate the journey.

I rooted into this truth to give myself courage for showing up more with my voice when I first started video blogging regularly. Just so we're clear, I do not like to be on camera. Highly introverted, I'd much prefer to sit quietly in my office and not be seen by the masses on the internet. But, I am also fiercely dedicated to pushing myself out of my comfort zone, so I challenged myself to video blog weekly for one year to see what I could discover.

Well, as you might suspect, it was hard, especially at first. And that first three-minute video probably took me well over four hours to make! But through my perseverance, I got much better at the craft the more I did it. More importantly, I had an opportunity to do a tremendous amount of self-inquiry around why it sometimes feels difficult for me to "be seen" by others. Indeed, there is a significant vulnerability in expressing yourself authentically and in a public way. But with that great risk, there can also be great reward. For me, the reward was not so much related to what other people thought of me. Instead, the reward was seeing that I could not only tolerate this level of vulnerability, but also learn to more fully accept myself, even with all my imperfections. Since that experiment, I am much more comfortable in my own skin in general, but also when I am in front of a camera. The experience continues to open me up to new levels of potential at this brilliance center, even today.

POSSIBILITY 4: You Own Your Negativity

When we are willing to fully own our negativity, we make ourselves available to greater integrity and optimization in the Brilliance Center of Communication.

I know it sounds strange when you first hear it. Why would you want to own your negativity if you are trying to own your brilliance? Remember that we are *not* on a quest to deny our humanity. That just leads us to the illusion of perfectionism. When you own your negativity, you are willing to admit that you have the same potential for all the not-so-pleasant behaviors that everyone else does too. You can be greedy, selfish, rude, lustful, shaming, self-righteous, judgmental, weak, lazy, controlling, and so on. The whole point of owning these aspects of yourself is so that they do not run amok and cause self-sabotage by being repressed and denied.

Owning your negativity doesn't mean acting from it. It just means you refuse to put on a saccharin mask of fakeness to appease others or hide your truth. You admit to your imperfections and allow yourself to create a more truthful and real relationship with yourself. When you truly own your negativity, you experience a feeling of becoming whole, a liberation from the lies you hide behind. You also give yourself permission not to be perfect. You dismiss the old beliefs that you are not allowed to have these negative aspects if you wish to be worthy of love. The truth is, we all have these aspects, and when we acknowledge them, we can stop the wild goose chase of trying to prove our self-worth.

Though it may seem counterintuitive, the reality is that when you own these negative aspects of yourself, they open the door to true authentic connection with others. Owning your negativity allows you to disengage from negative patterns like co-dependency, passive-aggressiveness, judgment, and even shame. Let's look at an example.

Owning one's negativity is such a crucial part of healthy communication dynamics that when I train and certify coaches, it's one of the first conversations I have with them. On our first day of training together, I open up the space and invite all the trainees to come forward to publicly "own their crap" in front of the whole group. To ease the tension, I'm the first to do the exercise. I stand up in front of the group and tell them that sometimes I can be really self-righteous. I do this to protect myself from having others see my faults. Other times, I can be co-dependent and modify my behavior so that I avoid conflict with others. I do this because sometimes outward displays of conflict scare me, and I don't want to get hurt.

At first, I felt a little embarrassed to share so openly with my students, but what I soon realized was that it was necessary to role model healthy ownership of my negativity so that I could create a safe space for our work together. Every time I've done this in training, I've seen it profoundly alter the sense of connection and community among the group members in a positive way. I've also noticed that the more I own my own negativity, the less often I engage in those behaviors. In other words, my negativity has a lot less power over me now that I've integrated it into my conscious understanding of myself.

POSSIBILITY 5: You Refuse to Play the "Blame and Shame" Game

An additional way we can maximize the potential of this brilliance center is to refuse to play the "blame and shame" game, even when we are in conflict with another. It is always easier to see the fault in the other before you see how you might be contributing to a negative situation. When you stop being defensive or critical of others, you open the door to authentic communication and connection. It may feel challenging because you will have to be vulnerable and honest, perhaps in ways that you have not been in the past. But refusing to blame or shame others or yourself opens the door for greater self-responsibility and further connection to your brilliance.

When I started coaching Cecilia, she was struggling in her relationship with her partner, Jim. She wanted to spend more quality time with Jim, but lately he'd just come home from work exhausted and veg out for hours in front of the television. Whenever she'd complain about this to him and suggest they spend more time together, he would shut down even more. When Cecilia told me about her experience, she said she was feeling angry at Jim for not showing up more intentionally. He'd even forgotten their anniversary the week before, and she was worried he might not love her anymore. This brought up a lot of fear in her and feelings of not being good enough.

I suggested to Cecilia that the next time she saw Jim on the couch and felt like blaming him for all the tensions and disconnect in their relationship, instead she lean in. Specifically, I invited her to approach Jim and tell him how she was feeling. I instructed her to stay focused on her experiences, not on criticizing or analyzing anything Jim did or didn't do. The idea was for Cecilia to practice being vulnerable and communicating fully and openly from her place of brilliance (or her deepest truth), even when it didn't feel entirely comfortable for her to do so.

In our next session, Cecilia reported back about what had happened when she'd dropped the blame-and-shame game and communicated honestly with Jim. She said that she had told him her fears that he might leave or that he didn't love her anymore, that she hoped this wasn't true, and that she sincerely wanted to work on improving their relationship but wasn't sure how to do that. Then, she invited him to share what he was feeling. Fortunately, Cecilia's willingness to be vulnerable softened Jim, and he confided that he was feeling inadequate at work because of a hypercritical new boss. When Cecilia criticized him at home too, it brought up even more feelings of inadequacy in Jim, and so he just shut down.

This conversation was the start of a new level of openness and honesty in their relationship, all because Cecilia was willing to be vulnerable and not give in to the defense tactics of blaming and shaming. They still had a lot of relationship work to do, but this conversation precipitated their starting couple's therapy, and they were once again on the path to supporting their individual and collective brilliance.

POSSIBILITY 6: You Listen to Understand, Not to Reply

A final example of optimization at the Brilliance Center of Communication is listening in order to *understand*, instead of just listening to *reply*.

Listening skills are essential in communication, but unfortunately, "listening" has often become synonymous with just focusing on what the other is saying long enough to formulate a response. When you align with brilliant communication, you create enough spaciousness in yourself to hear another's truth, even when it differs from yours. When you listen to the other, it's not just with your ears, it's with your whole body. You take a stance of receptivity and truly receive what the other has to say. This type of listening also helps you slow down enough to practice compassion and empathy. Often, you will learn more about yourself in the process too.

A remarkable example of brilliant listening is demonstrated on an episode of *StoryCorps*, an NPR program that records and shares discussions between people of all backgrounds and beliefs. The conversation was between Mary Johnson-Roy and her son's killer, Oshea Israel. Oshea had killed Mary's son when they were both teenagers, after a fight at a neighborhood party. At first, Mary was distraught and had a lot of anger toward Oshea. But after twelve years of grieving, she visited Oshea in prison to learn more about him and share more about her son with him too. She was seeking closure of some kind. The conversation that ensued was a profound example of what happens when we intentionally choose to speak *and* to listen from a place of brilliance.

In the program, Oshea recalls feeling that, as Mary shared memories about her son, he became "more human" to him, so much so that he felt called to hug Mary as the tears rolled down her face during the interview. Upon being hugged, Mary released her anger and started to see Oshea as human too. He was no longer the monster who had killed her son. From that point forward, the two struck up a powerful relationship. Mary now calls Oshea her "spiritual son" and looks forward to the day when he graduates from college and gets married, things she will never be able to see her own son do. Oshea says that Mary's belief in him, even after the tremendous pain he caused her, is what motivates him to be a better person. They live next door to each other, and Oshea was even a groomsman in Mary's wedding in 2015. Their story is incredibly inspiring.

Their ability to communicate with each other from the higher ground of brilliance not only allowed them to connect in ways never expected, but also facilitated a deep healing in both. It has perhaps even inspired deep healing in the countless others who have reflected on their example. Their ability to see past the assumptions, judgments, and strong feelings toward each other allowed each to embrace the humanity in the other. They were open and receptive to possibility, and abundant amounts of love and positivity have come from that decision. You'll be hard-pressed to find a more compelling example of brilliance in communication than this.

Obstacles to Brilliant Communication
....

For an even fuller picture of the Brilliance Center of Communication, let's explore some of the ways this area of our potential can be blocked. As you read through the common obstacles, make note if any of them feel like they may be an area of concern for you.

OBSTACLE 1: Difficulty Speaking Up

Sometime in the past, perhaps as far back as early childhood, you may have learned that it's not safe to express what you really feel or that your opinion doesn't really matter. Whatever the reason, many people develop a fear of speaking up. Becoming aware of this pattern is the first step to turning it around.

When I began coaching Patricia, one of her goals was to work on her self-esteem. She said she often found herself not speaking up in social gatherings or even at work because she was afraid she would say something wrong and feel humiliated. Other times, she just struggled to find the right words. Though an incredibly intelligent person, she was quite shy and would sometimes get choked up when she felt put on the spot.

Though Patricia and I worked with a lot of strategies to help her improve her self-esteem, one that gave her a jumpstart was visualizing that her soul was "behind the wheel" of the car instead of her ego. You may remember this strategy from chapter 6. In essence, when she imagined opening herself up to let brilliance speak *through* her instead of *from* her, she felt a lot less pressure to "perform" and say the right thing. Her ego was paralyzed behind the wheel, but once she tapped into her higher self, she could de-personalize things and let her natural gifts come forth.

OBSTACLE 2: Being Secretive

A healthy bit of privacy is a good thing, but a pattern of secrecy is another thing altogether. Usually, a pattern of secrecy, or a feeling that you *cannot* share something about yourself with others or there will be significant negative consequences, masks a feeling of shame. Secrecy contributes to low self-esteem issues, deep insecurities, and even self-hatred.

Sadly, the people who often resort to secrecy as a way of managing their vulnerability are frequently the most in need of social connection and support. For example, much research into drug addiction shows that the best way to help an addict recover is through social connection. Yet, just about everything in our approach to addiction recovery in the United States is about publicly shaming and punishing addicts in hopes of making them stop. They are labeled, judged, and even criminalized. Perhaps many addicts hide their behavior for so long in part because they are terrified of being made to feel more ashamed than they already do.

When we invite in our brilliance, no matter how vulnerable it may feel for us to do so, we are welcoming in an opportunity to heal the disenfranchised parts of ourselves. Doing so, we no longer feel the need for secrecy.

OBSTACLE 3: Gossiping

Gossip is a low-vibration kind of communication. It feeds off rumors and half-truths. When you partake in gossip, you cloud your mind and make it more difficult to root into your own truth. Sometimes, we hide behind gossip and use it to keep attention off ourselves or to stay numb so that we don't have to feel what's really going on inside. If you catch yourself in gossip mode, consider what you are feeling underneath the mindless talk. Is there a need there that you can address in a healthier manner? What might you be avoiding in yourself by focusing on others?

In my line of work, I go to a lot of women-only empowerment events. Ironically, there's a strong tendency to gossip at some of these events. I'm always deeply saddened by this. I believe that women collectively engaging in gossip is a surefire way to prevent all women, including yourself if you happen to be a woman, from connecting with our brilliance. In her book *Resurrecting Venus*, Cynthia Occelli eloquently speaks to this: "So long as women focus on ways to separate and disparage one another, the world is damned to a mother-less reign...As women, our power in the world is equivalent to the strength of our sisterhood." When we act from brilliance, we remember we are connected to the whole and that our actions (and our words) matter. And so, we refuse to partake in gossip.

OBSTACLE 4: Needing to Be Right

Owning your truth does not mean you have to make the other wrong. Sufi poet Rumi famously proclaims, "Beyond good and bad, there is a field. Meet me there." To me, that field represents a place of truth where you are free from judgments and comparing yourself to others. In that field, you are immersed in a deep kind of wisdom that supports you in being authentic. There, you do not feel compelled to preoccupy yourself with what others choose to believe. Instead, you focus on staying true to your inner compass and living from there. When you let go of the need to be right, you often experience a great sense of freedom to be who you really are. A great feeling of contentment comes with this self-acceptance.

When I came up against this obstacle in my own therapy and my self-righteousness ran amok, my therapist used to jokingly ask me, "Would you rather be right or be happy?" What she was pointing out to me was that by clinging so tightly to my story about being right and making others from my past wrong, I completely isolated myself. I had nothing to do but be alone with my pain. At first, this felt like a good thing to do because it protected me from more pain. But I eventually realized that if I wanted to feel my brilliance again, I would need to embrace being vulnerable and release the need to always be right.

OBSTACLE 5: Always Needing Attention

Sometimes imbalance at this brilliance center is not reflected in secrecy, but in the opposite. We might feel we always have to make ourselves heard to bolster a sense of self-worth. There is a fear that if we don't make ourselves seen or heard, then we will be forgotten or insignificant. Sadly, in this state, even though we are genuinely trying to connect with others, we are relating much more to our fear than to anything else.

When you were an infant, your survival depended on your guardian hearing your cries so that your needs could be met. As an adult, though, this type of behavior (or the adult version of this behavior, I should say) is far less impactful. It's important to learn ways to feel secure enough in your truth that you do not need approval from others to access your brilliance. You also need to learn how to ask for support without being sucked into the drama of being a victim.

OBSTACLE 6: Lying

Some of us are so afraid of conflict or looking "bad" in the eyes of others that we make a regular practice of lying. It might be small white lies, or perhaps we tend to creatively exaggerate the truth to our benefit. Other times, we may leave out some crucial information, convincing ourselves that we did not tell a lie, but rather just chose to share a partial truth. As you can imagine, this is a slippery slope.

Our social-media-obsessed world further exacerbates the tendency we humans have to show only what we deem the best and most enviable aspects of our lives, while hiding all the things we feel less than great about. Look at the average Facebook feed or Instagram account and you will see a carefully curated highlight reel that makes it look like we're all having the best day ever, all the time. This practice of showing only the good about ourselves, or perhaps even lying about what that is, sets incredibly unrealistic standards for success, beauty, and even brilliance.

When we say "yes" to lies in our communication, we are saying a big "no" to our truth. It is not a good habit to develop. If you catch yourself telling a little white lie here and there, press pause. Stay curious and see if you can investigate the motivation for lying. Are you trying to look good? Are you trying to avoid responsibility for something? Are you feeling insecure? What might feel like a little white lie, more often than not, is hiding a pretty significant deep truth. Avoid that truth long enough, and you will start to see real problems.

OBSTACLE 7: Inhibiting Creativity and Self-Expression

Have you ever had a great idea for a creative project but found yourself rejecting it before you got started? Have you found yourself censoring your words in group discussions because you are scared you will say something stupid? Have you been saying "yes" to something that you really want to say "no" to because you do not want to offend a loved one?

We self-censor in myriad ways. Of course, we all need a filter, and it's entirely appropriate at times to use discernment with what you share and what you keep to yourself. Yet, when it comes to our creative potential and our authentic truth, far more often than not our inner critic obliterates an idea before it even comes out of our mouths. Talk about limiting brilliance.

Aliya had challenges with celebrating her creativity in any significant way. Inside she felt she had bold visions and rich insights to share about her life, particularly through her writing. But she rarely ever shared her journal entries with others. When I asked her why, she explained that her mother had always told her to not get too excited or boast too much about anything she did. She called it unladylike and selfish. Aliya had been encouraged to stay quiet and polite and not ruffle any feathers.

Reclaiming her voice and creativity was a process for Aliyah. A lot of her old beliefs around this topic were tied up with her sense of safety, and it wasn't easy for her to challenge the way it had always been. Nonetheless, one strategy that was helpful for her was to notice all the times she unnecessarily apologized for voicing her opinion. Often, what others considered a perfectly reasonable comment from Aliya in her head felt like "too much" or a mistake to share. With increased self-awareness and a commitment to slow down in an effort to disengage from her typical response, she gradually learned to eliminate this behavior. It was an important first step on a journey to reclaiming her brilliance at this center.

Unleash Your Power at the Brilliance Center of Communication

Truly, a whole library of books could be written about how to improve your communications to align more fully with the potential of this brilliance center. Throughout this chapter, you've already seen useful strategies that have helped others, but indeed, there are still so many more. Here I touch on some helpful guidelines and suggestions to get you started.

STRATEGY 1: Take an Inventory of Honesty

It is time to get real. Your potential for true brilliance will be severely limited if you tolerate dishonesty in yourself and others. Set some time aside and do an inventory of honesty to look at how truthful you are. Here are a few questions you might consider asking yourself during your inventory:

- Am I honest with myself about the motives for my actions?
- To what do I say "no" or "yes" when my truth is the opposite?
- When do I lie so that I can keep getting away with an unhealthy or bad habit?
- What aren't I truthful about in my relationships, and why?
- What am I holding back from saying to others that I really want to say?
- What have I been putting off that I know I need to do?
- What am I putting up with that I'd rather be cutting out of my life?

STRATEGY 2: Be Conscious and Non-violent with Your Language

So much more connection could be established between individuals if we were just willing to slow it down and be more thoughtful with our language. Fortunately, there are many excellent resources out there to support us with this objective. If you have never before heard of the technique of non-violent communication, now's a great time to learn how to use it to up-level your game at the Brilliance Center of Communication. You can find book recommendations on this topic in the workbook, in the section called "Additional Resources."

Non-violent communication (NVC) teaches you how to express your clear, non-judgmental observations and own your feelings and needs, and to develop self-awareness about what's important to you. It also teaches you how to listen to others' observations, feelings, and needs in a way that you can really hear them. Being conscious and non-violent with our communication sets a precedent for us to be non-violent with our actions too. Just like anxiety and stress are contagious, so too is communicating consciously. By choosing to take more responsibility for what I call high-vibration communication, you inspire others to do the same too. This can expand brilliance exponentially.

STRATEGY 3: Be in a Deliberate Relationship with Creativity

In our busy lives, many of us find that our unbridled creativity is placed on the back burner. With our never-ending to-do lists always vying for our attention, making time to celebrate and nourish our creative side can feel like an indulgence. But as a quote attributed to the American songwriter Charlie Peacock reminds us, "It's not just about the creativity. It's also about the person you're becoming while you create." Creativity is like nourishment for the soul. Deny yourself it for too long and you may be able to continue to function in life, but on the inside, you'll feel empty, starved for experiences that give your life purpose and meaning. Without creativity, the potential for brilliance wilts.

To avoid this, try to determine at least four bold, creative goals. Choose things that will help activate your self-expression and supercharge the power of this brilliance center. For example, I want to grow a backyard garden, take a pottery class, join a dance group, and learn archery, for fun and to explore the pleasures of life. These are creative activities that will get me out of my mind and into my body. They will also require me to engage more with others around topics unrelated to work. I need to be challenged in both these ways to optimize my brilliance at this center. That's why I chose these particular activities. To see that I follow through on them, I set deadlines and found an accountability buddy for each activity. Now it's your turn. What will you choose?

STRATEGY 4: Practice Healthy Conflict Resolution

The purpose of conflict resolution is not to change the other person's mind or actions, though that may happen. The real goal is to set an intention that aligns you with your highest truth so that you can communicate from that place. Even if you falter at aligning with those values, simply setting that intention to come from a higher place will support you in showing up more authentically and non-violently. Practice this new orientation with smaller conflicts in your life first, and it will become easier for you then to engage this approach when bigger, more challenging conflicts arise.

Fellow coach Randi Buckley offers a helpful tip for conflict resolution. She suggests that when you are in conflict with another person and you are trying to connect with them, assume the other person is doing the best they can. This may or may not be true, but either way, you are going to experience a lot less stress if you take this stance. For more ways to improve your conflict resolution skills to support your brilliance, complete the "Healthy Conflict Resolution" exercise in the workbook.

STRATEGY 5: Determine Healthy Boundaries in Relationships

I know, easier said than done! Are you starting to see how pervasive the concepts of this brilliance center can be? Boundaries in relationships affect just about everything in our lives. When you have healthy boundaries, this is a sign of love and respect for yourself. A boundary is firm in its intention. It helps guide you and keep you connected to the values of your inner compass even when communications with others is complicated or confusing.

Tolerating other people's negative reactions to your boundaries, should they occur, can be challenging at first. They may feel hurt, disappointed, or disagreeable when you put up a boundary. Remind yourself that though it may feel difficult to tolerate a negative response to your boundary, not setting that boundary just to "keep the peace" is a more disempowering choice in the long run, for both you and the other party. Not honoring your truth around your limits in relationships and communication with others can lead to co-dependency, resentment, a loss of your sense of self, or even abuse.

Why might you resist your boundaries. Are you afraid you might hurt someone's feelings? Are you afraid you'll do it wrong? Do you not want to appear selfish or rude? Do you fear rejection, abandonment, or separateness? Before you can implement them, you need to know why you resist setting healthy boundaries. Explore this strategy more with the "Healthy Boundaries" exercise in the workbook.

♦ **SELF-INQUIRY EXERCISE: Your Communication**

Rather fittingly, there is so much more that could be said about communication and how it interfaces with our ability to bring our brilliance forth in the world. But, for right now, I invite you to take in what you've learned from this chapter and answer the following self-inquiry questions. They will undoubtedly offer you insight into where you can start upgrading your Brilliance Center of Communication.

1. Can you identify a lie that you've been telling yourself, one that influences the way you show up in the world? For example, a lie I lived by for many years was, "Life is always a struggle." Another was, "I am only worthy of love if I am contributing back to the greater good somehow." Now you try. If you were to expose this lie and reveal the truth that exists underneath it, what would you find out?

2. Use this inquiry to own your negativity more fully so it doesn't sabotage your ability to communicate and relate with others:
   - Take a moment to bring all your most negative aspects to the surface right now. (For example, think about the side of you that's selfish, petty, self-righteous, jealous, mean, lazy, or whatever!) Describe this version of you in your journal. Be honest. This can be for your eyes only if you like.
   - To practice self-compassion, write a love note to that version of you. What might you want to say to these parts of yourself? How could you be more loving and nurturing to these aspects of your being? Consider reading the letter aloud whenever you feel bad about yourself.

After completing this chapter and the previous self-inquiry exercises, you are steeped in wisdom about some of the ways you might self-sabotage your Brilliance Center of Communication. To upgrade your potential for brilliance at this center, it's time to put what you've learned into practice.

1. Review the insights you have gathered to identify a limiting belief that blocks your mastery of communication.

2. Return to the self-inquiry exercise "Upgrading Your Beliefs to Optimize Your Brilliance" on page 62, in chapter 4. Follow Steps 2 to 6 for clearing a limiting belief pattern and replacing it with a new vision, applying these to the limiting belief you've identified in your Brilliance Center of Communication.

If you feel stuck with identifying a limiting belief or would like some examples of common limiting beliefs in this area, please refer to the exercise "Optimize Your Brilliance Center of Communication" in the workbook for additional complimentary resources to support you.

Well done! Remember to say your new affirmation and *feel* your visualization every day in your body to reinforce this new pattern. Start implementing the action steps too. With each step, you are becoming more and more established in your brilliance. Keep it up!

CHAPTER 8

The Brilliance Center of Love and Connection

Awakening to oneness is the experience of big love.
Knowing you are one with all, you find yourself in love with all.
—*Timothy Freke and Peter Gandy,* The Laughing Jesus

Having embarked on the journey of finding your own voice, it's time to add another layer of complexity and explore the expansive and mysterious realm of the heart. Our next stop on the journey, the Brilliance Center of Love and Connection, is where you'll discover the unending web of relationships that exist in your life. It is the place where you feel the true essence that connects you with others on this earth.

The Brilliance Center of Love and Connection represents the midpoint of our journey. In the yoga tradition, it correlates to the heart chakra, or the *anahata* chakra. *Anahata* translates as "pure" or "unhurt." I liken this to the place inside you that is above the dramas of your life. It's the pure seat of your soul's yearning. It's the tender and wise knowing of your being that can transcend fragmentation of the self and provide a place of deep integration at the soul level. It's the part of you that truly knows that nothing is wrong with you and you are completely lovable even if your life is less than perfect.

The Brilliance Center of Love and Connection is this place within you that balances all the various aspects of your being. That is why when you feel balanced and happy in the heart, you can experience a very profound sense of wholeness, inner peace, and self-acceptance. Health at this center brings a feeling of steadiness and continuity to your life and your spiritual path.

The action statement that best describes brilliance at this level of your awareness is

I love.

It's important to note that here we are not referring to love in a romantic or sexual sense. Rather, love as it relates to the Brilliance Center of Love and Connection is the unifying force of brilliance. It is a constant and enduring love.

Love, in this sense, is not contingent on outside stimulation of any kind but is experienced as an inner feeling. It highlights our similarities, our universal self, rather than our differences. It is not a feeling of love based on any kind of need, but it is based on unconditional acceptance.

Optimizing the Brilliance Center of Love and Connection takes patience, courage, and understanding. We must surrender to forces larger than ourselves in order to open up to the power of the heart. As you embark on this part of the journey, it is a good time to remind yourself that exploring your brilliance centers is not about being perfect or discovering where you are wrong. Instead, it is a search for deeper truth. Keep that in mind as you unravel the incredible power of the heart and discover the magic of living and relating wholeheartedly.

Love and Brilliance
. . . .

L – O – V – E. Never has a four-letter word inspired so much joy and pain. Let's get right to the heart of the matter (pun intended) and address this mysterious, tantalizing, complex concept. Bear with me, as I'll need to get a little philosophical with this in order to set the stage for our work together in this chapter.

What is love? That's a daunting and possibly unanswerable question. Fortunately, we do not have to come up with the definitive answer for the ages. We are looking at love in terms of our journey to brilliance, and that, in and of itself, will feel challenging!

Love is a unifying force. It draws things together and keeps them in a relationship. Now, the "things" it draws together could be different aspects that exist within you, individuals who are drawn toward you, or components of your environment and you being drawn into an integrated whole. At the most essential level, the deepest connection possible through love reminds us of the fundamental truth that everything is one. I call this *absolute love:* Our feeling and experience of deep connectedness to the whole. What is the purpose of absolute love, and why is it important to our brilliance?

In her book *Wheels of Life*, author and teacher Anodea Judith describes absolute love as "a binding force [that] allows something to hold together long enough to evolve its patterns to deeper and more cohesive states. Love allows change and freedom, but keeps coherence at the center." In this sense, one important purpose of absolute love is that it reminds us of who we really are at our core, that we are brilliant, even when we don't *feel* that way. Remember our metaphor of simultaneously being the ocean and the wave? Absolute love allows us to remember our "ocean selves" even when our "wave lives" have caused us to forget.

In other words, absolute love helps us transcend our egos, make connections within ourselves and with others that bring us closer to our brilliance, and learn self-acceptance. Absolute love is a core necessity on our path to brilliance. It provides the ultimate context for our personal growth work and keeps us in touch with the big picture. It reminds us of who we really are. Sounds important, huh?

If absolute love is all-powerful, then why can't we feel this love all the time? And why do the ego-based experiences of love so often feel lacking, painful, or both? Complicated questions. To answer them, first we must understand this important fact: *absolute love is not a feeling or a state of being that can be forced by will.* It cannot even be created, because it is always there. Absolute love is what we sometimes call "supreme consciousness." In this sense, it is the very fabric of the universe. We may get glimpses of it or feel immersed in it during moments in nature or moments with an intimate partner or when we engage in our true passions. But in those moments, we are not the source of absolute love. Rather, it is a light, a brilliance, if you will, that shines through us.

Problems can arise on our path to brilliance when we attribute the source of absolute love to someone or something in particular. Consider the following statements:

- "No one makes me feel more loved than you do, John."
- "The beach is the only place I can feel this kind of love and connection."

- "I feel so whole and at peace when I am in the presence of my guru."

Nothing is inherently wrong with these proclamations. They might be quite true for you in the moment because these people or situations may have been gateways into your experience of absolute love. But when you equate them as the *source* of absolute love, then you set yourself up for potential suffering.

What happens when John changes his behavior or leaves? What if you can't live near the beach anymore? Or what if your guru ends up being a fraud? Does absolute love disappear?

We cause ourselves great suffering when we put expectations and limitations on absolute love and forget that the experience of absolute love is always available to us within. Let's look at an example.

After two years of being together, Kendra found out that her boyfriend, Darren, had been regularly cheating on her. She was devastated and in shock. All that she thought to be true about her relationship was not. In her eyes, this was the ultimate betrayal, and she felt completely undone. She wasn't even sure who she was anymore.

Through our work together, Kendra was able to see that she had unconsciously made Darren the *source* of absolute love in her life. So, when he left, it wasn't just a break up. To Kendra, it felt like a flat-out rejection of her core being. In other words, it led her to feel that something was wrong with her, that she wasn't lovable, and that no one would ever love her.

Kendra was *not* responsible for Darren's behavior or shortcomings. Nonetheless, with this insight, she could see how she had been negating her brilliance by making Darren the be-all and end-all of love in her life. With this perspective, she could step back and learn new ways to reconnect with her true sense of self, heal her wounds, and re-ignite her brilliance.

To summarize, absolute love is your feeling and experience of deep connectedness to the whole. It cannot be taken from you. It lives within you and all around you.

At this point you may be thinking, "That's all well and good, but I still want to be in a loving relationship. I still want to be loved by others. I still want to be a loving person and feel worthy of love. How does knowing this about absolute love help me with any of that?"

We do not live in this world as disembodied spirits. So, we need to learn practical skills and self-awareness to help us in our relationships. In this chapter, we'll explore these and I'll offer you some tools to create a life filled with love. Nonetheless, I can say with great certainty that no tactic, communication skill, or relationship technique will do you much good in the long run if you forget the essential truth that at the core of everything is absolute love.

Reflect for a moment on the conditions you might place on love for it to be a part of your life. Do you feel you do not have the right to be loved unless you do things perfectly, look good, weigh the right amount, or act a certain way? Do you withdraw love from another individual or even groups because they look different than you? To the extent that we filter absolute love through the lens of our ego self, we can cause distortion around the basic truth that all of us have the right to be loved and to love. All of us hold the source of love within ourselves, always. Please keep this in mind as we move into the nitty-gritty of the details. Our next step is to look at the importance of self-love.

Self-Love on the Path to Brilliance

Exploring matters of the heart requires bravery at the highest of levels. You must be willing to move forward even in the face of fear or pain if you want to stay true to your heart. Perhaps nowhere is this more relevant than when it comes to loving yourself.

So much has been written about learning to love yourself that it's hard not to sound clichéd when talking about it. I will do my best to stay away from the platitudes and speak authentically about such an important topic.

Something that has really helped me in learning how to love myself more is to let go of the idea that "loving myself" is some end state that I just have to work hard enough to reach, and one day I will finally be there. You do not simply wake up one morning and say, "I've got it all figured out. Now I love myself!"

Instead, loving yourself is as an ongoing process and evolution that occurs throughout the entirety of your life. In every moment, you have choices you can make. You can choose behaviors, thoughts, and ways of being that reflect self-love. Or, you can choose things that move you further away from that. Self-love is an active process that comes alive in how you choose to show up in the present moment.

Here are a few truths about self-love to keep in mind as you explore how to optimize this brilliance center within you.

TRUTH 1: Self-Love Requires Self-Awareness

Since self-love (or lack thereof) is an inside job, we need to have a system of frequently checking in with ourselves, questioning our assumptions and beliefs to see if they are helping or hurting our relationship to ourselves. Even if you feel like you are very self-aware already, I guarantee that you can always further increase your understanding. A great place to start is with a regular journaling practice. I provide some useful journal prompts to get you going in the workbook, in the exercise entitled "Journaling About Self-Love."

TRUTH 2: Self-Love Requires Responsibility for Your Feelings

It is very easy (and very human) to get caught in a story about how the others did us wrong. This way of thinking will only get you so far. At some point, if you are serious about learning to love yourself, you have to drop your obsession with the other. Learn to focus on you.

You may not be able to change what happened or what people did or didn't do. But as you learned in chapter 6, you always have a choice about what to focus on, what meaning to give it, and what action you want to take accordingly. Learning to take responsibility for how you choose to feel and be in the present is a huge part of learning to love yourself. Where might you be giving your power away by focusing too much on the other?

TRUTH 3: Self-Love Requires Regular Check-Ins

When you are uncertain whether you are acting in alignment with self-love, it can help to ask yourself, How would I act in this situation if I was in accordance with self-love? Give yourself opportunities to create new patterns in self-love as you go along. Do not expect to get it perfect every time, but know that it can help if you set yourself up to succeed with small wins moment to moment. This makes the bigger acts of self-love a little easier to manage when the time comes.

TRUTH 4: Self-Love Requires Making Peace with Pain

We all have a legacy of pain that has been passed down to us, and usually the beliefs we develop around love get wrapped up in this history. Maybe you have a memory of being loved for certain behaviors and being shamed for others, so you learned to deny aspects of yourself that you thought were unlovable. Maybe you felt abandoned as a child and never want to feel that pain again, so you shut yourself off from intimate relationships and feel like you are unworthy of such love. Whatever your story, denying it or trying to forget it will not work, certainly not in the long run. At some point, on the path to self-love, you have to travel through the "darkness." We have been taught to fear this darkness, thinking that we will not be strong enough to confront this pain head-on. Ironically, facing the pain and letting it move through you is what tenderizes your heart enough so you are able to love yourself.

I had a firsthand experience of this tenderizing of the heart when I moved to California. At the time, I was experiencing what the Spanish mystic and poet St. John of the Cross called a "dark night of the soul." I'd recently had a bad break-up, and I also lost my New York City apartment because of sky-rocketing rents. To make things even worse, I also lost nearly seventy-five percent of my business profits due to the 2008 market crash. I'd been a workaholic for years, and on top of feeling heartbroken and broke, I was incredibly exhausted. What's more, I felt like a complete fraud. Here I was, a life coach, and my life had fallen completely apart! I felt very lost. I knew if I was ever going to "find" myself again, I'd have to do a major reboot. So, I moved to California.

I had no master plan for how things were going to work once I arrived in Los Angeles. I just knew I needed to go. Those first few years were the roughest, but I will never forget the serendipitous moment when I wholeheartedly committed to love myself like I never had before. It was December 31, 2009, and there was a special blue moon lunar eclipse happening that night. I lived right by the beach, and I headed out to the water at sunset to do an end-of-the-year ceremony before the evening came.

I had only been in Los Angeles for six months at that point, and I had very few local friends, I had not much business to speak of, and I was still feeling down about myself. But, committed to my spiritual practice, I mustered the energy to do my ritual on the beach. When the sun finally set, I got up to walk back to my apartment, and in the sky, I saw the biggest, most beautiful full moon I had ever seen in my life. It was so breathtaking, it literally brought me to my knees.

I was so moved by this celestial beauty that I spontaneously decided to take off my Claddagh ring (an Irish "wedding band" my mother had given to me when I was a little girl), and I started to say vows to the moon. To this day, I don't know what came over me in that moment. Somehow, the moon had become an external representation of all the parts of myself that I had abandoned and treated poorly, and I knew I needed to proclaim to her, to myself, that I would never do that again. I vowed that I would always treat myself with love and respect, and that I would always have compassion for myself even when I screwed up or made the same mistake repeatedly. I promised that no other person or situation would ever get in the way of my commitment to myself again.

When I left the beach that night, there was no turning back. I had just had a commitment ceremony with myself! I affectionately refer to this now as the day I married the moon. But next came the hard part. I had to stay true to my commitment, and that meant really letting myself feel the pain of where I was at. Shortly after that night, I started regular therapy, began a new exercise regimen, took lots of beach walks, started eating healthier, and meditated more—all in the name of self-love.

It hasn't always been easy to remain committed, and facing the painful, wounded places within me has required more courage than I could have imagined. But on days when I falter, I remember that fateful night on the beach, and my commitment once again is renewed.

A Brilliant View of Relationships

The Brilliance Center of Love and Connection is not only the domain of self-love, but it is also where we encounter the power of relationships. Relationships of all kinds are a critical part of our process of awakening our brilliance. We humans are social creatures by nature, and so much of what we learn about ourselves comes through our experiences with others.

Relationships are a process of give and take. Our happiness, success, and fulfillment in them rests largely on how well we manage the balance of what we offer and what we receive. My mentor and friend Gail Straub describes this balance beautifully in her book *The Rhythm of Compassion*:

> I've come to think of this relationship between soul and society much like following the in-breath and the out-breath, as in meditation practice. There's a natural time for the in-breath of caring for self and family, and a natural time for the out-breath of caring for the needs of the world. The challenge is to become skillful in following our rhythm—knowing when it's time to [receive] and when it's time to [give].

Relationships are indeed an ebb and flow. Since the common denominator in all of them is you, one of the best ways to maintain the balance in your relationships with others is to first maintain balance within yourself. There are many kinds of balance, for example, between

- your body, mind, and spirit;
- your mental flexibility and stability;
- your masculine and feminine energies;
- your ego and your soul;
- responsibility and surrender;
- giving and receiving; and so on.

We are most effective in relationships when we move forward from the fullness in the heart, the part of us that can skillfully navigate the complexities of finding balance. When the heart center is strong, it allows us to achieve an inner equilibrium that supports all our relationships. Let's look at an example.

Jeremy came to me for business coaching, but after a few sessions, we discovered that a personal relationship was one of the major obstacles getting in the way of him being more successful at his entrepreneurial endeavors. Jeremy was the eldest of two children to a single mother. As his mother, Doris, was getting older, she began to experience health problems, and it was clear she could no longer live on her own. Jeremy didn't have the heart to "stick her in a nursing home," as he said, and Doris didn't want that either. So, Jeremy had decided to move her into his family's spare bedroom.

At first, it seemed to be going pretty well, but over time Doris became more demanding, wanting things to be exactly as they were for her in her own home. Jeremy started to feel resentment toward his mother, and the situation was affecting his marriage. Doris and Jeremy's wife, Sue, began regularly arguing about the "best way to do things" around the house. The situation had become unlivable, was distracting Jeremy from his work, and was throwing his life out of balance.

Though his "soul self" wanted to honor and respect his mother, Jeremy's "ego self" knew he needed to find another situation that would be more livable for him and his wife. He needed to find a compassionate way to transition his mother into a new living situation while conveying his love and respect for her. After some lengthy family discussions and exploration of options, Jeremy, his wife, and Doris decided on a new arrangement—an intergenerational living community nearby that would provide Doris with her own condo and full support on staff whenever she needed it. She felt good about this because it allowed her to keep some independence, and she was still close to her family. Jeremy and Sue reestablished balance in their lives and home.

But, perhaps most importantly, Jeremy lovingly expressed a boundary to his mother without being disrespectful or hurtful because he came from an intention of love. He was authentic and vulnerable in his communications with his mother, and she felt how sincere he was. That allowed her to soften her initial resistance. Jeremy mentioned to me that these conversations with his mother were, in his eyes, the most authentic and connecting that they had ever had. By honoring his truth in the relationship and finding the balance between his ego's needs and his soul's needs, Jeremy was able to come from a place of brilliance here, and everyone benefited. Furthermore, once he had attended to his personal matters, Jeremy could give renewed focus to his business, which struck another balance in his life.

What about you? Have you ever had a relationship where you lost sight of yourself by focusing too much on the needs and desires of another? Conversely, did you forget to be considerate and compassionate to another because you were too concerned with your own expectations? Sometimes, it's a little bit of both: you forgot to consider yourself and you forgot to consider the other.

In relationships, it's critical that we learn to establish a strong foundation within so that we are not reliant on external sources to provide our sense of ground and truth. When you move from a place of inner stability and self-acceptance (one might call this self-love), then you set the stage for much greater success in relationships with others. When you have self-love, you connect to others not out of neediness but from a sense of abundance. You truly relate to others with compassion and empathy. This naturally dissolves judgment and encourages your heart to open even more.

It is not always easy to open your heart in relationships. Fears easily obstruct brilliance and throw off your balance and inner rhythms. If you would like to explore more deeply what fears might be getting in the way of your brilliance, take a break from reading this chapter and explore the "Relationship Fears" exercise in the workbook.

Trusting Yourself in Relationships

Another important theme to address in the Brilliance Center of Love and Connection is the idea of trust. Without trust, healthy relationships cannot exist. We need to trust ourselves and others. Let's first take a close look at how we can do a better job of trusting ourselves.

We all "screw up" from time to time. It is part of being human. Making mistakes is not necessarily a problem. We can learn from them so that we can act in more aligned ways in the future. But, if we use our mistakes as evidence for why we should not trust ourselves, then we are keeping ourselves permanently stuck, halting any opportunity to move forward based solely on past behaviors. This perspective does not account for your evolution and that you can change and learn.

When you refuse to trust yourself, it's hard to engage in relationships wholeheartedly. It's like trying to dive into a pool, but only halfway. It just does not work that way. If we want to be in relationships wholeheartedly, we have to be willing to trust ourselves, even though we are imperfect creatures and may continue to make mistakes. Trusting yourself does not guarantee you will always get it right, but that you are willing to show up with an open heart and with presence so you can evolve from past mistakes and stay open enough to learn from any additional ones.

Remember, failure is a natural part of your learning and growing process and not a reason to condemn yourself. Thomas Edison made one thousand "not light bulbs" before he created one that worked. Oprah Winfrey was fired from one of her first TV jobs as an anchor in Baltimore. Steven Spielberg was rejected *twice* by the University of Southern California's School of Cinematic Arts. Michael Jordan didn't make his high school basketball team. Imagine how our world would be different if every time one of us failed, we just gave up completely.

Past behaviors are only indicative of what happened in the past. What you choose to do with that information now is what truly matters. Keep yourself grounded in the now, and forgive yourself for being human. You are in good company! All of us are imperfect; no one is exempt. Process your mistakes (with a professional, if you need to), and then know when it is time to let them go and move on.

When trying to build self-trust, it can also help to make new promises to yourself. Start small. Set yourself up to succeed, and keep a victory log. Every day, record the "wins" in your journal, no matter how small or insignificant they may seem. A new pattern is created with lots of small steps.

Finally, when you are trying to build self-trust, it's imperative that you learn to act in alignment with your values, even when you don't feel like it.

It is not always going to feel natural and easy to start a new pattern in you. You have to learn to source from a deeper place than just what feels good or natural, as that is not always indicative of what is most aligned with your brilliance. Slow down and check in with yourself to make sure you are orienting from what you know to be your highest truth. It will pay off in the long run, even if it does not feel so comfortable in the short run.

Trusting Others in Relationships

Trusting others can feel like a frightening prospect, especially if you have been hurt in the past. But successful relationships are built on trust, and trust is what allows us to have closeness and intimacy in our relationships. So, how do we manage to trust others when there are no guarantees in relationships?

There is no magic bullet when it comes to learning to trust others, but there are some helpful things to keep in mind that will make it easier for you to negotiate this vulnerable emotional terrain.

TIP 1: Become Aware of Your Beliefs

So many of your beliefs about trust were first formulated in early childhood, even before you could talk, and now those beliefs are cemented in your subconscious, ruling your behaviors whether you know it or not. There's a psychological model called attachment theory that specifically looks at how a person learned to behave in a relationship when they felt hurt. It can be helpful to learn your attachment type so that you can understand your patterns and create more secure attachments in the future. Remember, what happened in the past does not have to dictate what happens in the future. You can find book recommendations on this topic in the workbook, in the section called "Additional Resources."

TIP 2: Evaluate Your Patterns and Behaviors

After a betrayal of trust, it's so easy to go into the blame game. I do not recommend it. It is not a very good use of time, and it keeps you stuck in the hurt. Let yourself have your feelings. Move through the pain. Once the pain has been honored, start to look at your patterns that may have contributed to the situation. Consider the boundaries you held in the relationship. Did they honor you and your commitment to your highest self? Were they reflective of a belief that you are worthy of love and respect? Were there places where your intuition was telling you something was not right, but you ignored it? Were there places where you could have communicated your needs more accurately? I cannot stress enough that this type of self-inquiry is *not* about blaming or shaming yourself or the other. It is about taking responsibility for the journey ahead by choosing to look inward. Go forth with this lens, and you will be able to reap some important wisdom even from the most difficult times.

TIP 3: Go Slowly

If you are feeling shaky about trusting another, why not start with small extensions of trust? Give yourself a longer runway, so to speak, before taking flight into the realm of trusting someone with your most precious belongings, most intimate truths, or most vulnerable secrets. With more time, there are more opportunities for you to get the sense of a relationship to determine whether it feels appropriate to go forward.

When I first met Robin, she had completely given up on the prospect of finding a partner. She described how every time she opened her heart and started a relationship again, she would invariably get hurt. She just didn't think it was possible for her to trust men. And then she met Scott. Scott surprised her with his gentleness and his ability to speak openly and intelligently about his feelings. Though she was scared to admit it, Robin knew she wanted to start dating Scott, but she wasn't sure how to trust again.

Slowing it down for Robin meant setting clear boundaries for herself. She decided that she was going to limit the number of times she would hang out with Scott each week so she could still stay committed to her other interests and responsibilities. In the past, she tended to "lose herself" and no longer saw her friends or engaged in certain hobbies when she was dating someone new. She also decided that she would wait a lot longer than usual before she was physically intimate with Scott. This would provide her with more space and time to experience her emotional connection with Scott before taking it to the next level. Finally, she decided she would share her fears openly with him so that he could understand where she was at. This was a vulnerable process for Robin, but it allowed her to be in greater relationship with her own brilliance, which ultimately led to a better and stronger connection between her and Scott.

TIP 4: Be a Clear and Compassionate Communicator

Sometimes, trust is challenged in a relationship because we do not speak up about our fears and concerns as they arise. Instead, we let them simmer, and interpersonal tension builds. Aim to clear up any misunderstandings as soon as possible, so the relationship residue does not build up. Then, the energetic field can stay open for trust to build.

TIP 5: Refrain from Projecting Your Unresolved Pain onto Others

If someone triggers you, likely this will subconsciously bring up all the other times someone or something made you feel that trigger before. This can be sticky because you may start to project the pain of *all* your past experiences onto the one person you are having the triggering experience with in the present time.

Stay aware. Take responsibility for what is yours to resolve. Those feelings have nothing to do with the person you currently have a challenge with. This kind of self-awareness is essential if you want to avoid defaulting to a stance of distrust based on past experiences. Take, for example, what happened for my client Hannah.

Hannah had recently become a new mom, and her marriage, which had been rock solid before the baby, was now experiencing a lot of challenges. Specifically, Hannah was feeling increasingly aggravated with what she felt was her husband being lazy and not doing his part in the childcare. When I asked her to tell me more about this, she started to share some of the details about her husband, and I noticed she was weaving in some painful memories about her father too.

Hannah's father had left her mother when Hannah was just a little girl. What's more, Hannah grew up her whole life hearing stories about how lazy and irresponsible her dad, and all men, were. The more Hannah talked about this, the more she started to realize that although she and her husband were having problems, it was likely she was exaggerating the extent to which he was in fact being lazy. She realized she'd been projecting some of her unresolved pain about her dad leaving onto her husband. As a new mother, and feeling vulnerable about providing a safe and secure environment for her daughter, all her old fears came up. When she shared this new insight with her husband and took responsibility for her part in the conflicts, he felt less judged and threatened. As a result, he was able to own his part too, and they were able to find a better balance with the relationship responsibilities.

TIP 6: Make Peace with Risk

If you are truly committed to your brilliance and living fully, you are going to have to take risks. And taking risks means you will sometimes get hurt. Not all is lost, though, because a broken heart is also an open heart. Never forget that you have a choice about how to perceive things. And choosing to root into your higher understanding, even when things do not work out as you hoped, is an excellent way to create fertile ground for new, trustworthy relationships.

Optimization at the Brilliance Center of Love and Connection

We've already covered a lot of ground at this brilliance center by looking at the importance of self-love and some of the basic dynamics needed for healthy relationships. Here are additional ways you can thrive at your Brilliance Center of Love and Connection.

POSSIBILITY 1: You Embrace Living with an Open Heart, Even When It Hurts

One of my teachers, Andrew Harvey, in his book *The Return of the Mother*, writes, "Only a heart that breaks again and again can ever be strong enough to bear everything...A heart that consents to break again and again will be strengthened with each break...to become more and more open to empowering divine grace." I could not agree more. For sure, staying open is not always easy, and it takes a lot of bravery. But what a way to live! When you are bold in your desire to feel the full spectrum of life, you are given a chance to evolve on a soul level. Next time it hurts to stay open, remember this, and perhaps the sting will be a little less as you discover the new wonders that await you.

POSSIBILITY 2: You See Your Vulnerability as Your Strength

In her famous TED Talk entitled "The Power of Vulnerability," author and speaker Brené Brown reminds us that vulnerability is the birthplace of creativity. Here is a silly but effective example to demonstrate what she means. Have you ever seen hermit crabs on the beach? When they outgrow their shell, they must abandon it and search for a new one while totally "naked." How terrifying for them to be so vulnerable! But being "naked" is exactly what they must endure in order to grow into the new, stronger version of themselves. We humans are really no different. If we want growth and we want to step into new, stronger versions of our truth, we must be vulnerable. Can you find the exhilaration in that?

POSSIBILITY 3: You Are Willing to Process Grief and Move On

Grief. Even just saying the word can conjure up a feeling of heaviness in my body. When your heart has experienced a loss that it grieves, it can feel impossible to move on. There is no single way to handle grief, but it is important to know it does take time to heal. Also, like most emotions, it does not get processed in a linear fashion. Grief comes in waves. Some days are easier than others. If you experience deep grief, be sure not to isolate yourself, and seek out the support you need. Be extremely kind and compassionate to yourself while grieving. Regular, daily commitments to self-care will help to gently usher you out of the darkness and back into the world with new tenderness when your soul is ready.

Bridgit experienced tremendous grief after having multiple miscarriages. She and her husband had tried for years to have a child to no avail. They had decided to make peace with the fact that they were not able to have a biological child together. To honor their grief, they planned a trip to their ancestral country of Ireland. They visited old family sites on both sides of their family, and they even performed a special ceremony around saying "goodbye" to the child they were never able to have. Many tears were shed, and their hearts slowly started to mend over time.

Much to their surprise, a year later, after having adopted a son, Bridgit found herself pregnant again. This time, she gave birth to a healthy baby girl! Though there will never be any scientific way to prove it, Bridgit is quite sure that by honoring her grief and by being willing to fully let go of the possibility of having her own biological child, she energetically paved the way for her dream to come true.

POSSIBILITY 4: You Practice Seeing Yourself in the Other

Practice seeing yourself in the other, even when thinking about those people you just can't stand! We are all part of one human family, and, therefore, we are all subject to the same joys and challenges of a human existence. Next time you feel sure you are different from that "other" person, press pause. Maybe you do not express the same tendencies in the same way that they do, but in you still exists the same possibility for imperfections.

Another one of my spiritual teachers, Ram Dass, used to keep on his altar a picture of George W. Bush during his presidency. The photograph sat right alongside beautiful images of several deities and saints. When asked why he kept Bush's photo there too, he replied, "To all these saints and deities I can say, 'I love you.' The day I can say to George Bush, 'I love you,' I know that I will be a good person."

When we remember we are all human and choose to extend love no matter what, we open the door to more compassionate communication and empathy. We are in deep alignment with our brilliance and able to be a true expression of the power of absolute love.

POSSIBILITY 5: You Commit to a Practice of Gratitude

Gratitude is an expansive energy that opens the heart, and the great news is that it can be practiced no matter what is going on in your life currently. A *practice* of gratitude is different than just an *attitude* of gratitude. An attitude implies a surface-level belief, a pleasantry. Brené Brown describes in her e-course on "The Power of Vulnerability" how one can have an attitude of yoga by wearing yoga pants daily and owning a yoga mat, but that does not mean they have a practice of yoga.

It is similar with gratitude. When you have a practice of gratitude, you live in the world with an abundant outlook, and you act from that knowing. You tend to be more generous in spirit and inform all your relationships with a loving presence. Are there places where you can practice gratitude more fully in your life?

Obstacles to the Brilliance Center of Love and Connection

To round out our understanding of the Brilliance Center of Love and Connection, we need to be aware of some of the obstacles that could block our potential from blossoming. Here are some of the behaviors to look out for.

OBSTACLE 1: Privatizing Your Love

A lot of times, we take the bigness of our hearts' capacity to love and share it only with those in our immediate circles of family and friends. We forget that we can also extend love to strangers, even to people we do not "like." Granted, how that love gets expressed will look different depending on the person or the situation, but we always have an opportunity to act from love.

Take some time now to reflect on where you might currently privatize or limit your love. What would it look like for you to expand your love even further in big and small ways? How might you use your relationships as a launch pad for serving the world in bigger ways?

I had an opportunity to reflect more on this obstacle after I became a mother. As a highly introverted person, I'm likely to keep to myself or only make an effort to connect to a few close friends and family. If I don't check myself, this can lead to a significant privatization of my capacity to love.

After I had my daughter, however, that all changed. Little babies have a way of attracting attention wherever they go. So, whenever I took my daughter out in public, I found myself interacting with a lot more people than I used to. At first, I was a little uncomfortable with this, but then I chose to see it as an opportunity to give more love away. I started connecting with strangers about all kinds of things and even celebrating the miracle of life. This was an important lesson for me in how easy it can be for us to expand our net of love to include more. And I also learned that when I did that, I felt more connected to my brilliance and could receive more love myself.

OBSTACLE 2: Isolating from Community

When we are closed off in our hearts, we tend not to reach out as much to others for companionship, friendship, and community. As humans, one of the things we crave more than anything in this world is to feel like we belong, to overcome the fragmentation of our modern times and feel connected to other souls. If we lack community or fail to reach out to connect with others, we can lose our sense of humanity and be susceptible to deep loneliness. This can breed depression and further isolation. It's a nasty cycle.

I've noticed this obstacle happens a lot for people based in urban settings. There's a way that we can isolate ourselves even more when we're surrounded by millions of people. We just blend into the crowd and go unnoticed. If you tend to isolate yourself from others, it could help to, for example, engage in more small talk during your basic interactions with people, like when you are in a grocery store line or at the bank. From there, consider introducing yourself to your neighbors, if you haven't already, or inviting them to coffee if you've already met. You can build community slowly, but you must try if you wish to see a difference.

OBSTACLE 3: Feeling That Others Determine Your Self-Worth

Perhaps you feel unlovable unless you are in an intimate relationship with another. Or maybe you are overly focused on pleasing others. Or possibly you tend to lose yourself in relationships. When you are overly focused on the other, it is impossible to be truly present in the relationship. Instead, you are constantly living in a state of reactivity. This may work for a while, but eventually, this pattern is self-destructive. It is sometimes referred to as co-dependency—a dynamic in which you develop an excessive reliance on other people for approval and identity. Codependency is usually a learned behavior, and with diligence and the right support, it can also be unlearned. You can find book recommendations on codependency in the workbook, in the section called "Additional Resources."

OBSTACLE 4: Difficulty Forgiving

To be clear, forgiveness is not mandatory. It is always a choice. But it is helpful to look at our tendencies here to see where we might be keeping ourselves stuck. There's an old saying, "Not forgiving someone is like drinking poison and expecting the other person to die." It may sound harsh, but it does get the point across. When you do not forgive others, you perpetuate your own suffering.

You do not forgive to condone the actions or behaviors of others. You forgive so that you can have peace and move forward in a way that respects your truth. In other words, when you forgive someone else, you are ultimately doing it for *you*. Even if that other person is not able to receive your forgiveness for whatever reason, you can still offer it as a means to heal yourself.

Sometimes the person you need to forgive is yourself. In this case, the same idea applies. The more you can let go of the old way of relating to the hurtful story, the more you will be able to open up to new possibilities for connection and healing.

Unleash Your Power at the Brilliance Center of Love and Connection

We have already outlined a lot of success strategies for the Brilliance Center of Love and Connection. Here are a few more techniques to stay empowered at the heart level.

STRATEGY 1: Practice Vulnerability

Give yourself opportunities to practice vulnerability so that you can build up a tolerance for it. Then, if you ever find life thrusts you into a vulnerable situation, whether you like it or not, you will feel more prepared to handle it.

In my coach training, I ask the trainees to practice vulnerability not just verbally but also by eye-gazing. The group splits up into partners and spends time silently looking into each other's eyes. Undoubtedly, this can be an intense exercise! But it's important to learn how to be present to someone while still staying rooted in yourself as you encounter your own vulnerability. Perhaps you can try, in your own life, looking into people's eyes more intentionally as you speak to them.

STRATEGY 2: Proactively Create a Community

How do you create opportunity for *conscious* community in your life? Consider doing service work. Or maybe hold a potluck with acquaintances you would like to get to know better. Nowadays, with social media and meet-ups, there are clubs for just about everything out there.

For example, I occasionally host a community entrepreneurial mastermind potluck at my house for other women. I do not do this as part of my business, though it can help my business. Rather, I do it as a way of staying connected socially with others who have similar values. How could you bring more fun and connection into your life?

STRATEGY 3: Shower Others with Love

Once, when I lived in New York City, I found myself extra grumpy on a crowded, hot subway car. Rather than adding to the misery of the situation, I spontaneously and silently said blessings to every person I saw in the subway car. After each blessing, I'd close my eyes and imagine myself showering that person with rose petals in celebration of them.

I practiced this silent meditation all throughout the ride and quickly became happier and much more relaxed. Now I use this practice frequently, especially when I am feeling negative energy toward another. It is a simple but impactful way to energetically add more love to any situation.

STRATEGY 4: Take Your Inner Child on a Date

Still working on the self-love thing? Take your "inner child"—that part of you that sometimes feels unloved and wounded—on a date. Make it a day filled with nourishment of the greatest kind. Take naps. Play. Do the things you loved to do as a kid, but perhaps do not permit yourself to do anymore. Indulge your imagination and creativity. What would make you happy? If you really struggle with self-love and self-care, you may want to make this a regular thing.

Some of my clients have come up with creative ways to activate this strategy. Mary didn't just have a date with her inner child, but invited her husband along too. She planned a day for the two of them to celebrate all the quirky things about their childhood. As eighties babies, they filled their day with some of the classic music of the era, plus favorite childhood activities like building forts, roller skating, and going to the arcade. They finished off the day with a pizza dinner and ice cream for dessert! A bit kitschy and silly perhaps, but Mary and her husband, Tim, felt strongly reconnected to each other after the festivities, and Mary was feeling supercharged in her self-love too.

STRATEGY 5: Practice Breathing

What better way to embody a rhythm of balance and compassion in your life than to practice regulating your energy through the in- and out-breath? Breath practices drop us into the present moment where our power lies, and they provide a very real and tangible way to influence our energetic flow.

Feeling depleted? Focus more on the nourishment of the in-breath. Feeling scattered and overextended? Then focus more on letting go during the out-breath. Our breath is available to us at all times and is an excellent source of empowerment and healing. If you would like additional guidance on specific types of breath exercises, please refer to the "Working with the Breath" exercises included in the workbook.

STRATEGY 6: Practice Letting Go

If you are working on building trust, it usually helps to learn how to surrender the desire to control. Explore what it might look like to let things go, loosen up, or allow others to take charge where you traditionally like to be the one totally in control. You do not have to do it all at once. As with practicing vulnerability, take baby steps.

Learning to let go is the prerequisite for receiving. If you hold on too much in the way of expectations, it can be difficult to receive. Relationships need some ebb and flow. Notice where you might be restricting the process by holding too tightly. A helpful prayer to recite when working on letting go is the Serenity Prayer by St. Francis: "God grant me the serenity to accept the things I cannot change, the courage to change the things I can, and wisdom to know the difference."

STRATEGY 7: Receive Compliments and Say "Thank You"

A big part of mastering self-love is learning to tolerate your own wonderfulness! Can you resist the temptation to self-deprecate or qualify, deflect, or deny a compliment the next time someone gives you one? What would happen if you let yourself just receive the validation? Sometimes, allowing yourself to receive compliments can be the small building blocks to a foundation of healthy self-love.

♦ SELF-INQUIRY EXERCISE: Your Relationships

Now it's time to do a self-inquiry exercise about your own Brilliance Center of Love and Connection. Record your answers to the following questions in your journal:

1. Describe a time when you forgave another person. What did that feel like? What did you have to let go of to make that possible? How did your life change because of forgiving this other person? Are there other places in your life where you would like to forgive like this again? Spend at least thirty minutes writing about this so that you are forced to go deeper than you might otherwise.

2. Practice this three-part exercise about your relationship fears:
   A. Complete the following sentence five times, with a different ending each time: "When it comes to relationships, I am afraid that…"
   B. Complete the following sentence once: "But most of all, when it comes to relationships, I am afraid that…"
   C. Answer the next question in relation to the fear you listed in point B: In what ways, negative *and* positive, has having that fear affected my life?

◆ **SELF-INQUIRY EXERCISE: Optimize Your Brilliance Center of Love**

To upgrade your potential for brilliance at this center, it's time to put what you've learned into practice:

1. After completing the previous self-inquiry exercise, you have more clarity about some of the fears that might get in the way of you optimizing your Brilliance Center of Love and Connection. Review your answers and the other insights you gathered from this chapter to identify a limiting belief that you have at this center, perhaps focusing on a particular relationship that you'd like to work on to be more brilliant.

2. Return to the self-inquiry exercise "Upgrading Your Beliefs to Optimize Your Brilliance" on page 62, in chapter 4. Follow Steps 2 to 6 for clearing a limiting belief pattern and replacing it with a new vision, applying these to a limiting belief you've identified in your Brilliance Center of Love and Connection.

If you feel stuck with identifying a limiting belief or would like some examples of common limiting beliefs in this area, refer to the exercise "Optimize Your Brilliance Center of Love and Connection" in the workbook for additional complimentary resources to support you.

You did it! Good job. Remember to say your new affirmation and feel your visualization in your body every day to reinforce this new pattern. Start implementing the action steps too. Brilliance begets more brilliance. Let's keep going.

CHAPTER 9

The Brilliance Center of Personal Power

Sentiment without action is the ruin of the soul.
—*Edward Abbey,* A Voice Crying in the Wilderness

O ur next stop on the journey is the Brilliance Center of Personal Power. This is where you can turn your energy into action. It is the brilliance center concerned with your sense of ego, strength, and will. It is often known as the fire center because it's the place from which you *activate* your intention and make stuff happen. This brilliance center relates to the third chakra, the *manipura* chakra, in the yoga tradition. Here, we reveal the potential to discover, uncover, and use our power. The action statement that encapsulates this brilliance center is

I do.

For our purposes on the journey to brilliance, let's think of power as directed energy. As part of the universe, we each have an aspect of the universal energy running through us. How we direct that energy is how we exercise our personal power. In order to use our power in a way that supports our brilliance, we need to take a closer look at what gets in the way of doing that. Specifically, we need to look at our fears.

How Fear Can Get in the Way of Our Brilliance
. . . .

Fear is an emotional response induced by a perceived threat. We have many responses to fear, including to run, fight, hide, and freeze. Fear can make us feel out of control and unable to access our power. It does this largely by keeping us stuck in our minds.

When we are feeling fear, we worry about what may or may not happen in the future. We are no longer mindful of the present moment. This is a problem because the only place we have access to our power *is* the present moment. So, if we want to move past our fears and into alignment with our brilliance, we have to bring ourselves back into the "now."

One way to stay in the now moment is to learn to harness your fear and make it your ally. After all, fear is just another form of feedback. Your fear shows you that you are in territory where you feel vulnerable. As scary as that may feel, it is also an opportunity to learn how to be with your vulnerability in a new, more empowering way. Let's look at a few examples.

A New Way to Relate
Genevieve had a big fear of abandonment. In several past relationships, her partners had left her suddenly and unexpectedly and, as a result, whenever she started to feel close to someone she was dating, she shut down and became aloof. She was worried this pattern was going to sabotage her current relationship with Sean. To make fear her ally, Genevieve consciously recognized every time the fear of abandonment creeped up in her thoughts. When it did, she made a point of reaching out to Sean to connect with him. If she was in the same room with him, she might even go over and gently place her hand on his knee, and she would tell him she was feeling vulnerable about being abandoned. Much to her surprise, this only made Sean want to be closer to her. By making fear her ally, Genevieve was able to stay in the present moment instead of focusing on past traumas, and as a result she was able to cultivate a stronger connection of intimacy with Sean.

Taking a Leap
Paul was ready to quit his job as a graphic designer. He loved his work, but he'd been under the supervision of a senior designer for a while. And he really didn't like his boss. He thought he could do a lot better if he started his own graphic design business. As ready as he felt to make the break, he still had a lot

of fear. He had steady work at his current gig, and he wasn't sure he'd be able to handle all the new business management he'd need to tend to on his own.

Nonetheless, Paul decided to take the leap. Instead of letting his fear paralyze him, Paul embraced it as a motivator for showing up more fully. He channeled the energy behind his fear into an intention for personal excellence. His fear gave him heightened awareness, and that made him better at attending to all the fine details and strategic preparation he would need to master in order to succeed on his own. By harnessing the power behind his fear, Paul was able to show up wholeheartedly and make his new business a success.

Running With It

Claire's office, where she worked in Chicago, had just promoted her to a new position in Seattle. She was terrified to leave her known community. She didn't know anyone in Seattle, but she really wanted to take the job. When we talked about how she was experiencing fear on a day-to-day basis, she described feeling edgy and anxious, like she had ants crawling under her skin. I knew Claire was a runner, and I suggested she start training for that marathon she'd always wanted to do to give her an outlet to process some of that excess energy. Not only did Claire start training, but the marathon she chose was the Seattle marathon, in her soon-to-be hometown. Once she moved, she found a local group of runners who were training to run the marathon for charity. By using fear as her ally, Claire was able to accomplish a long-time personal goal and facilitate building a community of friends in her new home.

As these examples show, wherever there is fear, there is also power and opportunity to choose your brilliance. Here are some helpful tips to remember when you want to make fear your ally.

TIP 1: Stop Trying to Be the Superhero

In a lot of New Age spirituality material, there can be a push to be *fearless*, be bold, and go big. There is nothing wrong with wanting to go big and bold, but we do ourselves a disservice when we assume that we have to be fearless. It perpetuates a misconception that we have to feel totally confident and secure before we move forward with our dreams. Nothing could be further from the truth. If you are actively moving toward your dreams, you are very likely to be scared from time to time because you are pushing your edge. You are exploring new ground and new vulnerabilities. The goal is not to avoid fear or deny it, but rather to learn how to be with it in a different way—a way that empowers you instead of immobilizes you.

TIP 2: See Your Fear as Fuel

A tremendous amount of power is bottled up in your fear. In an episode of *MarieTV* called "The Power of Following Your Fear," coach Marie Forleo explains it like this: "Follow your fear. It's a GPS for where your soul wants you to go." Knowing this, if you can learn to feel the physical sensation of fear in your body without getting attached to the story of your fear that your mind wants to tell you, you can learn to channel that energy in a new direction. That's a powerful turnaround!

Next time you feel fear, press pause. Slow it down and feel what is happening in your body. Describe the physical sensations to yourself, and then decide where you would like that energy to go. Give yourself a clear and direct action you can take, no matter how small, that will move you in the direction you intend. A helpful question I ask myself when I am trying to reorient my fear is, "What would be the next best step to move me in the direction I want to go?"

TIP 3: Keep Good Company

Fear has a hard time keeping its grip on you if you are surrounded with others who already know and actively harness their fear as their ally. Naysayers, critics, cynics, and procrastinators tend to perpetuate a negative relationship with fear. Seek out others who are also trying to relate to their fear in a new way and support each other.

TIP 4: Investigate Limiting Beliefs around Fear

When fear has subsided, investigate what limiting beliefs may be contributing to your feelings. If we are not diligent with weeding out the beliefs that no longer serve us, when fear flares up again, it may feel challenging to reorient to a more positive way in the heat of the moment. Take the time to reflect on your fears and the beliefs they foster. Use the techniques you are learning in this book to help you proactively create a new story where fear is no longer your enemy, but your ally.

Learning to Believe in Yourself

We cannot talk about personal power without also discussing self-esteem. Even if you have all the personal power you could possibly ever want, if you do not believe in yourself, it is next to impossible to be motivated in any significant way. We know this, and still there are so many things that get in the way of us feeling confident about ourselves. Why?

It has a lot to do with what we have been taught. At a very young age, you start to learn "the rules" of society. You are taught to obey your parents or guardians first, then your teachers, bosses, government, and so on. In essence, you learn what are considered acceptable ways to behave, think, and look. You also learn that if you stray from what is considered the standard, even if it feels more authentic to you, you run the risk of not being accepted. You may even suffer other consequences. So, very often, we choose to conform.

Some level of conformity in society is important. For example, we all need to follow the same traffic laws so no one gets hurt. But when the need for conformity gets internalized in our minds to the extent that we feel we need to adjust the way we look, act, or speak just so we can be accepted, it's a breeding ground for insecurities, self-doubt, shame, or even self-loathing. We find ways to manage our "image," and we start to forfeit our power in big and small ways. Here are some examples of what this might look like.

Hiding His Identity

Michael was an extremely successful businessman and manager in the tech world. His reputation was so well known that newly graduated hiring prospects with lots of student debt were lining up to do unpaid internships with him just to be exposed to his brilliance. To the outside world, things looked grand for Michael. But inside, Michael felt quite compromised. He was a gay man, and he felt like he couldn't own this part of himself freely or he might suffer negative consequences in his professional circles. His job often required him to interact with a lot of conservative individuals, and Michael was sure there would be judgment, gossip, and perhaps even loss of business if some of them knew his truth. Rather than deal with that potential fallout, Michael, in his words, just decided to "suck it up," even though it made him feel bad about himself to do so.

Making Herself Small

Suzanne was taught to be the "good little girl." For as long as she could remember, it was modeled to her that women and girls were supposed to be pretty and polite and always do what they were told. A self-aware adult woman now, Suzanne knew she didn't have to buy into this old patriarchal view if she didn't want to. But still, she caught herself many times falling back into habits that aligned with this belief pattern anyway. For example, when her boyfriend, Trent, would ask her what she wanted to do that night, Suzanne would often catch herself saying, "I don't care. What would you like to do?" Even though she clearly had preferences, she would default to Trent's desires to avoid saying something that might make her appear "unacceptable." Every time this happened and Suzanne was aware of it, she felt foolish and bad about herself. Her inner critic would call her "lame" and "childish" for not speaking her truth, but she was still scared by the prospect of saying the wrong thing. So, she just kept engaging this pattern anyway.

When we start to entertain negative self-talk in our minds, we risk taking it as solid truth. Then, we start to question our sense of self-worth. It is as if we all downloaded some software program with a nasty virus on it, and it's causing us to forget who we really are. We forget our true nature—our brilliance. Of course, it is unlikely that we are going to feel good about ourselves all the time, but here are a few things we can do to enhance our confidence and remember our self-worth in those vulnerable moments.

TIP 1: Eliminate Excuses

You can use your mind to convince yourself of just about anything. A lot of times when you feel fear or lack of confidence, you use your self-talk to justify your lack of action.

- "I just don't have time."
- "It is not a good fit."
- "I can start my new exercise routine tomorrow."

If you want it, there will always be an excuse waiting for you. However, if you want to get a better grip on self-esteem, it helps to make a no-tolerance policy for excuses and instead choose a relationship of honesty with yourself. Instead of giving into the fear or lack of confidence, turn it around with an empowering declaration, just as you learned to do in chapter 4. For examples of helpful empowering declarations specifically for self-esteem, please see the "Bolstering Your Self-Esteem" exercise in the workbook.

TIP 2: Get Support to See Your Blind Spots

Because we are usually our own harshest critics, it can be challenging to see our own blind spots. Consider talking to a close friend, a mentor, or even a coach or therapist and share with them feelings you have about yourself. Ask for their perspective, not to receive their approval or even for them to make you feel better. Ask them to support you in determining if what you think about yourself is a distortion in your head, or if it holds actual truth. It is important to do this only with someone you trust. If you're not certain a friend or close loved one could do this for you, it's best to seek out a professional therapist.

TIP 3: Hold Mistakes Lightly

I can guarantee that if you are going forth on your path to brilliance, you will encounter times when you make mistakes. Try not to blow it out of proportion. Keep perspective and learn to laugh at your mistakes, or at least hold them lightly. You do not have to use them as another reason to beat yourself up. Over-seriousness has a way of breeding extra criticism.

My acupuncturist had a great technique for helping me make light of my inner critic. I once came into a session criticizing myself because I had just written a whole chapter of a book and then lost it instantly when I spilled my tea over my computer and fried my hard drive. He gave me a sweet smile and told me to close my eyes and imagine it happening again in my head. But this time, instead of me spilling the tea, I should imagine it was a bunch of circus monkeys. He told me we all have a "monkey mind" that likes to keep us on a circus wheel of negative thoughts constantly, but it's best we don't take that part too seriously. It was a silly image, and effective at breaking me out of my self-critical state.

TIP 4: Don't Make Yourself Special...In That Unhelpful Way

When we lack confidence, we have a way of singling ourselves out:

- "I'm the only one who always gets it wrong."
- "Everybody else has their life figured out."
- "A good relationship is just not possible for me. Something is wrong with me."

When we isolate ourselves like this, it makes us feel even worse. And most of the time, it's not even true. Everyone has down moments. Everyone has self-doubts, and everyone has bad feelings about themselves on occasion. I experienced a powerful example of this truth while leading an empowerment retreat for teenage girls. I had asked the girls to each anonymously write down a negative belief they had about themselves. I then took their responses and wrote all those negative beliefs up on a board. As they looked them over, I asked them to raise their hand if they had felt a belief on that board before, even though it wasn't the one they'd written down. Everyone raised their hand. Then I asked, "How many of you, at one time or another, have felt every belief you see on this board?" Sadly, every hand went up.

The reality is that part of the human condition is to be susceptible to negative thoughts about ourselves. But we don't have to choose that route. There is an old saying: "The grass is not greener on the other side. The grass is greener where you water it." Notice where you let your attention go, as that is what will take root in your mind.

TIP 5: Use Your Body

I mean this suggestion in two ways. Firstly, engaging in a regular exercise routine improves your hormone regulation, and that levels out your moods. A more emotionally balanced you means a more confident you. Secondly, when you feel less than good about yourself, sometimes it can help to position your body in a certain way to help boost your mood or mental disposition.

Have you ever noticed that when you're feeling depressed, it's hard to keep your chest open, your shoulders back, and your chin up? If you feel a bout of negativity coming on, try holding your body in an open position like this for a few minutes and see if it sparks a different mental outlet. Or, if you are feeling even more bold, maybe you can take a stance of a favorite archetype to supercharge your mood or outlook. For example, whenever I need an extra confidence boost, I take a "warrior II" yoga pose to feel a sense of confidence move through my body. Other times, I might take the classic "Wonder Woman" pose with my feet spread out and my hands on my hips. In truth, it doesn't really matter what the pose is, as long as it's one that makes you feel good. If you like, you can even put on music that pumps you up to get an extra boost with this technique. For examples of some power pose techniques, refer to the "Power Poses" exercise in the workbook.

TIP 6: Work Through Your Shame

Shame is a nasty thing. Guilt is what you feel when you think, "I did a bad thing." But with shame, you feel, "I *am* a bad person." It makes you feel faulty, damaged, unworthy, and broken. With shame, you start to believe "something is wrong with me." Shame keeps us trapped in the ego realm, and we feel cut off from the wise contextual view of our soul and our brilliance. Sometimes, we do not even want to admit to ourselves that we have shame because it might feel embarrassing to do so. What are we to do?

The first step to overcoming shame is to acknowledge it. This technique is sometimes called "Name It to Tame It." Once you have named it, it has less power over you. Then, you have an opportunity to drop into the present moment and re-script the inner dialogue to a healthier one. Please note that shame may take a long time to work through, and it could be very useful to work with a therapist if shame comes up a lot for you. I've put together a selection of helpful resources to work with on shame in the "Additional Resources" section of the workbook.

TIP 7: Be on Your Own Team

I struggled for years with low self-esteem, largely because I had such a harsh inner critic. My perfectionism and my high ambition kept me always pushing to go forward and do better. Somehow, I never felt enough. Then, one day, I was complaining to one of my sisters about how crappy I felt about myself, and she gave me some wise advice. She said, "Decide for once to be your own biggest cheerleader instead of your biggest critic." For some reason, that time it landed for me, and I changed the rules.

From then on, I was going to put all my ambition and drive into my dreams, but also into being the best friend to myself that I could be. I still have my moments when I falter, but as soon as I declared a new baseline of "cheerleader" instead of "critic," the outlook became much brighter.

Here's the simple truth: *No one on this planet (even your most cherished loved ones) are going to have more interest and investment in your happiness and well-being than you.* It is so incredibly simple that it's easy to forget. We need to be kind to ourselves, and our first priority needs to be showing up one hundred percent for ourselves. That is how we nourish our brilliance.

Making Choices That Align with Brilliance

Another area that falls under the realm of the Brilliance Center of Personal Power is that of willpower. In her book *Wheels of Life*, Anodea Judith describes will as "consciously controlled change." She explains how, as we make choices, we "[give] birth to the will." A healthy will can overcome the inertia of old patterns and negative habits to help you align more with your brilliance. But if you struggle with willpower, decision making could be a real problem area for you. Let's take a few examples.

Avoiding the Choice

You feel overweight and unhappy with your appearance. You know you could exercise more and eat healthier to bring the weight down, but you just cannot get motivated. You make excuses of not having time. You tell yourself you hate exercise. Deep inside, though, you know you are hurting. You want to feel motivated to take care of your health, but you feel ashamed and overwhelmed at the prospect of beginning. Rather than seek out support to work through the shame, you just keep ignoring the problem and putting it off for another day.

Lacking Motivation

Your marriage is on the rocks. You know this is largely due to your apathy around connecting intimately. You've been married nearly fifteen years, and you still love your spouse. But you feel so spent from your high-pressure job that by the time you get home from work, all you want to do is veg out. You're a good financial provider for the family, and you feel you should have the right to some down time. But "some down time" is turning into a regular pattern of numbing out and being totally unavailable for your partner and family. Your marriage is suffering, and you want to change it, but you just don't feel like you have the energy or motivation to do so.

Freezing Up

You are a passionate artist, and you make a reasonably good living. But you are experiencing a major creativity block. You've experienced these before, and you try all your old tricks to reboot, but nothing is working. So you feel like just giving up. Then you start thinking about how hard it is to do this as your profession. After all, the economy is bad, and our culture does not value the arts as much as it values other industries. You start to seriously consider taking that job at the family business that's been waiting for you as long as you can remember. You can hear your dad's voice in your head saying, "So, you're finally wising up and going to get yourself a real job!" That thought makes your stomach turn. You decide instead to just stay stuck right where you are, blocked, and do nothing, even though that feels like crap. You're paralyzed.

As these examples show, activating your will is no joke. So, what can you do to activate a healthy sense of will to support your brilliance in coming forth?

You need to be diligent about the choices you make. Most importantly, you need to choose very carefully where you let your energy go. That includes your mental, emotional, physical, and spiritual energy. Notice the story you use to describe your current situation. Is it a helpful one? If not, use the tools in this book to help you reframe it.

Sometimes, to activate our will and make choices, we need to drop into the specific details and determine our next action. I call this operating at the "30-foot level." Other times, it is appropriate to take a step back and consider the bigger picture before we choose our path. I call this the "30,000-foot level." We need both perspectives to make decisions that line up with our values and keep the momentum going in the here and now.

Flexibility is also essential, because we don't make decisions or activate our choices in a vacuum. The world around us will interact with our choices and affect the way things turn out. Remember Brilliance Principle #1: Be firm with intention and flexible with form.

It is also useful to remember what *not* to do when trying to make choices from an empowered place. Here are some tips.

TIP 1: Stop "Shoulding" Yourself

When we "should" ourselves, our actions start to feel like requirements. We are trying to make something happen out of force. Willpower coming solely out of forced action is much less effective because it is out of alignment with your personal energies. To inspire your actions, first intentionally connect to your soul's larger vision. Next, you can activate Brilliance Principle #3 and view your discipline as devotion to that vision. Then your actions are no longer coming from a place of "right" or "wrong" or "should" or "should not." Instead, they are coming from a place that says, "I choose to act in alignment with my soul, and that feels good even if this action is not necessarily the easiest one for me to take right now." For a simple word upgrade, every time you catch yourself saying "should," replace it with the word "choose" and see how your energy shifts around the matter.

TIP 2: Know When Not to Act

Your will is like a muscle. Use it often, and it will get stronger. There will be other times, however, when it will feel right to let that "muscle" take a back seat so that you can surrender your will to a higher truth. Perhaps you have been trying at something for a long time and it is just not working out. It can sometimes help to step back to gain some perspective. Maybe you have missed something by being so close to the situation the whole time. Remember that choosing not to act is also a choice.

To put it another way, being willful is not about being a stubborn bulldozer and plowing through things with no awareness about the circumstances around you. There's a give and take in exercising your will in a healthy manner. Sometimes it will feel right to go full throttle, and other times you may need to back off. Listen to your intuition, and be aware of the natural ebb and flow that is part of any process.

Personal Power through Livelihood
. . . .

Your livelihood, or what we often call "work" or "career," is another area of your life that falls under the realm of the Brilliance Center of Personal Power. This is one of the biggest areas in your life where your sense of personal power will come forth.

Livelihood can be a touchy subject. Throughout our lives, we receive a lot of messages about what warrants a worthy livelihood and what does not. It can be hard to ignore this as you try to follow your own inner compass. Furthermore, especially in the United States, we have been handed down the lore of the American Dream—work hard enough and long enough, and you will achieve success. And "success," by the way, looks like owning a house with a picket fence and having two kids and a dog by the time you're in your mid-thirties.

As outdated as that dream may seem, it still has an impact on our consciousness collectively and individually. Many of us begin to feel bad, lazy, or lame if we do not have a job that we are unbelievably passionate about. Or perhaps we feel we screwed up because we do not have as lucrative a livelihood as we had hoped for, and we think we never will. The opportunities to put ourselves down and beat ourselves up about our livelihoods are endless. Let's look at an example.

Priya was a practicing doctor in a family medicine office. She was the first in her family to go to college, and there had been a lot of pressure on her to go to medical school, become a doctor, and make a name for herself. She reasonably liked science, and she loved her parents. So, she went along with this ideal because it seemed like the best and most logical thing to do. Years into her career, however, Priya started to question her decision.

She discovered that she really didn't like the work as much as she had anticipated she would. There was a lot of bureaucracy and red tape she had to deal with daily that made her feel disillusioned and ineffectual at her job. She also felt irritated that the system was set up so that she would have minimal contact with patients and spend a lot more time in front of a computer screen than she had realized. The money was good, but her heart wasn't in it as much as she'd thought it would be.

Because it had taken a long time to get to this point in her career, and because so many people in her family were deeply proud of her accomplishment, Priya felt foolish and embarrassed to find herself in this position. Her inner critic was telling her she should have realized she didn't want to be a doctor *before* she went to medical school and spent all her parent's money on years of education. She had a lot of shame and guilt around her feelings, and she wasn't sure what she would want to do if she pursued another career.

Through our work together, Priya was able to step back from the outside pressures for a moment and check in with her inner compass. It took a lot of patience and self-compassion, but she discerned that she didn't mind being a doctor after all. But she didn't want to do it in the traditional way that her family expected. Instead, she wanted to be on the front lines, where her skills were vitally needed. She wanted more time with patients and less bureaucracy.

She followed this thread of inner wisdom and began exploring other options. She secured a job for herself with Doctors Without Borders, which allowed her to work in different countries and explore a passion for travel while connecting with patients and using her skills in ways that felt deeply meaningful to her. Her parents never fully embraced Priya's decision, but in her heart she knew it was the right thing for her to do. She felt that the best way she could honor her parents and the opportunities they had afforded her was to be true to her brilliance and serve from there. Years later, Priya is still a doctor, now happily practicing and living in the United States.

Like Priya, your adventures in the livelihood realm can become a lot less stressful if you learn to apply the following helpful insights.

TIP 1: Define Success on Your Own Terms

I have mentioned this concept before, and it is an extremely relevant one to keep in mind as you consider your choices regarding your livelihood. Are you crystal clear on what your definition of success is for your livelihood? For example, during my early days as a yoga teacher, I adopted the common belief that more money equals more success. And since I wanted to be successful, I worked more and more to bring in the money. But much to my surprise, I found my overall sense of happiness going down after a certain point. Sure, I had more money in the bank than I'd ever had before, but I also had no time to myself. I was working exhausting hours. I barely had time to relax, and my personal life was suffering. After a time, I reevaluated, clarifying what success meant to me, and decided to scale back my hours and move into a cheaper apartment. The following year, I made a lot less money, and I was a whole lot happier! Do not assume you know your definition of success. Write it out and get clear so that you can see where adjustments need to be made.

TIP 2: Let Go of the Fairytale

Now more than ever, with the invention of the internet, it's incredibly easy to be exposed to the common fairytale: "I have found the job of my dreams, and now I am living my best life!" I appreciate the impulse to encourage people to follow their passion and to inspire them by sharing a tale of victory. The downside to this, though, is that as a society we have begun to perpetuate the idea that following your passion always feels like some blissed-out experience. There's a belief that if you are willing to work hard enough, you most definitely will find a job that lights up your heart. In truth, it is more complex than that.

Following your passion does not always feel blissful. Sometimes, it pulls up your most vulnerable feelings. It challenges you. It makes you doubt yourself. It demands discipline, strength, bravery, and a willingness to fail. Of course, if we shared all that, those fairytale stories would not sound nearly as sexy. So, we hide those aspects or downplay them significantly. The truth is, if you are following your passion, you are going to constantly put yourself on new edges of growth, and that is likely to feel uncomfortable and unpleasant, at least some of the time.

It is also not always the case that someone's livelihood matches up perfectly with their greatest passions, nor is it a requirement that one have a passion-filled career in order to live a brilliant life. Where is it written that passion has to be restricted to livelihood? I know many brilliant souls who have jobs that they use as a means to an end so that they can pursue their passions outside work. I also know people who have multiple smaller jobs that allow them to pursue many passions simultaneously. And I also know people whose passion just happens to line up with the way they make money. But, no matter what type of situation the person is in, I notice the ones who feel most fulfilled and alive in their brilliance are those who have given up the fairytales they were told and explored finding the truth that worked best for them. They make conscious choices. They create inspiring narratives to tell themselves, no matter what their external circumstances. They stay flexible and learn more about themselves while the journey unfolds. And they always express gratitude for the process. Whatever their livelihood, they find a way to show up passionately, and that's what makes the difference.

TIP 3: Embrace Doing It Your Way

Your livelihood is ever-evolving, and there is no one right way to do this. This may seem obvious, but it is important to remind yourself of this as you pursue a livelihood that best supports your needs. Do you find yourself stuck in a job you can't stand just so you can pay the bills? Are you feeling like you are off track because you do not have the type of career you thought you would have at your age? Or do you feel disappointed because the job you trained for and absolutely thought you would love turned out to be a lot different than you expected?

Whatever the circumstance, if your current livelihood is less than desirable, remember to keep in mind the larger context. With each new decision you make moving forward in this area of your life, you will reach another point at which you understand more about what might work best for you as you move ahead. Stay positive and get clear on the vision you have for yourself. This will make it easier to keep going even when you are not feeling so enthused. To help you get started, you can access a guided visualization through the workbook entitled "Your Brilliant Livelihood" to take your first steps in designing your vision for brilliance as it relates to your career. Enjoy!

Optimization at the Brilliance Center of Personal Power
. . . .

What happens when your Brilliance Center of Personal Power truly flourishes? Though it never looks the same in anyone, here are some possibilities that you are likely to see.

POSSIBILITY 1: You Take Healthy Risks

Using fear as a form of fuel and feedback, we can assess risk and determine the best way to move ahead. We become strategic in our decision making and develop critical-thinking skills. When assessing a potential risk, we consider how taking that risk would or would not align with our core values and intentions.

We also consider what it will require to take this risk. We determine what would be the best- and worst-case scenarios that could result from taking this risk. Finally, we think about what we will be able to walk away with, even if the risk does not turn out as hoped.

POSSIBILITY 2: You "Go with the Flow" and Release Control

When we release control and go with the flow, we stop trying to manage our circumstances, to minimize our vulnerability, and to position ourselves for the most comfortable ride possible. Instead, we embrace the journey with open arms. We welcome the uncertainty as an opportunity to practice curiosity, mindfulness, and trust. It's not a passive experience. Rather, it's a conscious stepping into a place of receptivity as we respond to the cues of the universe.

Our actions are then guided by a heightened awareness within ourselves as we learn to be better listeners and receivers in all that we do. For me, the concept of "going with the flow" invokes the image of floating down the center of a river, letting the current gently guide me as I take in the fullness of my surroundings. If I encounter obstacles on the path, I am still able to respond and navigate my way around them. But I don't needlessly struggle to hold on to the banks of the river to control the pacing and flow of my journey. That would just make the experience more cumbersome and less effective, and it would cause me more suffering. Instead, I opt for trust and let myself surrender to the larger process at hand. I become a co-creator with the universe then, and I stay open to the river supporting me in aligning more fully with my brilliance.

POSSIBILITY 3: You Feel Positive and Confident

It's not always easy to stay positive in today's world. It is fashionable to be sarcastic and self-deprecating. It is very tempting to get sucked into all the media exposure telling you how you need to improve and change yourself to be that "perfect" being that is worthier of love than you are right now. Sigh. Even the most sophisticated and conscious souls can get pulled under by this illusion.

When you thrive at this brilliance center, you find yourself a lot less susceptible to the "noise" outside. Imagine you are a radio tower putting out a high-vibration signal. As your positive message beams out into the world, it attracts to you only that which is resonant. Keeping your thoughts and words positive brings in more of the same.

Often, confidence is not so much an end-state that we achieve one day. Rather, it is a choice we make repeatedly in the continuous stream of "now" moments. When we choose to say yes to ourselves, we build confidence. When we deflect or deny our light, we weaken this inner force.

POSSIBILITY 4: You Are Playful at Work

There is a kind of fluidity and gracefulness that comes when we feel optimized in this brilliance center. We no longer compartmentalize things so strictly in our minds. We see joy and playfulness even in the things we do to be productive. We have an overall enthusiasm for life, and we find enjoyment in whatever we do, even if it does not involve the most passionate of subjects.

The secret to unleashing this kind of vibrancy is to remember it is discovered in the little things we do far more often than we realize. You do not have to make massive, sweeping shifts in your life to awaken this passion. For example, when I had an incredibly monotonous temp job stuffing envelopes, I decided to make the best of it. Some days I made a game of it, racing against the other temp workers in the office. Other days I would engage in long discussions with my co-workers to pass the time. Use your creativity to find what is joyful even in the mundane.

POSSIBILITY 5: You Channel Anger into Creative Tension

Our center for personal power also houses our capacity for anger. Perhaps you've learned to suppress your anger because you were taught that it was not a suitable emotion to display. Or maybe you have occasional outbursts and find anger difficult to manage. Either way, just like fear, anger is a kind of fuel, an actual energy that exists in the body that can be channeled into all kinds of actions.

A very powerful way to use the fuel of anger is to turn it into creative tension. You do this by leveraging the story of your anger to create a more positive outcome. Often individuals who have suffered a tremendous loss do this. Instead of getting lost in their anger or grief, they pour their energy into a passion project.

That is how the organization M.A.D.D. (Mothers Against Drunk Driving) began. One mother lost her child to a drunk-driving accident. Now, decades later, the organization she started in the aftermath of her loss has become one of the most influential and widely supported non-profit organizations in the United States, helping victims of drunk-driving accidents and their loved ones. There is great power in anger, and it can be an incredibly creative force when directed strategically.

POSSIBILITY 6: You Have Enthusiasm and Passion for Living

When you stoke the fires of the Brilliance Center of Personal Power, it awakens a deep passion for life, one that is not reliant on external sources to burn bright. And once this fire is ignited, it can last a lifetime.

For many years in New York City, I taught yoga classes to Alzheimer's residents in a nursing home. Even though their mental capacities and ability to communicate were often challenged, the residents who had a natural passion and enthusiasm for life still stood out from the rest. I remember one woman, Marilyn, was such a positive and passionate individual that everyone on the unit benefited from her presence. She would "cha-cha" down the hallway while she hummed some of her favorite big band tunes from the old days. She would frequently give hugs to people, just because. No matter how bad the pain became in her body due to some of her physical ailments, she would always find a way to look at the bright side.

I once had the great fortune of meeting her family, and they told me that Marilyn had been like this her whole life. She was always full of passion and enthusiasm. No matter what life threw her way, she rode the waves with ease and grace, staying connected to her brilliance. A thriving Brilliance Center of Personal Power will afford you this kind of connection to your life force.

Obstacles to the Brilliance Center of Personal Power

Let's examine some of the obstacles we might encounter in this brilliance center. Suppose your Brilliance Center of Personal Power, your fire center, has been dampened down to a mere pilot light. Or perhaps it's starting to expand out of control, with flames raging on the edge of an explosion. How might these imbalances show up in your brilliance?

OBSTACLE 1: Defaulting to the Extremes of Power

You may default to the extremes of power and become submissive and passive at one side of the spectrum or overly controlling and aggressive at the other. Personal power exists on a spectrum. If you feel your inner fires are dampened, you may be more prone to submissiveness, passivity, and repression of anger. On the other extreme, when your inner fire is in overdrive, you may become domineering and aggressive. In both cases, the balance is out of whack.

Learning to balance your sense of personal power requires you to be self-aware first. A lot of the work we have been doing in this book until now has been directly related to your sense of personal power. If there are areas where you struggle with limiting beliefs, keep investigating them. Get the support you need to help uncover the opportunities that exist under those old belief patterns. Challenge your assumptions about yourself. Stay curious, and look for new growing edges. Balancing your personal power is an ongoing process that requires regular self-inquiry and commitment. Stay the course.

OBSTACLE 2: Comparing and Being Overly Competitive

The less confident you feel about yourself, the more likely you are to compare yourself to others. Comparison is a no-win situation. It robs you of your joy and keeps you oriented to outside perceptions instead of connecting with your inner wisdom. Imagine comparing a sunflower to a rose. One is not better than the other. They are just different, both beautiful and magnificent. It becomes easier to stop comparing yourself with others if you make a point of establishing a deliberate relationship with yourself. With daily meditation, I am much clearer now about what thoughts in my head are truth and which are just noise. When a richer inner dialogue takes place, comparison more readily falls away.

OBSTACLE 3: Suffering from Overambition and Workaholism

A personal power center in overdrive might seem appealing at first. "Wow! Look at how much I can get done, and look how rewarded I am for doing more…and more…" What may have initially started out as a healthy impulse can go awry if we neglect our boundaries, our health, and our well-being. In today's Western world especially, there is a big emphasis on livelihood and work. The most common question we are asked when we first meet someone is, "What do you do?" This cultural tendency to value livelihood and work above all else can often lead us to the belief that our work is the primary place where our self-worth comes from. For many, it is where they feel most capable, adept, and acknowledged. This, in part, has led to an epidemic of workaholism and ambition gone wild.

It is wonderful to feel accomplished at your work and proud of the job you do. It is also great to enjoy your work and to want to prioritize it. But, if you always choose work, or perhaps even hide behind it as a means of avoiding other parts of your life, press pause. Your self-worth does not come from your form of employment. You will limit your brilliance if you use your job as an excuse to avoid other parts of your life. Have an honest conversation with yourself about your work boundaries. Do you need to work as much as you do? Are you avoiding things by focusing on work all the time? Do you believe your only sense of worthiness comes from what you do? Challenge your assumptions and see what you discover.

OBSTACLE 4: Struggling to Motivate Yourself

We all have days when we feel less motivated. However, if you suffer from chronic lack of motivation and consistently procrastinate, you may be dealing with something a little more significant. Usually, when these behaviors ensue, you are avoiding or resisting something. It could help to ask yourself what you are afraid might happen if you were motivated and did what you intended. Are you afraid to fail? Are you afraid to succeed? Are you afraid to be vulnerable in some way? Get clear on what you are resisting, and that can help you shift the momentum in another direction.

Be forewarned that sometimes the limiting belief you are resisting is buried so deep in your subconscious that you do not even know you have it. Or, you may be embarrassed to admit it out loud because it may sound ridiculous to your rational mind. Remember that beliefs are often not based on rationalism but on feelings. So, it is important to be kind and compassionate to yourself as you develop greater self-awareness here.

Procrastination and apathy also tend to happen more when we are in a bad mood. Keeping things positive and light in general is often a way to sustain motivation. Another helpful tip is to set small benchmarks and reward yourself when you achieve a goal. As silly as it may seem, research has shown that the belief that we will be rewarded in some way is responsible for up to three-quarters of our actions! Finally, surround yourself with others who are motivated. It's far more challenging to be apathetic when surrounded by activated, positive souls.

Unleash Your Power at the Brilliance Center of Personal Power

Truly, everything in this book could be used as a strategy to boost personal power, and we have already covered so much in this chapter. Nonetheless, here are a few more strategies to help you boost this brilliance center.

STRATEGY 1: Get Moving!

Find something that works for you—dancing, running, yoga, swimming, or whatever else lights you up. The body loves to move. Sadly, so much of our lives nowadays (at least in the Western world) is sedentary. When you move, you create a direct channel to feel yourself as energy. This is so important for us, especially if you tend to get stuck in your head and overthink. Often, when you move, you find yourself having insights or aha moments that give you just the push you need to break out of old patterns.

I set my phone alarm to buzz once an hour so that it reminds me to get up from my computer on my long work days and take a dance break. Five minutes of dancing or stretching always perks me right up and literally reboots my brain with the endorphin release. I find this to be much more effective (and much more fun!) than a coffee break.

STRATEGY 2: Set SMART Goals

If you struggle with goal setting, time management, and general motivation, this could be a helpful trick. Ask yourself the following questions as you set a goal:

- Is it **S**pecific?
- Is it **M**easurable?
- Is it **A**chievable?
- Is it **R**ealistic?
- Is it **T**ime-Bound?

The SMART goals acronym was first presented by consultant George Doran in the 1980s, and it has since been added on to by other consultants to create SMARTER goals. The additional "E" adds the question, "How can I **E**valuate this goal?" and the "R" stands for, "How can I **R**eevaluate this goal?" These two added letters are an important reminder that setting and meeting goals is a continually evolving process and often not linear.

STRATEGY 3: Celebrate Yourself

Here's a little trick I use on those days when I feel less confident. I created something called an "Acknowledgement Folder." Over the years, I have collected nice things people have said about me in, for example, birthday cards, testimonials, voice mail messages, and even social media posts. I've also collected things that remind me of my successes and victories in life, both personally and professionally. Then, when I am having a down day, I pull it out and read through it. It reminds me to keep things in perspective, to stay positive, and to be kind to myself. It always leaves a smile on my face and keeps me moving forward with more positivity. Try it!

STRATEGY 4: Play!

In *The Ambiguity of Play*, play researcher Brian Sutton-Smith reminds us that the opposite of play is not work, but depression. If you want to explore your passions and enthusiasm for life and be more spontaneous, what better way to do it than by playing?

What is play? Play is time without purpose. It is anything you can do that makes you feel uninhibited. In other words, when engaging in play, you couldn't care less what others think of you. You're just having fun! When you play, you also lose track of time.

Play is not a luxury. It is a necessity. Without play, the very nectar of life can dry up. What does your play look like? Is it being outside playing sports?

Is it drawing? Is it reading a book? Not sure? If that's the case, then I definitely suggest you make a play date with yourself and start exploring some options. Have fun!

◆ **SELF-INQUIRY EXERCISE: Personal Power**

In your journal, record your answers to the following prompts:

1. Name a fear you currently experience, perhaps one getting in the way of you doing, being, or having something you really want. Reflect on this fear and brainstorm ways you could make your fear your ally to help you get closer to your desired result.

2. How well does your current livelihood support your brilliance? Are there ways it could support your brilliance more? Please describe.

◆ **SELF-INQUIRY EXERCISE: Optimize Your Brilliance Center of Personal Power**

After completing this chapter and the above self-inquiries, you have a lot more insight into the Brilliance Center of Personal Power. To upgrade your potential for brilliance at this center, it's time to put what you've learned into practice:

1. Review what you've learned in this chapter and see where you might want to dig a little deeper to create a new vision for this center of brilliance. You might choose to focus on a particular fear that you would like to make your ally. Or you may focus on improving a self-esteem-limiting belief. Or you may look more closely at your livelihood and how it can be better aligned to support your brilliance. Choose a limiting belief in whatever area feels most beneficial for your process right now.

2. Return to the self-inquiry exercise "Upgrading Your Beliefs to Optimize Your Brilliance" on page 62, in chapter 4. Follow Steps 2 to 6 for clearing a limiting belief pattern and replacing it with a new vision, applying

these to the limiting belief you've identified in your Brilliance Center of Personal Power.

If you feel stuck with identifying a limiting belief or would like some examples of common limiting beliefs in this area, refer to the exercise "Optimize Your Brilliance Center of Personal Power" in the workbook.

Great job! You've completed another powerful step on your journey. Remember to connect to your new vision daily and start implementing action steps now to put your brilliance to work.

CHAPTER 10

The Brilliance Center of Emotions

Our feelings are not there to be condemned or conquered. They're there to be engaged and expressed with imagination and intelligence. —T.K. Coleman, Your Funky Mood Is Creative

We've come a long way on our journey now, but we have a few more stops to go. Our next destination is the Brilliance Center of Emotions. This brilliance center is governed by our desires, pleasures, sensations, sexuality, creativity, and, of course, emotions. It is also the brilliance center of movement and change. In the yoga tradition, this correlates to the second chakra, *svadhisthana* (*swad-he-stah-nah*), which translates as "one's own abode."

You've probably heard the phrase "your body is your temple." Well, that's what this brilliance center reminds us. Your body is the "abode" of your soul. It's the vehicle through which you experience this earthly realm. You explore the world through your senses, and through your experiences you discover the world and everything in it is in constant flux. Things are always changing, including your own emotions.

The intelligence at this brilliance center gives us the ability to feel and flow with that constant change, hopefully in a graceful way. The action statement that captures the essence of this brilliance center is

I feel.

Working with this brilliance center can be challenging, but also incredibly exciting and fulfilling too. After all, it is the brilliance center that rules over all those juicy (and messy) parts of our lives, such as emotions and sexuality. It's from this brilliance center that we learn to move and reach beyond ourselves and make connections with others and the world around us.

This is also the brilliance center of opposites, of masculine and feminine energies coursing through your body in a way that is totally unique to your being. It is the place from which you start to understand and explore your attraction to masculine and feminine energies outside yourself. In order to understand the workings of the brilliance in this center, it's imperative that we first do a deeper dive into the meaning of emotions.

The Importance of Emotions

My mentors David Gershon and Gail Straub describe emotions as "energy in motion: e + motion." When we express emotions, we are moving the energy of our unconscious feelings into the conscious realm.

Emotions are instinctual and inherently tied to movement. Just look at young children who cannot yet express their feelings through words. They will emote through their body with movement, expressions, and sounds. You may have also noticed that when you suppress your emotions, you feel tenser and more restricted in your body. For example, an angry person might lock their jaw and tighten their fists. A depressed person may have a slumped posture with rounded shoulders as they physically block the emotions in their chest.

It takes energy to hold emotions inside, sometimes a lot of energy. In fact, an extensive body of research shows that suppression of toxic negative emotions like anger, grief, resentment, and hate increases cortisol (the stress hormone), which directly suppresses immune system function. In some cases, this has been found to link to higher incidences of heart disease and cancer. On the other hand, if you have a healthy practice of releasing and processing your emotions, this can greatly improve your well-being and may even reduce your physical tension and stress.

Whether we are aware of them or not, emotions clearly affect our health. So that we can be more aware about how emotions affect alignment with our brilliance, let's explore some of the ways emotional well-being (or lack thereof) can show up in our lives.

Overidentifying with Your Emotions

When you overidentify with your emotions, you are ruled rather than informed by them. This "ruling" usually comes in the form of aversion or attachment.

We live in a world where pain is demonized and feeling good, happy, and carefree is considered ideal. If something feels uncomfortable, we are not typically encouraged to explore it and see what insights and information it has to offer us. This is unfortunate because all our emotions, pleasant or unpleasant in nature, are just forms of feedback. To deny ourselves our negative emotions deprives us of a tremendous amount of inner wisdom that could bring us into greater alignment with our brilliance.

One way we avoid our feelings is to repress them. Please note that *repression* is different from *suppression*. We all suppress our feelings from time to time. Let's say you have a fight with your daughter before work, and you don't want to appear overly emotional in your morning board meeting. So, you temporarily avoid those feelings in order to go about your day in a professional way. That is *suppression*. Later, when you get home from work, you reconnect with your daughter so you can process your argument and freely express your emotions together at that more appropriate time.

Repression of emotions can be a lot more serious. Repression develops when you have hidden your feelings so far in your unconscious that you don't even know you have them. These are usually negative feelings (often from your childhood), such as grief, anger, resentment, and rage, which have been buried for so long, you have, in essence, disowned them. However, those feelings are still very much in your body and psyche, and they influence your ability to show up in an emotionally healthy way in your present-day life. Let's consider a few examples of repressed emotions wreaking havoc.

Repressing Anger

Janet had been dating Rob for a while, and it was going quite well. But then Rob made a silly sarcastic joke about Janet, and she didn't just get mad, she felt like she wanted to hit him. Hard. Taken aback by her feelings, she tried to ignore them. Rob immediately apologized and never did it again. But Janet kept thinking about it. Eventually, she made up some reason to break up with him. She felt numb inside, but she convinced herself the relationship wasn't going anywhere anyway.

Partying to Avoid Loneliness

Ted hated to be alone. He fancied himself the life of the party. He was always organizing the happy hours after work, and he was active on several dating websites so that he could keep his social life busy. If he had to be at home by himself, binge-watching television and drinking beer until it got so late that he passed out on the couch was always a good way to close out the night. Sometimes, he felt lonely and depressed, but usually just for a little bit. And he could ignore it if he just drank another beer and kept his buzz going.

Denying Unhealed Trauma

Ellen was a put-together, independent, and strong woman. Everybody thought so. She felt good about her life. She had a decent job and a nice relationship. But one day, her boss, Louis, and she had a disagreement, and Louis raised his voice at Ellen quite loudly. Ellen froze and suddenly felt as though she were a five-year-old girl again and her father was yelling at her. She didn't understand it because she was usually so articulate and able to clearly express her feelings. But in that moment, she wanted to burst into tears and hide under her bed. Going forward, Ellen vowed to avoid all conflict with Louis, but her work began to suffer. She put so much energy into trying to keep Louis happy to avoid that uncomfortable feeling his anger aroused that she lost perspective on her strengths and capabilities.

As the examples show, for a while, we can function quite normally with repressed emotions. But eventually, those feelings will surface again in the body and demand our attention one way or another. If they are not dealt with intentionally, they may start to manifest as physical ailments. With repressed emotions, it's often quite challenging to connect with your brilliance because they create unconscious blocks in your energetic system.

Another way we avoid our feelings is by projecting them onto others. Projection is a psychological defense mechanism. When we project, we attribute characteristics that we find unacceptable in ourselves onto another person. This is often done unconsciously too. Let's look at a few more examples so we can start to see where we might be projecting.

Judging Others

Anna was out dancing with her girlfriends when she saw some female club performers on the stage. She immediately started gossiping with her friends about how slutty and ditzy the club girls must be. Even though she felt a strong dislike for them and the way they dressed and moved, she still couldn't take her eyes off them. She didn't like to admit it, but seeing them made her feel a whole lot of shame about her own body. Rather than feel that, it was easier to judge them.

Controlling Others

Jake was always pushing his son, Rick, to practice his football skills. He made him do extra drills after practice and enforced a strict curfew so that Rick could get ample rest before the big game days. Because of a knee injury, Jake was never able to get the college football scholarship he had badly wanted. And now, he was certainly not going to let his son miss that opportunity. Jake wished his dad had been as diligent with him as he was being with Rick. Had he been, Jake might not have failed and his life could have been totally different. He wasn't going to let Rick be a failure too.

Disliking Others

Mica was taught to like everyone, but when she met Valerie, a fellow editor at her magazine job, she felt jealous and annoyed by her. Valerie seemed so much smarter and better able to handle the stresses of work. Rather than admit her dislike, Mica decided that Valerie was the one who didn't like her. Valerie was kind of uppity, after all, and Mica convinced herself that Valerie must have thought she was better than everybody else. It felt better to think that than to feel the insecurities she was having.

These examples show how projection might create a temporary fix for dealing with uncomfortable emotions, but if you make a habit of it, you just postpone the inevitable. As long as you deny your negative emotions by projecting them onto others, you are unable to receive the feedback those emotions have to share with you in a healthy way. When we are willing to truly accept them, we can then process those emotions and align more fully with our brilliance.

The other way we overidentify with our emotions is to develop an attachment to them. Do you always seek that next high? Are you worried something might be wrong if you do not feel happy all the time? Do you incessantly seek out self-gratification and things that make you feel pleasure? Or, less extremely, maybe you are very attached to certain things in your life feeling a specific way. Here are some examples of unhealthy attachments to emotions.

Needing This One to Be "The One"

Skyler had only been dating Keith for a month, but she just knew he was the one. They were so compatible, and they always had a good time together. Keith "checked all the right boxes" in her vision for a life partner, and she consistently felt happy and loved around him. He was perfect. Though Skyler was aware she had a pattern of getting involved too quickly with people and, in the past, these situations ended badly, she was sure this time was different. Besides, she couldn't be alone anymore. She was already thirty and thought she really ought to be married by now.

Getting the Next Adrenaline High

Dre always sought that next adrenaline rush. He loved the high he got from that next big risk, that next challenge to conquer. He tried it all. He skydived, bungee jumped, surfed the biggest waves he could find, and scuba dove with sharks. His need for an adrenaline fix was getting harder and harder to meet daily, and his "regular" life was starting to feel flat and dull. He couldn't stand it. He was always looking for that next rush when he could really feel alive.

Excessive Attention Seeking

Charlotte loved the way she felt when she was the center of attention and all eyes were on her. She loved the powerful feeling that rushed over her in those moments. That was the only time in her life when she was sure she mattered. Getting a big, dramatic response out of people made her feel seen, like she couldn't be ignored. It didn't even matter how she did it. Whether it was by wearing provocative clothes or saying something irreverent or making a scene with a big emotional display, Charlotte was hooked on getting attention.

As these examples show, emotional attachments, like aversion strategies, aim to keep us feeling only the pleasant emotions so that we don't have to process painful or out-of-control feelings. Attachments and aversions often get developed within us because we were taught specific ways to be with our feelings when we were young. Much of this teaching was not direct, but implied. We were rewarded, maybe with a hug, smile, or some other sign of approval, when we expressed acceptable emotions. When we expressed undesirable emotions, we may have been ridiculed, shamed, or even punished. We may have received some verbal messages around these implied teachings too:

- "Good girls don't get angry."
- "Real men don't cry."
- "It is not ladylike to show too much enthusiasm."
- "It is impolite to say no."
- "You shouldn't act too sensual. Men will get the wrong message."
- "It's weak to show your feelings. Stop being such a little girl."

Even well into adulthood, these beliefs and patterns are perpetuated. For example, in many work environments, we are advised not to get "too emotional." Or in relationships, there are countless books telling us just how to behave to attract your mate: "Don't appear too eager"; "Laugh more"; "Don't be contradictory"; and so on. It's as if we were trying to fit these "messy and inconvenient" emotions into neat little boxes and make them behave. But emotions are not neat or convenient. A more helpful way to think about emotions is by considering the element that symbolically represents the energy of this brilliance center—water.

The Power of Water
. . . .

Water is an amazing element, and a very appropriate one to associate with the Brilliance Center of Emotions. In his book *Sensitive Chaos*, scientist Theodor Schwenk calls water the "cosmic sense organ of the earth." How appropriate!

Water takes part in all metabolic processes on earth and within living creatures. Water also holds a tremendous amount of sensitivity, shifting or changing constantly to respond to the energy around it. Watch how water moves when you drop something in it, when wind blows across it, or when things move within it. It reflects the energy it experiences in the world. Similarly, our emotions reflect the energy we experience inside ourselves as a result of being in this world.

Water is receptive, and it can take on any shape that it is offered. It embraces or mixes with whatever is dropped into it. It does not stop flowing when an obstacle is in its path. Rather, it moves through it or around it and keeps going. If we were to be more like this with our emotions and just let them "move through us," then we would be able to unlock the energy behind our feelings. Sadly, we frequently get stuck in the "story" of the emotion and prevent the natural flow of energy from coming through.

Chemically, water is neutral and holds a multitude of possibilities in how it may connect or mix with other things to create new forms. Behind the stories attached to our emotions, the energy is also neutral, and we can use it to create any variety of outcomes to support our brilliance if we know how to skillfully work with that energy. Water can refresh, purify, heal, cleanse, revive, and clarify, just like emotions can when we let them run their natural course through our bodies. Indeed, both water and our emotions contain a plethora of possibilities for transformation when we choose to be with them intelligently. It may be helpful to remember this metaphor as you read the rest of this chapter and learn various ways to support your potential at the Brilliance Center of Emotions.

Emotional Intelligence

How do we work with our emotions skillfully? A popular phrase nowadays is "emotional intelligence." This buzz word was created in response to the concept of IQ. Your IQ, or intelligence quotient, measures your ability to think and reason. Your EQ, or emotional quotient, measures your ability to identify, use, understand, and manage your emotions in positive ways that support your brilliance.

More and more research is proving that our emotional intelligence is a huge factor in determining our ability to attain success in life and career. In their book *Emotional Intelligence 2.0*, Travis Bradberry and Jean Greaves discuss how emotional intelligence can be the single biggest predictor of performance in the workplace and the strongest driver of leadership and personal excellence. They describe four key components to emotional intelligence.

COMPONENT 1: Self-Awareness

You have a lot of autonomy in how you want to react to an emotion, but first you must be aware that you even have it! Developing greater self-awareness of emotions requires you to tolerate the discomfort of focusing on feelings that you previously were not conscious of or were purposefully avoiding because they felt difficult.

If you have been unaware of your feeling for a long time, it may be quite challenging to put words to them. *Remember that beneath each emotion lies the physical sensations that express it in the body.* So, if you are not yet able to talk in terms of "I feel sad, glad, mad," and so on, then start with the sensations:

"I feel my jaw locking"; "My palms are sweaty"; "My breath is slowing down." Once you familiarize yourself with the sensations, the fuller picture of the emotion will begin to reveal itself to you.

COMPONENT 2: Self-Management

Self-management is how you act once you become aware of your emotions. You'll know you're making progress here when you are able to initiate behaviors aligned with your brilliance, even when you don't feel like it. For example, can you choose healthy foods and exercise even when you feel lazy and depressed? You have been learning many self-management and self-awareness techniques throughout this book, so you're on the right track!

COMPONENT 3: Social Awareness

Social awareness is your ability to accurately interpret emotional cues from others. This can support you greatly in effective communication. Interestingly, as your self-awareness skills around your emotions improve, you may also become more skilled at observing emotions in others. Both kinds of awareness require that we slow down and avoid making assumptions.

When practicing social awareness, be mindful not to assume that emotions look or feel the same for everybody. If you are not sure about how someone is feeling, if you sense it would be appropriate to ask them for input, go for it. I still do this occasionally, even with people I know very well, because I never want to assume I know the "right" interpretation.

COMPONENT 4: Relationship Management

Relationship management looks at your ability to manage your interactions successfully based on the other three components of your EQ. This is probably the toughest of the four components to master. We've already discussed several relationship strategies in chapter 8, and this chapter will provide more techniques for further expanding your repertoire.

Bradberry and Greaves point out one additional fact I'd like you to consider when thinking about how emotions affect our ability to align with brilliance: *we feel something before we think about it.* The way information enters your body through your senses is like an electrical impulse. The first place that impulse enters your brain is through the base of your spinal cord. Then it travels through the frontal lobe (behind your forehead), or the limbic system, which is where your emotions are produced. Only then, after the emotion has been experienced, does the impulse travel to the rational side of the brain. So, when we look at it on a basic biology level, we see why it is not enough to just *think* new thoughts to change our life. We must practice *feeling* new thoughts. Consider an example of putting this into practice to support our brilliance.

Sasha was a social worker in her mid-thirties. She was a well-adjusted, intelligent, and responsible young adult with a good job, a reasonable salary, and a nice circle of friends. Overall, she felt content with her life, and she had a promising future. The only area where she felt stuck was in relationships. Sasha had trouble trusting men. After doing a lot of self-inquiry work, she understood that this was related to an abandonment issue she had because her father left her family when Sasha was only six years old. She hadn't had any significant relationship with her father since, and what little she did hear about him wasn't positive.

Despite her best efforts to heal her wound around her father's leaving, she kept repeating the pattern of abandonment in her adult relationships with men. First, there was Brett. They were engaged, until Brett left her for another woman. She found out he'd been cheating on her for months. Then, there was Steve. They were on the track to marriage, but then Steve got offered a promotion in a law office in Miami that he just couldn't refuse. So, he left too. Finally, there was Brandon.

Sasha thought that for sure she'd finally worked through her "daddy issues" before linking up with Brandon. After all, she'd read just about every self-help book on the topic she could. She meditated. She went to talk therapy. She did forgiveness ceremonies, affirmations, vision boards, and reiki healing too. But after a year of being with Brandon, Sasha was in the same boat. Brandon rekindled an old flame with someone he felt was "the one," and he left Sasha too. She was crushed yet again.

Out of desperation to figure this pattern out once and for all, Sasha found a therapist, but this time one that worked somatically. This is a kind of body-centered therapy that looks at the connection between the mind and the body and uses both psychotherapy and physical therapies to help someone connect with and release the blocked emotions they hold in their body from past traumas.

Once they free up these old emotions, they are then able to truly *feel* new thoughts for the reality they want to create. Sasha didn't know if this would work for her, but she knew she had tried to *think* her way out of this pattern for years, and it wasn't working. If she had to get "messy" and do a deep dive into her old pain to clear it once and for all, she was ready.

For Sasha, this was the missing piece she needed. Like many young, well-educated women, Sasha tended to overintellectualize and analyze her problems. Until she really let herself feel, process, and release the pain from the past, it wasn't possible for her to create and feel a new reality. No matter what vision boards or affirmations she created, as long as the old emotional imprint was in her body, she was going to get the same old result.

It's important to note that this wasn't a quick fix for Sasha by any means. But after committing to the work and being willing to go to the vulnerable places inside herself to finally release the pain, Sasha made a lot of progress. She's started to date a whole other "type of guy." She's more aware of her blind spots now too, and she chooses potential mates much more wisely. And if it doesn't work out, it's not the feeling of deep despair or trauma that she experienced before. She's on her way to healing this part of herself so that she can create the relationship she really wants.

As we can see from this example, no matter how hard we try to ignore it, we are indeed emotionally wired creatures. Remember this as you move through the coming pages. Even if you are not inclined to the touchy-feely stuff of emotions, do yourself a favor and stay open minded. What you learn about your emotions can help you hugely in leading a more brilliant life. Next, we need to take a closer look at the warehouse of the emotions—the body.

The Wisdom of the Body

In our hyper-rational world, we commonly think that the intellect is the powerhouse of wisdom, but the body houses so much knowledge and understanding itself. *Your body holds the emotional imprints of all your experiences.* That is why, even if your mind has "moved on," as we saw in the last example, your body can hold unresolved emotions that may sabotage your plans for brilliance.

Your body understands the world largely through your senses. So, we cannot talk about the body without also talking about sensuality.

Sensuality. It is a loaded concept for many people. It so often gets linked to sex and pleasure, but it encompasses much more than that. Just think about your senses for a moment and how they open you up to so many wonderful experiences throughout your day:

- the delicious taste of your favorite home-cooked meal as it comes fresh out of the oven
- how a flannel robe or a silk shirt feel soft and smooth against your skin
- the way the colors of freshly bloomed flowers delight your eyes on a spring day
- the tantalizing smell of your favorite scent
- the relaxing sound of your favorite song soothing you on your drive home

Our days are filled with opportunities for us to connect to our sensuality, should we choose to. Unfortunately, a lot of us received less than helpful programming about how to be with our senses, and more specifically how to be with our *pleasure*.

Though we all have unique mental programming around pleasure based on our cultures, religions, upbringing, gender, and so on, many of the beliefs we learned about pleasure distort our relationship with it in some way. Some sources may have taught you that it is best to repress or fear pleasure. You may have heard things like, "Indulging in pleasure is not spiritual." Or, "It's not appropriate for a woman to have a big sex drive." Or maybe you heard, "There are more important things to do than tend to pleasures."

On the other side of the spectrum, people may encourage us to indulge in pleasure at all costs, regardless of the negative consequences. Perhaps it was suggested, "You only live once. You should do what feels good." Or, "More is better. You can never have enough" fame, sex, money, and so on.

Distortion around pleasure shows up in our society in many ways. First, there seems to be an epidemic of chronic workaholism, especially in the Western world. In this case, our priorities are efficiency and effectiveness above all else, and pleasure is left at the wayside. Inevitably, this leads to health problems, and it greatly influences family structures in our society too. In addition, our society's propensity to warp all messaging related to sex and our bodies has contributed to a huge problem with body-shame issues and eating disorders, among other concerns. Furthermore, addictions to drugs, alcohol, sex, pornography, and material things are all examples of how our views around pleasure can get grossly out of balance and lead to some very serious problems.

Clearly, we need to come to terms with how to have a healthy approach to our bodies, our sensuality, and our need for pleasure. One way to make progress here is to remember that indeed our bodies are our temples. If we reconnected to them in that light and established a relationship with them that reflects that level of respect, we would find things naturally returning to a place of healthy balance. Let's look at an example.

Mark liked to feel good and look good all the time. He worked hard as a consultant and made a good enough salary to buy all the right brand-name labels for his look. He spent much of his free time lifting weights at the gym so that he could keep up his appearance, and he'd even work through injuries to make sure he wouldn't lose his edge. He was on three different dating sites so he would always have a "hot" date by his side when he went out with his friends. To the outside world, Mark looked like he had it all together.

On the inside, though, Mark felt awful. He wasn't depressed, per se; more like numb. He felt his life was lame. He didn't have any close friends he could talk to about important things, and he wasn't sure he would know how to talk about those things if he did. He didn't have a girlfriend he loved or one who loved him. And his job was okay, but he was eventually going to top out salary-wise, and he didn't like the thought of that. Buying expensive clothes, dating, sleeping with attractive women, and gloating about these things were just about the only things that made him feel "alive." If he couldn't secure these usual pleasures to boost his mood, he would smoke weed and forget about life for a while.

Then one of his internet dates convinced him to go to a yoga class. Much to his surprise, Mark loved the class. It challenged him physically, more than he thought it would, and at the end of the class, after relaxation, Mark felt a wave of serenity like he hadn't felt in years, maybe ever, wash over him. He was curious enough to go back again on his own. And again. I happened to be teaching that first class, and Mark eventually asked me to start coaching him as well.

Fast-forward years later, and Mark is no longer a consultant. He's a yoga teacher! He leads retreats and chanting circles all over the world, and he has a men's group in which he teaches other men how to connect in healthy ways with their pleasure and emotions. It may seem like quite a transformation for Mark, especially if you knew him in his former life. But the reality is, once he had access to the tools and support that could help him develop self-awareness, he was able to completely change his relationship to his emotions and his need for pleasure. It was a long road for Mark, and he had to get honest with himself and vulnerable in ways that he never had before. But with patience and self-compassion, he was able to commit to a new balanced and healthy self-care regimen for his body, mind, and spirit—one that made it possible for him to find his true path to brilliance.

Mark's example shows us that we can detach from our bodies and only check in with them when we are using them as a means to an end, to seek out pleasure. Our mind-oriented world encourages us to think of our bodies as an afterthought. We neglect and abuse them, sometimes by eating less than ideal foods, not exercising enough, or pushing them too hard; other times by overtaxing them with extreme exercise and diet regimens to keep them looking a certain way.

Sadly, body abuse (or at a minimum, body neglect) is the standard for many of us. But what if you could think of your body as something more than just the vehicle that carries your brain around from one place to another? What if you could indeed treat your body as if it were *sacred*? Because it is! To support you in developing a more brilliant relationship with your body, I've included the "Brilliant Self-Care" self-inquiry exercise in the workbook. Be sure to carve out some time to do this important exercise as a first step in implementing a healthier self-care regimen for your body.

Sexuality

. . . .

Another area where the Brilliance Center of Emotions comes to life is in our sexuality. Of course, if you look at how pleasure gets distorted in our consciousness, you can imagine what happens when we start to talk about sexuality! As a society, instead of embracing a healthy emotional attitude toward sexuality and our bodies, we have managed to compartmentalize that aspect of our consciousness and subject it to all kinds of misrepresentation. It is commonplace to see messages of sexuality being intertwined with violence and objectification of bodies, especially women's bodies. This has been standard practice for generations. And now, damaging and dangerous media messages about sexuality only seem to be on the rise with the popularity of social media. No doubt, it is heavy to think about all of this, and just by being members of this society, we are inevitably affected by these messages.

Sexuality is one of the most primal forces in the body. It can be the means to help us generate a new life. But even if we never engage in procreation, our sexuality still offers us a way to open up to greater levels of passion and creativity in our beings. True sexuality is not about having sex with another or even making a child. It's about aligning with the fullness of our life force and living from there.

Though you may choose to engage in sexual relationships with others, you do not need to be in relation to another to feel and celebrate your own sexuality. When sexuality gets relegated to only intercourse or orgasm, we miss the mark. As feminist Judith Plaskow describes in her book, *Standing Again at Sinai*, "If sexuality is one dimension of our ability to live passionately, then in cutting off our sexual feelings, we diminish our overall power to feel, know, and value deeply." Whether you engage in sexual acts or not, your sexuality is still a hugely important force of brilliance within you that can inform many other parts of your life as well.

Most of what we believe about our sexuality we learned from others—our parents or guardians, religion, pop culture, social media, friends, colleagues, and so forth. There is a good chance that at least some of those beliefs that got filtered into your consciousness are less than helpful and are inhibiting you from having a more empowered relationship with your sexuality.

For example, Pamela is an incredibly talented artist and dancer, and you can see the full force of her sexuality come out in her artistic offerings. You feel alive in her presence just watching her perform. However, for Pamela, the stage was the only place she used to feel safe expressing her sexuality. She felt like she had some extra boundary of protection when she shared this part of herself in a performance.

If you were to meet Pamela off stage, she would appear quite shy and as though she was uncomfortable in her own skin at times. She mentioned this to me in our work together, and we started to explore her feelings around sexuality. Through our conversations, we uncovered that because of many different implied messages in her childhood, she had learned to believe that it was not safe to own her sexuality. The creative being that she was had a hard time accepting this, though. So, unconsciously, she had found a way to have the experience of this life force running through her body by channeling it into her artistic craft. It worked, for a while, to separate it out like this. After all, she had become quite an accomplished dancer. But the older she got, the more she felt like a fraud. How could she feel so good and confident in her body on stage but so scared and timid off stage? Who was her "real self"?

For Pamela, connecting to choice was important. She needed to remind herself that she could choose the extent to which she wanted to experience her sexuality, both on and off the stage. There were no expectations about how she was supposed to do this. I reminded her that her sexuality was for her alone, and that the rules about what she wanted to think and feel about this part of herself were up to her. I invited her to imagine her sexual life force as an adjustable flame inside her that she could turn up or down according to her desires and comfort level. I also encouraged her to think about the whole of life as one big "dance" so that she could break down any artificial boundaries that determined her sexuality could only happen on stage. Finally, I suggested she work with a therapist around old traumas that were influencing her ability to feel safe in her body.

With these approaches, tools, and support, Pamela began to create a new, more confident reality for herself around her sexuality. And, as one might suspect, this overflowed into other areas of her life as well. As she steps into the power of this life force, her business, her performances, her relationships, and her finances are all blossoming in positive ways.

Because our bodies are complex and contain all our emotional imprints, these types of transformations in perception may take quite some time, and they will require a fair bit of trust, faith, and courage from you, should you seek to explore a different way of being with your sexuality. If you are curious to learn more about the limiting beliefs you may have inherited around sexuality and how you can turn them around, please check out the self-inquiry exercise "Creating Empowering Beliefs about Sexuality" in the workbook.

Optimization at the Brilliance Center of Emotions

After looking at emotions, the body, and sexuality, you already have a strong grasp on what a healthy Brilliance Center of Emotions looks like. Here are a few other ways you can recognize when this center is optimized for you.

POSSIBILITY 1: You Embrace Change Gracefully

Remember our water imagery for this brilliance center? Water flows. It embraces the obstacles in the path or merges with them, but it does not let the obstacles stop the flow. I have noticed that people who are particularly good at flowing with change stay mindful and focus on the positive in the present moment. They do not waste much energy on worrying about the future or regretting the past. Instead, they stay focused on intention and how they want to show up in the now.

They also tend to take deeper breaths and think before they speak. They seem to have a regular practice of inner connection that allows them to be less reactive in life and more grounded in the knowledge of their core truth. This may sound a little too nice and neat, I know, but most of the time these individuals have worked at making a conscious choice to show up in this way. It takes practice before we can create a new habit. Stay committed and give yourself time to learn this new way of being "in the flow."

POSSIBILITY 2: You Balance Masculine and Feminine Energies

When I say "masculine" and "feminine" here, I am not referring to gender. Rather, in the yoga tradition, they describe a polarity between two types of energies. This polarity is also described in other traditions. The masculine energy tends to be fierier. It is linear, fast, direct, hard, robust, and hot. It has a catalytic power to it and is usually associated with *doing*. The feminine energy is cooler, more disperse, slower, and far more organic. It is nonlinear and has a soft and receptive quality. It is usually associated with the quality of *being*. It is more about the holding of space rather than any catalytic process. We need both these qualities to feel balanced. If we are more dominant in one, this sometimes creates challenges for us, individually and in our relationships with others. It's like the in-breath and the out-breath. Both are critical to our function.

Where do you think your natural tendencies lean—toward the feminine or the masculine energy? Remember, this has nothing to do with your gender. Generally, individuals find they have a tendency toward one type of energy over the other. I invite you to explore spending more time in the energy that is *not* your most dominant. Do you have stronger masculine energy? Practice being more receptive in your relationships. Are you more feminine in your energy? Explore what it feels like to be the initiator in your interactions. It will probably feel awkward, and you may resist this practice, at least a little bit if not a lot. Remind yourself that it is worth challenging your comfort zone to discover new aspects of yourself so you can show up even more brilliantly in life.

POSSIBILITY 3: You Nurture Yourself and Others

When you are truly in your brilliance in this center, you are comfortable in your own skin, and you sincerely nourish yourself with your words, thoughts, and actions. Your brilliance here awakens a healthy expression of the caregiver within. This self-nourishment also supports you in showing up in the world with a generosity of spirit that nourishes your relationships. It is like sweet nectar flowing out from an abundant well of goodness within.

In a world where anxiety is as contagious as the common cold, it is easy to forget that kindness is contagious too. It would be a mistake to think of kindness as a trivial afterthought or a weak offering. There's a saying, "Kindness is difficult to give away because it keeps coming back." Indeed, kindness has an expanding quality that opens us up more to new possibilities to shine. When you take a stance of kindness, it has a way of giving back to you tenfold.

POSSIBILITY 4: You Have Healthy Boundaries

It is hard to overstate how important healthy boundaries are. We discussed this in chapter 8 when we looked at relationships. Boundaries are the container for the life you want to live. Setting healthy boundaries is intricately tied to how you feel about and treat yourself. Boundaries also help you develop healthy emotional regulation so that you can avoid things like repression or projection. They provide you with safety, nourishment, and a place to rest and restore.

A boundary is not a wall or a rigid stance on how things have to be. A wall limits all positive outcomes. Steven Arterburn, founder and chairman of New Life Ministries, articulates it like this: "A wall confines you to a past that cannot be changed and to a future of more of the same." A boundary, however, is firm in intention but flexible in form, allowing for a future of hope and healing.

POSSIBILITY 5: You Feel Embodied

When you feel connected to all aspects of yourself—body, mind, and soul—and are present to the "now" moment, you are experiencing embodiment. Learning embodiment is a critical skill. When you live in an embodied way, you are much more able to identify your needs and feelings, and you can provide yourself with self-soothing. You are also much more likely to recognize and course-correct when your thoughts are reflective of limiting beliefs.

If embodiment (staying aware of and connected to your body) is not something that comes easily to you, here is a simple suggestion to consider. Whenever you are performing daily essential tasks to keep your body functioning, bring your full attention to them. For example, when you are brushing your teeth, really notice how the bristles feel against your teeth and gums. Notice the taste of the toothpaste. Listen to the sounds you make while brushing your teeth. Make it a heightened sensory experience. It may seem trivial when you are doing it, but it has a way of increasing your awareness and connection to your body and your emotions. You can begin to feel more present, grounded, and appreciative of your whole self. Conveniently, this can also help reduce stress because your attention is fully immersed in the here and now rather than in the past or future.

Obstacles to the Brilliance Center of Emotions

Obstacles to the Brilliance Center of Emotions can lead to imbalances in our relationship with our bodies and emotions and in our understanding of our sexuality. Here are a few things that may arise.

OBSTACLE 1: Fostering Addictions

Earlier we talked about aversion and attachment in relation to our emotions. When we are inclined to a compulsive and exaggerated form of attachment, we may develop a type of addiction. Addiction can come in many forms— drugs, alcohol, or sex, for example. You could be addicted to incessant buying of material things or to eating, gambling, or serial monogamy. It is possible you are addicted to more esoteric things like receiving compliments and attention on social media. You could even be addicted to your own suffer- ing—thinking that holding on to your old story of the pain is the only way you can feel alive.

Each of us has the capacity for addiction. Sadly, though, addiction is stig- matized in our society, and many feel ashamed about their addictive behaviors. If you feel stuck in the shame, the cycle will just continue. If you are suffering from addiction, it is so important to be kind and compassionate with yourself as you seek out support from a doctor or therapist. The journey happens one step at a time, and your strength will build as you continue forward. If you are currently seeking guidance around an addiction, you can find more support in the "Additional Resources" section of to the workbook.

OBSTACLE 2: Having Excessive Mood Swings

Each of us is wired differently. Some of us are even-keeled, and others feel things more to the extreme. So many things influence our moods: genetics, hormones, diet, cultural conditioning…the list goes on. There is no one right way for your feelings and moods to fluctuate. Nor is it required that you feel things at any particular level of intensity. Yet it is helpful to notice if your mood swings or sensitivity to emotions affect your ability to live in a vibrant and healthy way, day to day.

If you feel like a prisoner to the erratic and uncertain nature of your moods or frequently feel overwhelmed by sensory input from your environment, you may be more sensitive to your inner balance of energies. In that case, it may help to seek out some additional support. Remember, having a unique sensitivity to your energy balance or mood rhythms does not mean anything is "wrong" with you. But, if this condition is making your life uncomfortable or even unmanageable, perhaps it would be wise to seek out professional guidance from a doctor or therapist to discover the options for more support around this.

OBSTACLE 3: Being Rigid in Your Body, Beliefs, or Behavior

Sometimes, we are so overwhelmed by the emotions or sensory feedback in our lives that we develop a strategy of shutting down to keep everything out. Sometimes this is done unconsciously or at such a young age that it may feel like you had no choice in the matter. And now you have a pattern. You may have learned that it was safer to hide your feelings, keep to yourself, and not let others in. This is often accompanied by a strong desire to be in control so that you can manage your vulnerability. Your behaviors and beliefs become rigid, and you may even find your body holding certain rigid postures or patterns, such as locking your jaw or tightening your fists. This strategy might work quite well for a while, but it can be exhausting to keep up your guard like that all the time. If you find you have a tendency for rigidity in your emotional, physical, or mental patterns and it is causing you suffering or isolation, remember that this is just a learned pattern. It can be unlearned.

Once again, working with a coach or therapist can be helpful. You might also benefit from engaging in movement activities that encourage more fluidity. Another way you can explore this dynamic in yourself is to first "praise the pattern" to acknowledge all the ways it has supported you in the past. For example, maybe it was a good form of protection for you and kept you safe from further pain. Then identify all the ways the pattern of rigidity no longer serves you. Perhaps it prevents you from developing closer relationships with others as an adult. Once you look over these two lists, you are ready to envision what "2.0" will look like. How could you improve upon the current pattern to make it more aligned with your brilliance?

Unleash Your Power at the Brilliance Center of Emotions

To round out our chapter, here are a few more strategies you can use to awaken your brilliance at this center.

STRATEGY 1: Pleasure Your Senses Daily

It is easy to get stuck in "go" mode and focus so intently on your to-do list that you forget there are small things you can do to greatly increase the pleasure factor as you go about your daily tasks. Try playing soothing music in the background as you pay your bills. Or maybe put a vase of flowers on your bedside table to bring a little extra spice into the bedroom. One of my friends suggested to me once to "dress up for my dreams" and buy some silky or soft pajamas to make sleeping that much more enjoyable. Even if you have absolutely no time in your life right now for additional play, rest, or more involved pleasures like a vacation, there are still many small adjustments you can make that will make your senses "pop" and greatly increase the nourishment that your soul feels on a daily basis. No excuses. Just make the choice to live more sensually and go for it.

STRATEGY 2: Regularly Journal for Better EQ

Even if you feel quite competent in the area of emotional intelligence, it never hurts to actively explore your emotional realm. There have been times when I have felt stuck in a certain relationship dynamic or repeatedly challenged by an inner struggle, so I have taken out my journal to write about what was going on inside me. Sometimes, I would write a dialogue between my higher self and the part of me that felt stuck. Other times, I might write out a hypothetical conversation between me and a person I was in conflict with, in order to help get clear on what I wanted to say—and to develop more empathy for the other person. With the endless stream of self-help materials available online, there are many excellent "journal prompts" and "self-inquiry questions" out there to guide you. It is not so important what type of inquiry practice you choose to get more familiar with your emotional terrain; it just matters that you do. Explore your inner landscape. To get you started on journaling, refer to the self-inquiry exercise entitled "Journaling about Emotions" in the workbook.

STRATEGY 3: Embrace Uncertainty and Tap into Its Exhilaration

If you are a conscious explorer of brilliance continually seeking that next edge of growth in your life, then you will be repeatedly exposed to uncertainty. Most of us can accept that. But at what point do you learn to not just accept that fact but enjoy it? How amazing that we get to be in a position to push ourselves in such a self-gratifying way!

The CEO of Social Jukebox, Tim Fargo, insightfully tweeted, "Your mind is your prison when you focus on your fear." The opportunity to focus on the negative will always be available. It is the low-hanging fruit on the tree. It may take that extra pause in your thoughts to reorient toward enthusiasm, curiosity, and excitement, but the opportunity is ever-present. The space between the trapeze bars is a vital one indeed. Remember that if you get tripped up in the story that your ego tells you about uncertainty, then forget the details. Instead, connect to the raw energy of the sensations in the body and choose how you want to direct it from there.

STRATEGY 4: Explore Possibilities for Authentic Relating

Did you know that there are all kinds of social clubs, meetup groups, classes, and events for the specific purpose of helping people learn more conscious ways to relate to each other? It is an exciting time to be involved in consciousness-raising on a societal level.

For example, there are tantra classes that teach individuals about masculine and feminine polarities and how they affect our communication with others. (And by the way, tantra practices are not exclusively about sex. Tantra is about balancing opposite energies for a unified whole.) There are social clubs that focus on teaching people techniques for authentic relating. There are workshops, classes, trainings, and retreats that can teach you so many wonderful skills and tools for learning better embodiment, emotional intelligence, and conscious communication.

Be adventurous. Try something new. Even if you do not like it at first, I imagine you will learn something powerful, simply by challenging yourself to move past your comfort zone. A growing movement of people out there want a more peaceful and harmonious world where empathy, kindness, and compassion reign. Open your eyes and see where there may be possibilities to get involved.

♦ SELF-INQUIRY EXERCISE: Your Body and Sexuality

Remember, your body is the warehouse of all your emotions and holds a lot of wisdom. In this exercise, we take a moment to check in with this great source of knowledge.

1. Set a timer for fifteen minutes. In your journal, write your "life story" from the perspective of your body. What does it have to say about its experiences in this lifetime? Has it enjoyed this life? Are there ways it would like to improve things? How is it feeling after all this time?

2. Sexuality is one area of life where our beliefs can become greatly distorted by ideas that were passed down to us from others. What were you taught about sexuality as you grew up? How has this affected your behaviors and beliefs around your sexuality? Is there anything you would like to change here?

♦ SELF-INQUIRY EXERCISE: Optimize Your Brilliance Center of Emotions

To upgrade your potential for brilliance at this center, it's time to put what you've learned into practice.

1. The Brilliance Center of Emotions rules over our desires, pleasures, sensations, and sexuality; our feelings about our bodies; and how we understand and connect with our emotions. As you reflect on these areas, is there any place where you want to explore a little deeper? Is there a place where you feel stuck or challenged in your brilliance? Is there a certain belief around your body or sexuality that you would like to change? Are there attitudes about pleasure, sensuality, or emotions that could use an upgrade? Choose a limiting belief in one of these areas and complete the following steps for each belief you've identified that you'd like to explore.

2. Return to the self-inquiry exercise "Upgrading Your Beliefs to Optimize Your Brilliance" on page 62, in chapter 4. Follow Steps 2 to 6 for clearing a limiting belief pattern and replacing it with a new vision, applying

these to the limiting belief you've identified in your Brilliance Center of Emotions.

If you feel stuck with identifying a limiting belief or would like some examples of common limiting beliefs in this area, refer to the exercise "Optimize Your Brilliance Center of Emotions" in the workbook for additional complimentary resources to support you.

Nice job! Remember, these new beliefs only stick if you make the effort to connect to them in a meaningful way every day. Also, start taking small action steps to promote an even quicker connection to your dreams for brilliance. Good luck!

CHAPTER 11

The Brilliance Center of Grounding

If you have built castles in the air, your work need not be lost;
that is where they should be. Now put the foundations
under them. —Henry David Thoreau, Walden

At last, we've made it to the Brilliance Center of Grounding. In many ways, this brilliance center acts as a foundation for the rest of the brilliance centers. In the yoga tradition, the Brilliance Center of Grounding correlates with the first chakra, or *muladhara* (*moo-lah-dhar-ah*), which means "root support."

Energetically, this brilliance center acts like the deep roots of a tree, the foundation of a temple, or the anchor of a boat. Without it, we would go adrift in our purpose or lose our footing in this world. Things get a lot more tangible at this brilliance center because we are working with aspects of our physical realm. This chapter looks at how your brilliance shows up in your finances and in your choices regarding your home and physical environment.

Working with the Brilliance Center of Grounding is about going into the experiences of life, not just thinking about them. Here, we literally ground into reality. Grounding is the ability to maintain connection and presence with your body, the earth, and the world around you. When we are not grounded, we may lose our stability emotionally, mentally, and perhaps even spiritually. We become diluted and ineffectual in our ability to "show up," let alone pursue our brilliance. We are not present and mindful. In this state, we can often feel powerless and disconnected from our true path.

On a psychological level, this brilliance center is associated with the survival instinct and the will to live. It is concerned with basic health and vitality.

This is where you find your sense of individuality. Therefore, the action statement that encapsulates the brilliance in this center is the declaration

I am.

When you are grounded, you have a sense of inner safety, and this helps you manifest your dreams. That which has roots will endure. Being grounded also means you'll be more able to truly experience the full spectrum of life from an embodied perspective. You'll be able to really own your human experience and all that it has to offer.

Grounding also limits us, and that can be a very helpful thing. In her book *Wheels of Life*, Anodea Judith points out, "Grounding is a simplifying force. We are bringing our consciousness into the body which, for all practical purposes, exists in one space and time only—the here and now. Our thoughts, by contrast, are much more versatile, extending outside of space and time." When we are grounded in the here and now, we cannot do everything all at once. We are forced to make decisions and determine where to focus our energy. In this way, grounding inspires a necessary creative principle: To manifest successfully, we must get specific about what ideas we want to bring to fruition.

We must limit. This is scary sometimes because we are afraid we may not pick the "right thing" to focus on. Nonetheless, we still must proceed, and we must recognize that choosing to do nothing is a choice in and of itself. Life keeps happening whether we like it or not. To be grounded means you have to show up in the present moment and consciously choose how to be in your brilliance. How you make that decision in each moment is what determines the quality of the life you lead.

Your Brilliance Rests upon Certain Rights

It is all well and good to talk about brilliance, but none of it means anything if we do not fully accept the most fundamental rights we have as human beings—the right to be here and the right to have.

The Right to Be Here

The right to be here is about being comfortable fully occupying your body and living the way you feel is best for you. It is also about being comfortable taking up space—physically, emotionally, mentally, and spiritually—and not pretending to be someone you are not just to "fit in" better with the world around you. People uncomfortable with this right may apologize for simple things, such as sharing their opinion or asking a question in the normal flow of a conversation. Or, if someone is not fully claiming this right, they may feel the need to prove they have earned it through certain behaviors or actions.

I have personal experience with this. Growing up in a single-mother household of five sisters, taking up space was always a challenge, physically and otherwise. Money was tight, and my mother was stressed and working two full-time jobs. Unconsciously, I always had the thought, "I'd better do my part and help out, or I am just another mouth to feed and problem to solve. And I do not want to cause my mom any more stress." None of my sisters nor my mom suggested I had to "earn my keep" in this way. They were all incredibly loving to me. I was very fortunate in that way.

But, I was only five years old, and I did not know any better. I misinterpreted the uncertainty and stress my family had around money to mean that if I did not show up and "do my part," then maybe I would get kicked out of the family. It was far from reality, but that's where my little five-year-old mind went! I felt I had to prove my worth and earn my right to stick around.

Fortunately, I no longer believe that, but those childhood beliefs manifested in all sorts of unhelpful ways in my adult life, until I worked through them to see the truth. Before I figured it out, though, I suffered for many years as a workaholic in my twenties when I started my business as a yoga teacher. I worked an unhealthy number of hours to prove my self-worth and to "earn" my right to take up space in this world, which I felt I could only do if I was contributing back to the greater good somehow.

At one point I even taught yoga to nursing assistants at local hospitals on all three shifts, which meant I had classes at noon, 4 pm, and 2 am, all on one day! And that was on top of teaching my regular private clients and other public classes outside the hospital. I was literally an around-the-clock yoga teacher. Though a lot of wonderful experiences came from such an immersion in my passion, it was not a grounding or sustainable way to run my business. I learned quickly that I had to make some significant adjustments in my work/life balance to continue this type of career.

Through my own self-inquiry and work with a therapist and a coach, I saw how these negative work habits had been rooted in this very old belief around my right to be here. As educated and self-aware as I was at the time, I still had a big blind spot affecting my brilliance. If you would like to investigate more of your childhood beliefs around your right to be here, complete the self-inquiry exercise "Your Right to Be Here" in the workbook.

The Right to Have

The second fundamental right that brilliance rests upon is the right to have. The right to have is concerned with your need to survive, and not just with the basic needs such as food, water, and shelter. It also refers to your right to have things like success, prosperity, time to yourself, pleasure, adventures, friends, well-being, and so forth. As you expand your acceptance of your right to have, it will become easier to receive abundance in its many forms. Let's look at an example.

Lauren grew up in a poor family, and frugality was the law of the land. When her family had a bit of money, her mother was very generous at the church collection basket. The family never seemed to keep the extra money for themselves. Lauren grew up wearing hand-me-down clothes from her big brothers, and other girls at school often made fun of her. Over time, she started to resent the girls who had new clothes and looked "prettier and more feminine" than she did.

When Lauren got older, these childhood experiences and the beliefs they perpetuated translated into her developing a poverty consciousness. Even though, as an adult, she earned a good salary working at a communications firm, she still flinched whenever she saw wastefulness of any kind. She always made her own lunch and brought it to work. She refused to buy a car and only traveled by bike, and she bought all her clothes at thrift shops. It was true that many of these behaviors were in alignment with her environmental values, but Lauren also held a lot of secret resentment and judgment of others who weren't as responsible with money as she was. Why were they allowed to splurge on that new dress when she had to be extra frugal and only buy pre-worn clothes? Why did others get to relax and have down time when she had to work extra hours wherever she could so that she could help support her parents in their retirement?

To uproot these stubborn beliefs around her right to have, Lauren had to develop a lot of self-awareness of when these thoughts came up. Then, if she noticed a thought, she had to consciously check in with herself to ask, "What do I really know to be true?" In other words, she had to press pause long enough to connect to the reality of today, to remind herself that she was no longer the little kid wearing her brothers' hand-me-downs. I suggested she also start a gratitude journal, since gratitude is an expansive energy and would get her out of the constant state of contraction that poverty consciousness can cause. Finally, I knew Lauren was a socially conscious person, and I asked her to reflect on how she might be able to show up in the world in an even bigger way if she were to truly own her right to have.

Over time, with continued coaching, and some therapy too, Lauren was able to craft a new reality that more accurately reflected her truth—that she was frugal and she preferred not to have too many material things; but that she could also soften and relax into what she believed to be an abundant universe. As she worked with this new vision, she took more vacation time for herself. She socialized more and didn't worry so much about watching every penny. She also became less judgmental toward others and more curious. She started volunteering at a soup kitchen because she wasn't working as many hours and had more free time. She felt happier and more relaxed in general.

It continues to be an evolution for Lauren, but by connecting to her right to have, she transformed her life on many levels. If you want to explore more about your beliefs around your right to have, complete the self-inquiry exercise "Your Right to Have" in the workbook.

Where Brilliance Intersects with Money

So much has been written on the topic of money and personal empowerment, discussing how it relates to our well-being and our ability to succeed and show up in this world. There is usually an obvious feedback loop in the actions we take around money. We experience our income going up or down. We see the numbers in our bank account fluctuate at the push of a button. The response is immediate, and we feel the impact.

Money is a small portion of a larger idea called abundance. When I act from an abundant mindset to support my brilliance, I believe that there is enough to go around and I can partake in that prosperity. Embracing this idea of abundance can immediately get sticky, however. All you have to do is think about all the starving people on the planet and wonder, "How could the world possibly be an abundant place if all these people are living in lack and suffering?"

That thought alone is enough to break your heart and trigger an inner dialogue of guilt or shame around having money, even a little bit of it. It is easy to get lost in all the distorted beliefs our world has created around money. When we think of the people starving, though, it is important to know that hunger is caused by poverty and inequality, not by scarcity. Did you know we already grow enough food on this planet to feed ten billion people? There is enough to go around. It is just not equally distributed, and a *lot* gets wasted and thrown out.

Knowing this might make it easier to see through the falseness of the scarcity argument, but we are still left to deal with the ugly reality of the unjust way in which resources are distributed. It is very tempting to go to a mindset of anger, cynicism, despair, and hopelessness. You might think:

- "The system is rigged and unfair."
- "I'll never be prosperous."
- "The world does not value my gifts the same as others. I can't make money."
- "Money is evil."
- "Our world is run by greed."
- "If I start to make a lot of money, I will become obsessed with losing it and always need to earn more."
- "It is not spiritual to want money."
- "I have to struggle to make money."
- "Money and all it involves is just a big sham."
- "Money is magical. Only some are lucky enough to get it, and I am not one of them."
- "Rich people are jerks and selfish."
- "Rich people are better/smarter/worthier than the rest of us."

I get it. I am not going to try to candy-coat the real and painful realities regarding resources or lack thereof. Many are suffering due to the world we have collectively created. In her book *The Law of Divine Compensation*, Marianne Williamson points out:

Starving children are not poor in Africa because their consciousness is unaligned with love; they're poor because ours is… When we collectively make love our bottom line—making humanitarian values rather than

short term economics the organizing principle of human civilization—
then the situation will indeed miraculously change.

We all play a part, and that includes you too. No matter how small or
insignificant you may think your part is, I can tell you this: you matter. Your
choices will have an impact on the whole, even if you do not always see how
they do. I cannot claim to have the solution for the global problem of poverty,
nor do I expect you to. But I do know that continuing to hold onto limiting
beliefs about money and abundance is going to severely limit our ability to
show up in the world in a brilliant way and be part of a solution we wish to
bring to the world to help others.

Giving in to cynicism and focusing on what does not work will leave us
stuck in the problems. It is high time to get over whatever holds us back from
being an active player in creating our abundance—both for ourselves and
for the greater whole. African-American theologian and civil rights leader
Howard Thurman reportedly said, "Don't ask what the world needs. Ask
what makes you come alive and go do it, because what the world needs is
people who have come alive."

Along that same vein, allow yourself to "come alive" as you pursue your
abundance. Do it for yourself first. And if you do that in a way that holds
integrity and a commitment to your brilliance, you are naturally going to
want to share that abundance with others. Just watch.

Here are a few other useful insights I want to share with you about money.

INSIGHT 1: You Define Success and Abundance

Is more or less money better? What annual salary do you want to make? How
important is money to your overall well-being and success? Guess what? You
get to decide! There is no cookie-cutter answer to anything regarding personal
empowerment, especially when it concerns money and abundance.

In my coaching practice, I've worked with clients in all financial ranges,
and you know what I've discovered? Abundance is a mindset. It has nothing
to do with how much money you have in the bank. If you choose an abundant mindset, you invite the expansive energy of brilliance into your life, and
everything improves.

INSIGHT 2: Money Is a Neutral Energy

Money is not inherently evil or anti-spiritual. Nor is it always the thing that "makes the world go 'round." Money is a tangible but neutral energy. You choose what power to give your money. You can use it for good, purchasing things from companies that support your values and the health of our world. You can use it to advance your brilliance in many creative ways. Or you can use it to reinforce more of what you do not want in your life and in the world. It is up to you.

Know that money also tends to amplify your natural tendencies. If you are generous in spirit before becoming abundant, you will likely be even more generous in spirit and wealth after you have money. If you were anxious and controlling before you became abundant, you may find having more money just makes you more prone to anxiety and control issues. So, we must stay mindful and aware, aligning our abundance with the vibration that best reflects our truth.

INSIGHT 3: Working Is Different than Struggling

Most people have to work to earn a living, and sometimes this means taking a job that may not be your dream job. Having to do that job does not mean you must struggle, though. The attitude you bring to your work will in large part set the tone and determine what type of experience you have. Take, for example, these two perspectives:

Perspective 1: "I hate this crappy job, and it pays me nothing. I have to get out of here. This sucks."

Perspective 2: "Even though I do not like this job and it really challenges my patience some days, I choose to remember that I show up here every day so that I can pay my bills on time. This job allows me to buy some time while I look for one that better suits my skills. I know it is not the most ideal situation, but it is the best I can do for now, and that is all I can ask of myself. I am going to do everything in my power to keep this as fun and easy as possible until my next job is secured."

Feel the difference? How we choose to perceive of things in our life, including our abundance, is always up to us. And your perception is largely what's going to color your experience. Here are a few examples of how some of my clients have shifted their perceptions around abundance.

Abundance as Fulfillment

Beth was an investment advisor and doing very well financially. She had every-thing she needed to take care of her expenses and then some. Though Beth liked her job and was proud of herself for working so hard to achieve success, she couldn't help but feel like something was missing from her life. She was happily married, but her husband worked just as hard as she did, and they didn't have a big social life or a lot of friends. Both their families lived out of town, and they didn't have children. Sometimes after a long day at work, Beth would feel lonely and wonder, "There has to be more to life than just this."

It wasn't until Beth reframed her understanding of abundance that things started to change for her. For Beth, all the money she had was of no use if she felt alone. There was nothing fulfilling about it for her, and she felt uncom-fortable having so much when others had so little. In our work together, Beth created a new vision of abundance, one that included not just financial wealth but also a community of friends, connection, philanthropy, and a sense of belonging. She knew she wanted these things, but she wasn't sure how to get them. After creative brainstorming in our sessions, Beth devised a plan to cre-ate a women's philanthropy collective, inviting ten of her female colleagues who were also wealthy to join.

Each member of the collective would be required to make a yearly dona-tion of $10,000 to support a cause. But there was more. The group would get together monthly for social potlucks and to discuss what they believed should be the cause for that year. The first year, they gave the $100,000 to a local shelter for abused women and children. Several members of the collective met with women at the shelter, offering them financial and business advice as they negotiated getting out of abusive relationships.

Beth's life completely transformed. She had new girlfriends and an even larger community in her life through their networks. But it wasn't just friends or a community. A sense of purpose had infused the entirety of her life. She and her husband now had a much better work/life balance and engaged in more social activities for both professional and personal reasons. And Beth felt like she was discovering new leadership strengths and passions through her philanthropy work. Now that her financial wealth was being used strate-gically to connect her in meaningful ways with others and to contribute back to the greater good, Beth felt a sense of fulfillment that was her true vision for abundance.

Abundance as an Evolving Idea

Kenny was sick of having a "day job," working as a manager at a local grocery store chain, so that he could pursue his passion work as a musician in his rock band. The job gave him just enough to get by, and he always had his evenings free for gigs. But his double life was wearing on him. Perpetually tired, he couldn't book any out-of-town gigs because he couldn't afford to miss work. He knew he needed to change things up, but he wasn't sure how.

In our work together, Kenny felt clear that he had an old limiting belief that he couldn't make a living doing what he loved. Abundance felt like a "thing that other people could have but not him." Kenny was a confident guy, but when it came to this belief, he just felt defeated and stuck. I asked him to write out a list of all his strengths and good qualities. Among other things, he wrote that he was creative, passionate, diligent, and resourceful. After all, he'd been managing two jobs for years now, and he was making it work even if it was tough.

Reconnected to his strengths, Kenny now felt more confident that he could create an alternate reality around his idea for abundance, so he crafted a new vision. He clarified that he wanted enough freedom to be able to travel and do gigs in other towns. He also wanted to feel like money was abundant without requiring too much mental energy from him to do whatever his work would be. He needed to protect his creative headspace so he could be inspired to create more music. He also wanted his new job to feel fun, and not like a J-O-B.

The more we talked, the more it became clear that Kenny had the skill sets and the motivation to start a business offering guitar instruction. To free up his time, he created an online course with pre-recorded videos that he could market continuously and earn money from without needing to be present. He also picked up some private teaching gigs on the weekends even though he was still working at the grocery store. He gave himself a year deadline to get his new business up and running. Along the way he discovered that he had a knack for online marketing, so he started tinkering around with a few other online business ideas unrelated to guitar instruction. His efforts were lucrative enough that after fifteen months, he quit the job at the grocery store and stopped teaching private clients. His online businesses were now sustaining him completely, and he was earning $20,000 more than he had at the grocery store, and that was only in the first year.

Ultimately, his new profession looked different than he thought it would, but it fit even better than the one he had envisioned. Kenny's new vision for abundance came to fruition through focused intention, a strategic plan, and a willingness to stay committed and explore the unknown one step at a time. His motivation to follow through came not just from connecting to his passion for music, but also from connecting to his strengths and remembering his power to perceive. This is what allowed him to tune out the old beliefs about jobs having to look traditional in order to make money.

What about you? If you're ready to start cultivating a new vision for your own abundance, including your finances, complete the self-inquiry exercise "Your Brilliant Vision for Abundance" in the workbook. Your future awaits!

Home, Brilliant Home

In addition to governing our ideas of abundance, this brilliance center is also concerned with everything related to our physical environments, including our homes. "Home" can refer to both the very literal space in which you live and your sense of place in the world. Whatever way you think about it, your home plays an important role in your ability to show up in your brilliance.

In her book *All God's Children Need Traveling Shoes,* Maya Angelou describes "the ache for home lives in all of us, the safe place where we can go as we are and not be questioned." Indeed, when an actual physical home feels nourishing, comforting, and peaceful, we can thrive. With a literal strong foundation under our feet, we can feel safe to "fly" in our lives and follow our dreams, because we know we always have a place to land.

Our physical homes reflect our consciousness too. If I am not feeling grounded and am doing too much, my physical environment will reflect that. My desk will be disorganized and covered with papers from all sorts of projects. It does not feel particularly good to see my desk this way. I know by now that if I take the time and care needed to treat my physical environment like a sanctuary and tend to it as such, then it will become a vehicle and a container to support my brilliance in coming forth.

Marissa was a serious nature lover and thought she'd never leave the mountains of her home state Colorado. But she landed a dream job at a top environmental nonprofit in New York City, and she couldn't refuse the opportunity. To help ease the transition to her new urban environment, she made a serious commitment to herself to treat her home as her sanctuary. What's more, she decided the theme for her sanctuary would be "nature."

She built a high shelf along the perimeter of the living room ceiling, and on it she placed at least twenty houseplants of the long-hanging variety. When you walked into her living room, it was as if you were transported to the Costa Rican jungle. In addition to the greenery, she had multiple brightly colored orchids in each room, a running water fountain, a fish tank, and an aromatherapy machine infusing the sweet smell of roses throughout her space. Her furniture was minimal, and most of it was made from bamboo. She also had a melodic soundtrack of classical music playing in the background. It was truly a delight for the senses! Marissa showed me that no matter where you live or how small your home may be, if you have a powerful intention and some inspiration, you can create a sanctuary for yourself and your brilliance.

If you're ready to upgrade your home to "sanctuary" status, take a moment now to complete the self-inquiry exercise "Your Brilliant Home" in the workbook.

Home as a Sense of Place

Singer Lyle Lovett once said in an interview, "When you have a solid upbringing and a strong sense of place, that sustains you. My sense of home never leaves me." How true that is. Regardless of your physical home environment, inside your heart lives a "sense of home" that you can take with you wherever you go. That feeling can inspire a sense of belonging in the world. And just as we can all ache for the feeling of home, we can all yearn for a sense of belonging too. As Peter Block writes in his book *Community*:

> Belonging can also be thought of as a longing to be. Being is our
> capacity to find our deeper purpose in all that we do. It is the capacity
> to be present, and to discover our authenticity and whole selves…
> Community is the container within which our [belonging] is fulfilled.

As Block suggests, community is a necessity to feel a sense of belonging. Without community, we can feel a bit untethered from this world and unable to fully embody our brilliance. We are social creatures, we humans, and we need each other to grow and learn on our paths. As my teacher, Ram Dass, used to say, "We are all just walking each other home" in this lifetime.

I often work with clients on intentionally creating communities to support their brilliance. Invariably, some themes always seem to arise in this exercise. First, I often notice that people need in their community more individuals who will genuinely support their brilliance. Sometimes these can be friends or family, but more often than not, it's also helpful to have mentors, spiritual teachers, and fellow pilgrims on the path to brilliance in your circle.

Next, I also notice that there's an unfortunate tendency for many of us to lack diversity of all kinds in our communities. It seems we tend to hang out with people just like us. In my experience, the more my community has grown to include people of different generations, ethnicities, economic statuses, sexual orientations, and political views, the better I am able to show up as a citizen of this world. My life becomes so much richer. I am more educated about different perspectives. I am less likely to make assumptions. And interestingly, I've started to feel a deeper and deeper sense of belonging in the world no matter where I go.

The third thing I notice many of my clients lack in their communities is individuals *they* can mentor and support in whatever way they are best suited. When you regularly get to be a stand for other people's brilliance, you set yourself up for bringing out the best in you too.

If you'd like to do some more self-inquiry around building community, complete the self-inquiry exercise "Creating a Brilliant Community" in the workbook.

Optimization at the Brilliance Center of Grounding

Now that we have an overview of some of the life areas that are directly affected by the Brilliance Center of Grounding, let's take a closer look at how it might look when you are thriving in this area.

POSSIBILITY 1: You Feel at Home in Your Body

Your first home is not anywhere outside of yourself, it is in your own being— your body! When you feel at home in your body, the full vibrancy of your soul can attune to the physical world through the safe vessel of your being. It allows you an actual place in space and time from which you can experience the world and explore your consciousness through form.

The body is truly a miracle. In her book *Women, Food and God*, author Geneen Roth puts it this way: "Your body is the piece of the universe you've been given." Celebrate it and love it! And if you are not quite "there" yet mentally when it comes to loving yourself, take small positive steps toward self-appreciation every day.

POSSIBILITY 2: You Feel Safe

A lot of times, individuals get stuck on the path to brilliance because they do not feel safe. Sometimes, I think we confuse safety with security. Safety is an inner feeling, whereas security is an outer condition that we use to protect ourselves from being vulnerable. I will explain it another way, using the metaphor of a peach.

Think for a moment about the pit of the peach. It is hard and solid. Even if the juicy peach was entirely devoured, that strong pit would remain unharmed. Not only that, but the pit also holds all the genetic information needed to create a whole new peach tree. Its essence is intact even if the fruit is eaten or damaged. That pit represents our soul, and when we remember we *are* the pit, we have a strong inner feeling of *safety*. When we feel safe, we know that even if things don't go our way or we get hurt on life's adventures, deep inside where it counts we are going to be okay, a whole and intact soul, just like the pit of that peach.

The fleshy part of the peach, however, represents our ego. And, as you know, our egos can easily get bruised, beaten up, and hurt. If I don't want my ego to be harmed, I might take some precautions to protect it. These precautions are what we call *security*. If I were to lock the peach up in a box so that no one could touch it, it certainly would remain unharmed. But, if I left it there alone in the box, it would eventually dry up, get moldy, and rot. Similarly, if I put a metaphorical "box" around myself to prevent myself from getting hurt by others (for example, refusing to date because I've been hurt in the past and don't want that to happen again), I will stay secure. But life won't be very fulfilling. Certainly, we need to have some level of security, in the form of healthy boundaries. But if you go into overdrive with your security measures because you're scared, it might help to remind yourself that your sense of safety is not reliant on your security measures. It relies on you remembering who you really are—your soul.

POSSIBILITY 3: You Own Your Definition of Abundance

To fully own my truth, I have to give up the idea that I am anything other than myself. I have to take full responsibility for my beliefs and feelings. I choose what success looks like for me, even if it means I have to tolerate being misunderstood or rejected by others because of choosing my truth.

It requires bravery and boldness to own your truth, especially when it comes to money. Our society has so much to say about what financial success looks like, and we often feel that pressure. When I decided to become a professional yoga teacher and quit my nine-to-five job after going to college and graduate school to get all the right degrees for a prestigious career in environmentalism, not everyone understood or approved of my decision. Nonetheless, owning my truth allowed me to pursue what I deemed fulfilling and successful, and my life completely changed for the better. I felt so much more authentic.

It may require a leap of faith and some boldness and bravery on your part, but when you choose to say yes to your dream even if others just do not get it, that act deeply affirms your sense of self-worth.

POSSIBILITY 4: You Feel Connected to the Human Family and the Earth

One of the most beautiful benefits of feeling your brilliance in this center is that you remember your connection to the whole. The poet Kahlil Gibran wrote in "A Poet's Voice XV," "The universe is my country, and the human family is my tribe." Imagine how different our world would be if we oriented to that thought more than thoughts of our separateness. Would we have more love in the world? More peace? More compassion and empathy? I believe so. We probably would also have a very different relationship to our earth—one that celebrated and respected it in a balanced and thoughtful way. We may not be able to change how our collective family has related to each other and the world at large until now, but moving ahead, we can choose to take our consciousness—our little piece of the greater whole—and use it to affirm more of what we would like to see in the world.

One of my former yoga students, Valarie Kaur, beautifully represents this possibility with her work around revolutionary love. Kaur is an American civil rights activist, documentary filmmaker, lawyer, educator, and faith leader. She is also a Sikh woman. When a family friend of hers was the first to be killed in a hate crime after 9/11, Valarie started to document hate crimes against Sikh and Muslim Americans. Her work took her into prisons, to sites of mass shootings, and even to Guantanamo Bay. Though she had every temptation to go to a place of hate or even rage after seeing and documenting some of the things she did, Valarie chose instead to find more love in her heart, even for those who may appear to be her enemy.

In her work, she identified love as a potent tool for social change, and she started the Revolutionary Love Project to champion that effort. Love is a *unifying* force, and Valarie's work with this project has looked at how to mobilize that force to bring about more peace and harmony. By tapping into her brilliance, Valarie could see past her hurt and despair and remember in her heart that she is connected to the whole, that we are all one. And as such, she knew she had an opportunity to make it better by doing her part. To be deeply inspired and learn more about Valarie's work, go to ValarieKaur.com.

Obstacles to the Brilliance Center of Grounding

For an even more comprehensive picture of the Brilliance Center of Grounding, let's look at what happens when we are out of alignment with our root energy. Here are a few obstacles that might arise:

OBSTACLE 1: Feeling Constant Fear or Anxiety

Without an inner feeling of safety, your thoughts can be dominated by fear, anxiety, and worry. Of course, we all have moments where these things arise, but if you are plagued by them consistently, you may be out of touch with your sense of "home" within yourself.

A lot of times when you feel great fear or anxiety, it is because you are too much "in your head," and that's why you don't feel at home in your *body*. If this is happening to you, try thinking less and being more. Sometimes, there is nothing to figure out. Sometimes, we just need to surrender and let go into the present moment. Dance. Exercise. Go for a walk. Take a yoga class. Let your body help your mind get to a better place.

OBSTACLE 2: Fixating on the Material World

Sometimes, an obstacle at the Brilliance Center of Grounding may look like an excessive preoccupation with material things. This could be an obsession with shopping or finding the best "deals." It could also manifest as extreme behavior like hoarding. The belief may be, "If I have or accumulate these things, I will feel better, more complete, and more at home." Often this obsession with the outer world is used to mask some inner pain or trauma that a person is trying to ignore. It's very common to do this unconsciously.

There is nothing inherently wrong with wanting beautiful things or even enjoying accumulating them, but if it is being done largely to avoid something else going on inside of you, it may be a form of self-sabotage. It helps to be aware of why we want the things we want, so we can align our choices with what feels like our highest truth.

OBSTACLE 3: Always Feeling Lost, Alone, or Isolated

If we spend a lot of time living in our heads, we can disassociate from our bodies and disconnect from this earthly realm. When we become more aware of this pattern of disengagement, we notice all the ways we block ourselves from real connection with others—one of the main ways we feel a sense of belonging.

Start to notice if there are times where you "check out" or "float away." See if you can figure out what causes you to do that. Is there something you are trying to avoid? What might that be? Please note this kind of self-investigation takes time, and you may have some blind spots here. Be patient and compassionate with yourself as you explore.

Unleash Your Power at the Brilliance Center of Grounding

To keep the Brilliance Center of Grounding in right alignment, here are a few additional strategies you can employ.

STRATEGY 1: Lend a Helping Hand

If you are feeling ungrounded, poor, unhappy, or disconnected in this world, go out and do some service work. When you are feeling down and out, few things have the power to pick you up as successfully as making yourself available to serve another. There is actual scientific research on this, but perhaps you have personal experience with it too. When we focus on serving others, especially when we do not feel good about ourselves, we remember all that is good and capable about ourselves. We say yes to the light within us even when we may be feeling pretty dark inside. It is an exercise in faith and hope, and it affirms the positive within us. Sometimes that is all we need to change the direction of our momentum.

STRATEGY 2: Spend More Time in Nature

Besides the fact that there are all kinds of medical reasons it benefits us to spend more time in nature (research shows time in nature improves our happiness, immunity, and emotional resilience), there is also a deeper reason it is important. When we spend time in nature, it is the ultimate "returning home." We remember our primal connection to all life on earth. Being in nature produces brain waves that are similar to those experienced while meditating. In other words, it ignites within us a cellular memory of our deep belonging and connection to the earth itself. This is deeply healing and soothing to the soul.

If you have not played in nature for a long while, it may take some getting used to. Our society has sanitized our expectations, often creating a desire for everything to be nice and neat. Nature is not neat. Nature is organic and messy—in the most beautiful way, of course! Do not give up if your first excursion or two back into nature does not feel so sublime. Keep exploring different environments or go with a friend. Stay curious and see what connections can arise.

STRATEGY 3: Get Clear on Your Budget and Financial Goals

Are you working on becoming more brilliant with your money? It helps to have a clear view of where you are starting from and where it is you want to go. This may seem obvious, but a lot of people self-sabotage here by staying confused or vague so that they do not have to take responsibility for their abundance. Become very aware of your money habits—what comes in and what goes out, and where is it going. Once an honest and open relationship has been established with yourself around money, then you can start to evaluate if you want to make any changes.

STRATEGY 4: Appreciate the Little Things in Life

This brilliance center is about the earth energy. As a force of energy, the earth is slow, heavy, and solid. Our world in general glosses right over that rhythm and highlights the much quicker and more frenetic pace that technology supports. So, if you are feeling a little ungrounded or not present, try slowing it down.

Take an hour each day away from technology. Start to remember what it is like to connect to someone without texting or posting something online. Look into someone's eyes. Unplug and connect. Remember the simple joys of exchanging a smile with a loved one or smelling a flower on an afternoon walk. Frequently, the things that truly make us happy have nothing to do with money or materialism. They have to do with connection. We just have to take the time to pause and remember this truth.

♦ SELF-INQUIRY EXERCISE: Your Abundance and Belonging

In your journal, respond to the following questions and prompts about abundance and belonging:

1. Reflect on your relationship with abundance. Describe your relationship with money and abundance in five words or fewer. How would you like this relationship to look in five years? What beliefs might you have to change to make that happen?

2. Reflect on your sense of place in this world. Do you feel at home in your body, your current living environment, and your community? Why or why not?

♦ SELF-INQUIRY EXERCISE: Optimize Your Brilliance Center of Grounding

The Brilliance Center of Grounding lays the foundation for how we show up in the world. To upgrade your potential for brilliance at this center, it's time to put what you've learned into practice:

1. As you look over your answers to your self-inquiry questions and the topics we discussed in this chapter—your right to be here, your right to have, and your ideas around money, abundance, community, home, and sense of place—decide what area you would like to dig a little deeper into to align more fully with your brilliance. Where do you feel stuck or challenged in the Brilliance Center of Grounding? Is there a certain belief that you would like to change? Are there attitudes you have here that could use an upgrade?

2. Having identified a limiting belief in this center, return to the self-inquiry exercise "Upgrading Your Beliefs to Optimize Your Brilliance" on page 62, in chapter 4. Follow Steps 2 to 6 for clearing a limiting belief pattern and replacing it with a new vision, applying these to the limiting belief you've identified in your Brilliance Center of Grounding.

If you feel stuck with identifying a limiting belief or would like some examples of common limiting beliefs in this area, refer to the exercise "Optimize Your Brilliance Center of Grounding" in the workbook for additional complimentary resources to support you.

You did it! You've completed a deep dive into each of your brilliance centers. Fantastic job! Of course, the journey is far from over. You are always learning and growing, but this is an excellent time to take a pause and congratulate yourself for what you have learned thus far. When you are ready, go to the next chapter, and we will discuss how to put it all together.

PART THREE

CHAPTER 12

Putting It All Together

Writing a book about brilliance and how to recognize it at every level of your being can be challenging at times because you have to talk about it in a linear way, and there is nothing linear about this experience. Brilliance is not an end goal that you move toward. Rather, it is an ongoing process of awakening and activating one's potential within for use in the betterment of your own life and the lives of others, and even for the well-being of our world. It is a choice available to you in any instant. With each breath you take, there is an opportunity to choose brilliance in myriad ways. Perhaps you have already started to experience this as you have worked through the exercises in this book.

On this inner adventure, you have made many new self-discoveries, uncovered and eliminated self-sabotages, identified growing edges, evaluated and upgraded your belief system, and realized new ways to optimize your brilliance at every level. Congratulations! Getting to this point is no small feat. Of course, as I mentioned at the beginning of this book, you will not feel "perfect" at this point. For one thing, brilliance is not about perfection, as you know. Also, the journey never truly ends. This is just the conclusion of a particularly deep dive into your process. There is always more room to learn and grow.

And just in case you're feeling a little down on yourself because you aren't where you think you should be at this point in the journey, here's a bit of wisdom from one of my clients, Linda, as she reflects on her experience: "Just because I felt resistant or shut down sometimes during the reading doesn't mean there wasn't progress. Sometimes things just needed time to marinate and settle in. It took me two months, for instance, to start meditating consistently."

Linda also shared with me how her journey was more about the subtleties than any big transitions: "For me, when brilliance shows up, it is more like flow than fireworks. It feels both simple and profound and very ordinary. It's sort of like, 'Nothing to see here, it's just the universe surging through me and connecting me with everyone else while I'm in my pajamas.'"

Your Unique Journey to Brilliance

Everyone has a different experience of their brilliance, and it's important to trust your journey and how it is unfolding for you. As with Linda, the shifts you experience may be subtle. For others, like Alexis, the shifts could be dramatic: "When I reconnected to my brilliance, it gave me the clarity and the courage to leave my job, my city, and my relationship. I had known for some time that these changes were on my horizon, but it wasn't until I learned to stop living in conflict with my inner knowing that I was able to make these shifts. The brilliance principles, along with my core values, have become my anchor in times of trouble and give me the courage to move forward more confidently."

It's possible that the impact of your brilliance journey could be felt mostly in how you perceive of yourself. For instance, Sharna noticed, "Nothing about myself is as I thought. I have seen how strong an imprint was left on me by my early family experience. I see also that when I look at this in the old way, I judge. But when I look at it from a place of brilliance, I see only events that occurred, which then led to other events, like a vine growing through the forest. The imprint begins to fade, and the brilliant stone underneath shines through. The brilliance is always there and ready to emerge. The effort for me is in seeing through and clearing away the layers."

Others start to notice their brilliance primarily in how it shows up in their relationships. After reconnecting to her brilliance, Abby noticed, "Somewhere along the way, my boundaries have changed. More often, I say no when I mean no. I show up for people I care about even if I don't totally feel ready or know how. I just show up. And being allowed to show up feels intimate. And screwing up and being able to just keep trying feels intimate too."

Maybe your experience of brilliance has been about developing a deeper sense of trust in the universe. This is what happened for Joshua, who said, "There's a time for everything, and from what I know now, the timing for the most important things in life does not seem to be set by sheer willpower.

Brilliance has taught me that the journey is everything. It's all a perpetual practice, and if I just relax into that practice, things have a way of flowing and unfolding in their own time, and it's okay for me to let go and not try to control it all. It doesn't have to be that hard."

Still for others, the brilliance journey has mainly been about reconnecting with choice. This insight was a game-changer for Peter, who reported, "The idea and practice of choosing how I feel about people, places, and things has had a dramatic impact on my everyday life and my overall mental and emotional well-being. I have developed affirmations that I use frequently that constantly reset me to a more positive mind set. I simply don't allow myself to stay in a negative state of mind for as long as I used to. I now believe that you can view the world as a fundamentally hostile place or a fundamentally friendly place. I used to always choose the former, but now I choose the latter. And with that comes an ease and acceptance in all that I do."

The gifts of reconnecting with your brilliance are truly limitless, and my hope is that this book has provided you with the inspiration, tools, and courage you need to keep forging ahead on your path one step at a time. I encourage you to revisit the materials in this book or on the website with regularity to keep your mind and spirit sharp, especially during times when you feel you could use a little extra support.

Sustaining Your Brilliance

Have you noticed already how there is a rhythm to your brilliance? Sometimes you will feel deeply connected to it, and other times it may feel less vibrant. Sometimes you may be able to express your brilliance outwardly in a very concrete and robust way. Other times, it may act more quietly on the inside. These fluctuations in intensity and rhythm are natural and to be expected in any evolutionary process of growth. Whatever its current form or expression, though, your brilliance is always there within. Here are a few strategies to remember for sustaining your brilliance.

STRATEGY 1: Own What You've Learned

When we talk about something as personal as your brilliance, it is hard to find ways to describe it that will perfectly resonate with everyone. We are all unique, and different things make us tick.

Review what you have learned in this book. Take from it only what you want and need to keep going wholeheartedly on your path ahead. Are there words you need to change to make it feel more "you"? Are there concepts we discussed that were not entirely relevant to your experience? Leave them behind. That's to be expected and is all part of the process.

Use this book and the experiences it has brought to you as a launch pad for taking charge of your journey. When you dare to own your brilliance in this way, you stop trying to conform to the outside world and start connecting again to your truth. Stay open-minded and curious, yes, but commit only to what brings forth your brilliance in a truthful way for you.

STRATEGY 2: Commit to Regular Self-Inquiry

If there is only one thing you take away from this book, I hope it is this: *Always maintain an active relationship of inquiry with yourself.* You are an ever-evolving being with so much potential to do amazing things in your life and in this world. But so much of that will not have a chance to be discovered if you don't take the time and make the effort to connect to yourself in a meaningful, consistent way.

Self-inquiry is not about self-importance. It's about discovering your authenticity so that you can bring it fully to the world for the benefit of all. As Ramana Maharshi reportedly said, "Our self-realization is the greatest service we can render the world." Take a moment and be honest with yourself right now. How deliberate is your inner relationship with self? Do you give in to habits even though you know they don't serve you anymore? Stay curious and compassionate, and always look inward to those new discoveries that await you.

STRATEGY 3: Pay Attention to Your Resistance

Did you resist some suggestion or concept that we covered in this book? I hope so! Let me explain. In his book *The War of Art,* author Steven Pressfield describes, "The more important a call or action is to our soul's evolution, the more resistance we will feel toward pursuing it." That is a bold statement, and one people do not often like to hear, but there is truth in it. If something in this book got under your skin, it could very well be pointing to an area that's worth investigating further. Perhaps a new growing edge is being uncovered.

It is not my goal for you to blindly adopt or accept whatever I have written in this book as truth. The goal instead is for you to stay present and pay attention to the things that trigger you because your strong reaction is an important form of feedback. Use the trigger of resistance as a launch pad to investigate what is underneath. Here are a few questions you could ask yourself:

- Why do I have such a strong reaction to this idea, concept, or suggestion? What feelings does it bring up in me? When have I felt these feelings before?

- If I were to let go of my resistance, what might happen? Is there something I am avoiding?

- Is there a larger lesson or truth my resistance is trying to show me? What might that be?

I understand that these may not be the easiest questions to ask yourself, and sometimes they may not even resolve the resistance. But my hope is that they will give you a place to start investigating a little more deeply.

If you struggle a lot with resistance, it could be valuable for you to work with a therapist or a coach who will support you in making your way through some of this terrain. On the other side of resistance is usually a ton of creativity and potential to be explored.

STRATEGY 4: Build a Support Network

Brilliance thrives when you surround yourself with others who want you to succeed. What support do you need around you in order not just to survive but to thrive? You may not be able to create this support network overnight, but getting clear on what it is you desire helps you to know exactly where the gaps are and what steps to take in order to get the support you need. To get you started here, I've provided a self-inquiry exercise, "Building a Brilliant Support Network," in the workbook.

Using Brilliance to Support the Greater Good

When we started this journey, I mentioned that brilliance is about far more than achieving personal fulfillment. True brilliance awakens when we feel inspired to support the greater good through our thoughts, behaviors, and actions. But it's more than that, really.

To uncover our brilliance at all, we have to surrender fully to the humanness of our experience, and we often cannot do that on our own. My client

Alice describes this point beautifully: "Perhaps this is a no-brainer for some people, but I've learned we need each other. Like really. The ones that say or act as if they don't, they need others the most. I learned that we are where we are today because of the legacy of generations of people, from family to strangers. Our conflicts and struggles and desires and dreams are never ours alone. And so to resolve, to evolve, and to strive to create the world we want to live in, we need each other. We need each other to keep on making our every moment a conscious one."

Yes indeed. To come into the fullness of our brilliance requires us to be vulnerable with each other. Another client, Amy, shares her experience of this: "I've learned that I must radically accept my vulnerability if I want to grow and develop whatever magic I have to share with the world. And I think I have something to share, even if I don't know what it is yet. And that means making tons of mistakes pretty much on a regular basis. But what I found out is that I don't have to use every mistake I make as evidence of my future failings. That is my choice, my preprogrammed choice, but still my choice. The point isn't to obliterate any feeling of vulnerability, but instead change my relationship to it entirely."

So, assuming we are willing to be vulnerable with others and engage fully in our human-ness so our brilliance can blossom, how do we recognize and engage the unique ways we are able to contribute back to the greater good? What does that look like?

There is no one answer to these questions. Your ability to contribute back to the whole will continually evolve throughout your entire life. But you can do certain things to stay open and willing to fully embrace your capacity to be a force for good in the world. Here are some tips to keep in mind.

TIP 1: Consistently Commit to Your Personal Process

There's no bypassing here. Any professional or public contribution you wish to make, whether through your business or another initiative, will require you to keep a steady and firm commitment to your own personal path to brilliance. In other words, you must maintain your commitment to your personal growth and self-inquiry.

Your commitment to personal growth is the foundation upon which all your other offerings will lay. Without it intact, nothing will last. You cannot circumvent this part of the process. Speak to any recovering workaholic or do-gooder that's ever suffered from burnout, myself included. At some point or another, the jig will be up. Don't use your desire to help support others as an excuse to not to support yourself.

TIP 2: Get Clear on Your "Brilliance Point"

We all have certain gifts to bring to the world. We all also have our unique passions that light us up. Where your gifts and your passions intersect with what the world needs is your Brilliance Point.

Your Brilliance Point is a peak of leverage where you are well-situated to serve the greater whole. Your Brilliance Point will deeply engage your interest. Your passions will be clearly identified, and your competency and ability to serve will be strong, too, because you'll have determined the gifts you will be activating. Finally, you'll be offering something relevant and of great value because you will have taken the time to clarify specific worldly needs that you would like to address.

Take, for example, Jim, who is a coach, yoga teacher, and nutritionist. His talents and knowledge in the wellness field are vast. He's clear he would like to engage these gifts even more than he already does so he can be an even greater force for good in this world.

Jim's passions are many, but as he reflected on his Brilliance Point, he homed in on his love for sports and hanging out with his guy friends for a game of pickup basketball. Finally, when it came time for Jim to identify a need area in which he would like to serve, he identified Big Brothers Big Sisters, an organization that pairs professional adults with at-risk youth to provide an ongoing mentoring relationship for children experiencing adversity. He'd already been a "big brother" role model and mentor for a young teenager in his area for years, and he'd seen the positive impact it could have.

So now with his gifts, passions, and area of need identified, Jim crafted a plan for making his Brilliance Point come to life. He coordinated with the Big Brothers Big Sisters organization in his town to organize a pickup basketball game for local big brothers and their "littles." After the game, the group would stay for a healthy picnic in the park. Jim would provide the food, along with healthy eating tips for young men. Jim knew youth, especially teen boys, were not always well educated about what was best to eat to support their bodies in growing strong and healthy. With his skill set as a nutritionist and coach, he felt confident he could package this information in a creative way that would speak to the group. He also partnered with local grocery stores to provide free samples of healthy food that the teens could take home to their families.

The event was a big success, and it has led to Jim leading regular well-ness-related offerings through the Big Brothers Big Sisters organization in his town. If you would like to identify how you can best serve others, go to the workbook and complete the self-inquiry exercise "Finding Your Brilliance Point."

TIP 3: Do It Without the Need for Results

Whatever way you decide to be a force for good in the world, understand that you may not ever see the full effect of your offering. Do it anyway. In my experience, the best way to approach being of service is to offer it up with no expectations. Don't do it to be praised or noticed. Don't do it because you think it's the "right" thing to do. Don't even do it because you want or need to see that you're making a real impact. In his journal *Young India*, Mahatma Gandhi wrote, "That service is the noblest which is rendered for its own sake."

Just do it, for its own sake. Do it because you can. Do it because if you don't offer up what you can in your unique way, no one else will. Just offer it all up, and then watch. You will see the magic that happens when we give from a place of serene non-attachment.

TIP 4: Don't Try to Change People's Minds

You can provide information, vision, motivation, education, support, com-passion, and inspiration to others, but please don't offer up your brilliance with the expectation of changing anyone's mind. You know from reading this book that you alone are responsible for your beliefs and choices. The same holds true for everybody else. Respect other people's need to process and receive things in the way that is best for them. It is not for you to decide how, when, or if they make shifts in their path to brilliance. Be clear on that, and you will save yourself a lot of heartache and be able to give from a more authentic place.

TIP 5: Don't Expect Everyone to Come Along for the Ride

If you are really pushing yourself in new and big ways as you endeavor to share your brilliance with others, it's likely not everyone around you is going to understand what you're up to. You may encounter misunderstandings, criticism, and even disagreements from time to time. It's all good.

Keep an open mind and hear what others have to say, but be mindful not to set an expectation that others are going to feel as passionately about this stuff as you do or that they will even understand it. Similar to the last tip, be clear on your intention for offering your brilliance up, and let it be at that. The rest is not up to you.

TIP 6: Start Small and Experiment with Scope

Brilliance happens at every level: first in how you treat yourself, then rippling out into your immediate circles of contact, and from there reaching nearby circles of connection, your community at large, and so on, to eventually include the whole planet—and even the whole cosmos!

Start small. Lest you think you need to go out and do something monumental in scope in order to contribute, know that I've seen some of the most dramatic offerings of brilliance come from people really learning to love themselves for the first time and role-modeling that to their children, for example. I've been experiencing this as I raise my daughter, Savannah. I can't think of a greater offering of service for her than to teach her how to love and accept herself by role-modeling doing that for myself. In many ways, for me, this is a much more profound and harder act of service to fulfill than some of my large-scale business ventures. Watch out for the trap that says "bigger is better." That is not always the case. To learn more about how your brilliance can show up at different levels in your life, go to the workbook to complete the self-inquiry exercise entitled "The Scope of Your Brilliance."

TIP 7: Expect Mistakes and Be Ready to Pivot

If you're playing on your edge of your growth, which you will be doing if you're showing up wholeheartedly with your brilliance in the world, expect to make mistakes and get ready to regroup and try again. Nothing about the brilliance journey is linear. It is much more organic in nature. And like nature, it will appear messy, perhaps even chaotic at times. But the beauty, simplicity, and elegance are still there. One of my teachers, Nita Rubio, used to say that on the path we need to be "inwardly disciplined and outwardly untamed, just like nature." In many ways, this recalls the first brilliance principle: "Be firm with intention and flexible with form."

Stay curious and make it an adventure. Part of the joy of being on the path to brilliance is in the not knowing. For me, finding my way one step at a time and trusting the larger processes at work has always felt like a way to consciously commune with the universe. There is something exhilarating about not knowing the myriad ways that my experience of brilliance will unfold to serve others. The more I embrace this, the more effective I have become in bringing more light into the world.

TIP 8: Connect with Other Change Agents

Surround yourself with others on the path to brilliance too. Don't know anybody doing that? Well, you can expose it to them and get them involved. Or find mentors, role models, teachers, and fellow pilgrims who will be there to share with you in the ups and downs, the twists and turns of your journey.

What you expose yourself to will influence your perception of what's possible. Find people who are up to things that inspire you and be with them. If you can't physically be with them, read their books and their blogs, follow them on social media, and learn about what they're doing in whatever way you can. Raise the vibration around you, and you'll start to shift to resonate with it.

TIP 9: Welcome Resistance

We've already talked about listening to resistance on your own personal path to brilliance. Why would you want to welcome in resistance from you or others when using your brilliance to serve the world? Well, for one thing, if you're experiencing resistance, it means you're likely challenging the status quo. You're being vulnerable, and you're in the realm of innovation, and that's where new ideas get birthed! That's not a bad thing. You could be on the verge of offering up something truly new and valuable to the whole.

Don't fear the resistance. Use it as feedback to help guide you further on the path ahead. Listen to its cues to help you adjust your pacing or the intensity of things. Remember that resistance is a good sign that you are in unchartered territory that needs conscious exploration.

TIP 10: Realize the Trip May Be Long and Not Always Illuminating

Victoria had some wonderful insights to share about this as she explored how to bring her brilliance to the world: "It's thrilling to think about all the magic I get to create from what I've learned, but the everyday grind does not seem all that magical, which is why I need this formula. This is a huge one for me to remember and something I will pass on to everyone I will have the privilege to walk this path with. Brilliance is real-time! It's streaming live from me to you to everyone, but it won't always be so obvious to me that it's there. I have to find faith, and trust, and stay the course."

At first, Victoria thought that bringing her brilliance to the world might mean a major overhaul of her life, including leaving her job and perhaps even her marriage. But, as she put it, "using this formula" allowed her to slow things down, integrate the principles, and take the time she needed to let the right path reveal itself to her. Much to her surprise, she stayed in her job and her marriage and found ways to do her service from there.

In her marriage, she focused on letting go of the need for her husband to change in any way in order for the marriage to work. For years, she'd been wanting him to take more interest in his personal growth and well-being, but he never did, and she felt them growing apart. She decided to let go of that expectation completely and extend to him the deepest compassion she could. She also fully committed to her own path of brilliance, only to discover that by doing both these things, she motivated her husband to change. He felt her compassion and the sincerity of Victoria's inner work and saw how it was positively changing her life. And this naturally stimulated his curiosity to learn more about how to change his own. As a couple, they turned over a new leaf, going to yoga classes and meditation retreats together.

As for her work, Victoria thought she would need to leave her job in scientific research to find a place that would be more aligned with her new spiritual understanding of herself and what she had to offer the world. But after some reconsideration, she took a chance by starting a mentorship circle for women at her company. Being in a highly male-dominated field, Victoria knew the women in her office could deeply benefit from some additional support and camaraderie. For their monthly meetings, she adapted some of the material from this book to share personal empowerment concepts and ideas in a way that speaks to women in her profession. For Victoria, staying the course has meant not expecting everything to feel good or easy, or even to look the way she thought it would. That is important and relevant wisdom for us all.

Shining Bright: Being a Leader of Brilliance

Even if you create no conscious plan about how to use your brilliance to serve the greater good, by default of being actively on this path, you are going to positively influence others. Whether you recognize it or not, right now in your everyday life you have the capacity to be a leader of brilliance.

When you are a leader of brilliance, you hold space for the brilliance in others to come forth. More often than not, this happens in subtle ways and is communicated by how you hold yourself, treat others, live from your core values, and lead by example. Here are a few tips that can support you in becoming a conscious and willing leader of brilliance.

TIP 1: Own Your Humanity

Good leaders are far more practiced at being vulnerable than others. They understand that they need to be vulnerable in order to energetically engage in life. They understand that new growth within themselves and within those they are leading comes forth only when they are willing to let their guard down and be authentic. In his book *Barefoot Doctor's Guide to the Tao*, Stephen Russell captures this idea when he says

> Vulnerability is the only authentic state. Being vulnerable means being open for wounding, but also for pleasure. Being open to the wounds of life means also being open to the beauty and the bounty. Don't mask or deny your vulnerability; it is your greatest asset. Be vulnerable; quake and shake in your boots with it. The new goodness coming to you, in the form of people, situations, and things, can only come to you when you are vulnerable, i.e., open.

Tip 2: Embrace Paradox

When we embrace paradox, we move past the limitations of either/or thinking, and we can appreciate and respect the complexities of life. Holding the possibility of truth for both sides of a paradox allows us to see things from a more contextual angle. This larger perspective also makes solutions visible to us where others just see chaos. When you are willing to let go of the part of you that wants to see things as black and white, you can see the subtler wisdom and truths that exist in any given situation. This is where true leadership arises in a world that is all too often deeply committed to the divides.

Some examples of how you might hold paradox as a leader can be found just in the way you choose to show up. For instance, could you be a model to others for how to speak with both candor and diplomacy while in a disagreement? Or perhaps you can role model how to be simultaneously confident and humble or grounded and visionary. Or maybe you lead by showing how to successfully care for others and for yourself at the same time. The possibilities are endless.

To find where you can embrace the paradox to take it to the next level, notice where you bump up against either/or thinking and explore how you can turn it into both/and thinking.

TIP 3: Affirm the Positive

Sometimes I wonder what would have happened if leaders like Mahatma Gandhi or Martin Luther King Jr. had decided to give up one day because they were exposed to so much negativity and ugliness in the human condition. Imagine if they said, "I quit. This is too hard. I may not succeed, and too much is going up against me." How would our world be different?

Being brilliant is not always easy, and being a leader of brilliance takes even more courage. You have to tap into something bigger than just the ego's desires in order to stay committed and continue to see the light in what are sometimes pretty dark situations.

And, so we are crystal clear, being a leader does not always mean you are the head of a global social movement inspiring massive change. Sometimes leadership shows up more quietly. An anonymous quote captures this idea beautifully: "Sometimes the strength within you is not a big fiery flame for all to see. It is just a tiny spark that whispers ever so softly, 'You got this. Keep going.'"

TIP 4: Be a Good Listener

Being a leader is a lot less about knowing the answers and a lot more about being observant, aware, and open enough to put your assumptions aside, listen to others, and make space for their brilliance to come forth. Sometimes, brilliance might be shared in their words, but other times it is hiding beneath the surface, and we will miss it if we don't pay close enough attention.

When we cultivate true inner awareness, we establish presence. With presence, our energetic quality alone inspires others to bring forth their best because they can feel that they are going to be received.

Lucy was on a women's spiritual retreat where one of the other participants was quite shy and socially awkward with the group. Lucy observed her from a distance, since the woman pointedly sat alone at lunch. Lucy's intuition told her that this woman did want to connect with others, but she wasn't sure how to do it. So, Lucy wrote this woman a sweet note and slipped it to her as she left the lunch room. In the note, she complimented her eyes and invited her to "play" in the field that afternoon on the break. She said she'd be there waiting if she'd like to join.

Lucy's small gesture led not only to the woman showing up in the field for a fun nature hike, but also to the beginning of a wonderful friendship that still exists years later. By taking the time to sincerely observe, listen, and be sensitive to another's experience, Lucy had significantly changed her life, and that of her new friend, for the better. How might your life change if you became a better listener in all your relationships? What beauty might you inspire to come forth?

TIP 5: Expose Yourself to Alternate Ways of Being

In his book *Blessed Unrest*, author and activist Paul Hawken explains, "What we already know frames what we see, and what we see frames what we understand." A true leader understands the importance of exposing him or herself to things not yet known or understood.

There's the old saying that "you can never cross the ocean if you are not willing to lose sight of the shore." Our evolution requires that we explore the unknown, and sometimes that we do so boldly. Be willing to go toward that which is not in your comfort zone. For example, when Catherine adopted this principle, she discovered that "there were hidden ways that I gave up choice, and it only became clear to me once I stepped out of my comfort zone and started observing how others did things differently than me. Since I've realized this, I've been opting for choice more and more and discovering little places where I was still playing a victim. Places that I thought I could never change have shifted."

Claiming Your Truth and Igniting Your Brilliance
. . . .

Now, you are primed to go back into your life with an even richer understanding of your brilliance. I invite you to do this next self-inquiry exercise to envision what being a force for good in this world will look like for you.

♦ SELF-INQUIRY EXERCISE: Being a Force for Good

In your journal, record your answers to the following prompts:

1. Write down the values that define your inner compass. How can you

express these values in the world in a way that will help you be a leader of brilliance for others in your everyday life?

2. Think about a place in your life where you would like to show up as a leader of brilliance. Describe at least three specific ways you can start to make this a reality.

3. Review question 2. Answer it again, but take a bigger step out of your comfort zone and identify an area that feels a little more edgy to you when you think about bringing your brilliance forth. Describe what you can do to make it happen.

Great work! Don't forget to visit my website to download your workbook, which will help you organize all the insights and discoveries you've made on the journey to help you on the path ahead. It's truly just the beginning!

CONCLUSION

A Life of Brilliance

Here we are at the conclusion of our journey! It would not feel appropriate to end this adventure together without taking some time to express my sincere gratitude to you for reading this book and committing the time and energy to do the exercises within this text and in the workbook. It is my sincere hope that this journey has been transformational for you, or has at least offered a glimmer of light and hope. Perhaps your brilliance is now sparkling bright like a diamond. In any case, I celebrate you!

Whether we like it or not, a lot of energetic momentum in the world promotes the negative, reinforcing pathology and honoring excuses for a lack of integrity and authenticity. Whenever possible, I choose to root into a story of brilliance instead. I try to think of the vast collection of change makers and impassioned souls emerging the world over—committed individuals who are dedicated to improving life for everyone by letting their unique form of brilliance shine forth. I think of these individuals collectively as the Brilliance Movement.

One of my favorite authors, Paul Hawken, describes this type of movement in his book, *Blessed Unrest*:

> This is the story without apologies of what is going right on this planet, narratives of imagination and conviction, not defeatist accounts about the limits... Inspiration is not garnered from the recitation of what is flawed; it resides rather, in humanity's willingness to restore, redress, reform, rebuild, recover, reimagine, and reconsider...It is a massive enterprise undertaken by ordinary citizens everywhere.

We each have a part to play in this Brilliance Movement, and whether you feel it or not, it's happening everywhere, all over the world right now. Every day, countless people bravely step into their authenticity for the first time, ready to explore their vulnerability so they can let their inner light shine a little brighter in this world. It is with great confidence that I can say this is happening because in my line of work, I interact with these people every single day. The Brilliance Movement is real, and it is powerful beyond measure. Don't let the evening news convince you otherwise.

The inner work you have done over the course of this book is not just for your benefit; it is for the benefit of all sentient beings. I salute you for doing your part and giving it your all. And I sincerely thank you for letting me be a part of your journey. It is a privilege to be included. May you go forth with ease and grace and always endeavor to play in the field of possibility. Keep shining bright!

To your brilliance,
Amy

ACKNOWLEDGEMENTS

Getting to the point where I am writing the acknowledgements to my first book has been no small feat, and I have many people to thank for their support in helping me get here.

I send my heartfelt thanks to all of my teachers, mentors, and guides for showing me the way forward on the path to brilliance, especially during those times when it didn't feel possible. Special gratitude goes to Gail Straub, David Gershon, Lois Barth, Nita Rubio, and Patricia Haman.

I also wish to thank my brave, trusting, and open-hearted students and clients that have blessed me with the privilege of being part of their processes of self-discovery, healing, and transformation. I am deeply honored to have had the opportunity to witness the awakening of your brilliance and to share in the celebration of you bringing yourselves more fully to the world in all that you do.

A special bow of gratitude to Alice Wang, Pete Rizzi, Amy Kessler, Sharna Fabiano, Jillian Arena, and Linda Abbott. Together, we piloted innovations in being and doing, and I am so deeply touched by your ongoing support of each other and of me, my family, and my work. Deep bow.

And to my other fellow travelers on the path to brilliance, thank you for your unconditional friendship, for your belief in me, and for cheering me on through thick and thin. You know who you are.

A huge thank you to Maggie Langrick and the team at LifeTree Media for believing in me and believing in *Brilliance*. I specifically want to thank Sarah Brohman and Kendra Ward for their fantastic editing and moral support. It has been such a gift to work with this wonderful team to bring this book to fruition.

And of course, so much of what I know and have learned about brilliance has come from my four amazing sisters, Maria, Elizabeth, Caroline, and Jennifer, and my unbelievably strong and loving mother, Alice. I love all of you so much and feel eternally blessed to have been born into this tribe of exceptional women.

And finally to my husband, Glenn, and to my daughter, Savannah: you two more than anyone else have been with me on this journey from the very beginning. Savannah, this book was deeply inspired by you, as it first came to existence on the page when you were growing in my belly. I felt your presence with each word I wrote, and every day since you have made me so proud to be your mother. I love you immeasurably, my dear daughter. And Glenn, our partnership has always been a laboratory for learning and exploring our edges of conscious evolution together. Thank you for always bringing out the brilliance in me, even when I don't know how to do it myself. I love you so much and am infinitely grateful to have you by my side through this adventure we call life.

BIBLIOGRAPHY

Angelou, Maya. *All God's Children Need Traveling Shoes.* London: Virago Press, 1987.

Arterburn, Steve. *Walking into Walls: 5 Blind Spots that Block God's Work in You.* Brentwood, TN: Worthy Publishing, 2011.

Block, Peter. *Community: The Structure of Belonging.* San Francisco: Berrett-Koehler Publishers, 2008.

Brown, Brené. *The Gifts of Imperfection: Let Go of Who You Think You're Supposed to Be and Embrace Who You Are.* Center City, MN: Hazelden Publishing, 2010.

———. "The Power of Vulnerability." TED Talk, Houston, TX. June 2010. www.ted.com/talks/brene_brown_on_vulnerability.

Forleo, Marie. "The Power of Following Your Fear." *MarieTV.* Marie Forleo (website), March 1, 2016. www.marieforleo.com/2016/03/follow-your-fear.

Gibran, Kahlil. *A Tear and a Smile.* CreateSpace Independent Publishing Platform, 2018.

Gilbert, Elizabeth. *Big Magic: Creative Living Beyond Fear.* New York: Riverhead Books, 2015.

Greaves, Jean, and Travis Bradberry. *Emotional Intelligence 2.0.* San Diego, CA: Talent Smart, 2009.

Harvey, Andrew. *The Hope: A Guide to Sacred Activism.* Carlsbad, CA: Hay House, 2009.

———. *The Return of the Mother.* New York: Tarcher/Putnam, 2001.

Hawken, Paul. *Blessed Unrest: How the Largest Social Movement in History is Restoring Grace, Justice, and Beauty to the World.* New York: Penguin Books, 2008.

Judith, Anodea. *Wheels of Life: A User's Guide to the Chakra System.* St. Paul, MN: Llewellyn Publications, 1987.

Kabat-Zinn, Jon. *Wherever You Go, There You Are: Mindfulness Meditation in Everyday Life*. New York: Hyperion, 1994.

"Mary Johnson and Oshea Israel," *StoryCorps*, NPR, May 20, 2011, https://storycorps.org/listen/mary-johnson-and-oshea-israel.

Maxwell, John C. *Everyone Communicates, Few Connect: What the Most Effective People Do Differently*. Nashville, TN: Thomas Nelson, 2010

Occelli, Cynthia. *Resurrecting Venus: A Woman's Guide to Love, Work, Motherhood, and Soothing the Sacred Ache*. Carlsbad, CA: Hay House, 2012.

Osho. *Intuition: Knowing Beyond Logic*. New York: St. Martin's Press, 2001.

Plaskow, Judith. *Standing Again at Sinai: Judaism from a Feminist Perspective*. New York: HarperCollins, 1990.

Pressfield, Steven. *The War of Art: Break Through Blocks and Win Your Inner Creative Battles*. New York: Black Irish Entertainment, 2002.

Ray, Amit. *Meditation: Insights and Inspirations*. Inner Light Publishers, 2015.

Roth, Geneen. *Women, Food and God: An Unexpected Path to Almost Everything*. New York: Scribner, 2010.

Russell, Stephen. *Barefoot Doctor's Guide to the Tao: A Spiritual Handbook for the Urban Warrior*. New York: Harmony Books, 1999.

Schwenk, Theodor. *Sensitive Chaos: The Creation of Flowing Forms in Water and Air*. Forest Row, UK: Rudolph Steiner Press, 1965.

Straub, Gail. *The Rhythm of Compassion: Caring for Self, Connecting to Society*. Boston: Journey Editions, 2000.

Straub, Gail, and David Gershon. *Empowerment: The Art of Creating Your Life as You Want It*. West Hurley, NY: High Point, 1989.

Sutton-Smith, Brian. *The Ambiguity of Play*. Cambridge, MA: Harvard University Press, 1998.

Tolle, Eckhart. *A New Earth: Awakening to Your Life's Purpose*. New York: Plume, 2006.

Williamson, Marianne. *The Law of Divine Compensation: On Work, Money, and Miracles*. New York: Harper One, 2012.

INDEX